D1090004

How an Average Man Lived an Adventurous Life

*Includes Lists of the Best Things in the World &
Six Tropical Paradises Where You Can Live for
$500 a Month*

by

JOHN LINNEMEIER

authorHOUSE®

AuthorHouse™
1663 Liberty Drive, Suite 200
Bloomington, IN 47403
www.authorhouse.com
Phone: 1-800-839-8640

©2008 John Linnemeier. All rights reserved.

No part of this book may be reproduced, stored in a retrieval system, or transmitted by any means without the written permission of the author.

First published by AuthorHouse 12/15/2008

ISBN: 978-1-4389-1280-6 (sc)
ISBN: 978-1-4389-1279-0 (hc)

Library of Congress Control Number: 2008909639

Printed in the United States of America
Bloomington, Indiana

This book is printed on acid-free paper.

My Lord, my God, my light and staff and shield,
My true Guide upon this earth's dark face,
Judge me not by what my deeds should yield.
Judge me, Lord, according to thy grace.

From the Yom Kippur service

Dedicated to my beloved Guru, Baba Hardev Singh

Table of Contents

Foreword	1
Longest Night	3
Getting Holy in McLeod Ganj	7
Advice to Travelers: Walk toward the Music	9
Best Things in the World	11
Elephants 1	13
Elephants 2	15
Elephants 3	16
Best Things in the World	18
Amazing Grace (Part I)	21
The Dogon Country	24
C-U-P	27
Opporknockitty	28
Advice to Travelers: Pick Up One Piece of Trash	30
The Trees Were Weeping	32
Best Thing in the World	34
Stage Fright	36
Trouble at Tilicho Pass	38
Impeccable Gentlemen	40
Hard Traveling	42
Hyperinflation: A Lesson in Economics	44
Birdlife	46
Best Things in the World	48
S and M in NYC	50

Sous Les Ponts De Paris   52
Now It Is Clean   53
Advice to Travelers: Teach Me a Song   55
Scattered Memories of Vietnam   56
Get Out   59
Yucking it up in the World's Saddest Country   60
Two Way Street   64
I Remember   66
The Tower of Gao   68
Cyclone Tracy   70
The Worst Thing I Ever Did   72
Best Things in the World   73
Amazing Grace (Part II)   75
Little Old Ladies in Tennis Shoes Who Know How to Live   77
Advice to Travelers: Try Every New Fruit   79
Friendly Fire   81
It Is Forbidden   83
Best Things in the World   85
Beanheads Eating Smack-Sized Bites   87
The White Rose   91
Advice to Travelers: Dig Deeper   93
Everything You've Heard About the Sixties is (Mostly) True   96
Fire in the Hole   98
The Mayor of Fifth Street   100
Homesick Down Under   103
The Man in the Culvert   105
Best Things in the World   107
Amazing Grace (Part III)   109
Didn't You Learn Anything?   113
Advice to Travelers: Trekking In the Himalayas   115
The Chicago Marathon   116
Bleak Moscow   118
I Remember   120
Friendliest Country in the World   122
Ikebana in Tegucigalpa   123

A Tour of Duty in Vietnam 125

Best Things in the World 127

Up the Niger Beyond Timbuktu 129

Saved by Dolphins 132

Life in the White Cocoon 134

Advice to Travelers: Bargaining 137

The Art of War 138

Why I Love Holland 140

Why I Love India 142

Best Things in the World 146

Driving a Cab 148

Fishing in Goa 150

Drugs 152

Advice to Travelers: Don't Give Out Sweets 155

The Jericho Bar House 156

Racing At Sweet Owen Speedway 157

Best Things in the World 160

Fear and Greed: Playing the Stock Market 162

I'm an Angel 172

Cultural Adjustments 175

Best Things in the World 177

Advice to Travelers: Get Off the Rabbit Run 179

Ram Rahim Nagar 180

Three Warnings 182

Best Things in the World 183

Professor J.S. Puri 185

Dev Das 187

Slipshod Manor 189

I Remember 190

My Life as a Hooker 192

Returning to Vietnam 194

The One Who Brings Light 197

Riding the Rails 199

Advice to Travelers: Get a Haircut 204

Be Careful of Nicaragua 205

More to Life in Hong Kong 207

Best Things in the World 208

A Fish Story 210

The War through Vietnamese Eyes 212

Muy Hombre 215

Panty Raids 218

The Splendid Splinter 220

Best Things in the World 223

It Takes a Village 225

The Jaguar Birdman 227

The Fetishist 231

Three Churches 232

Trying to Die in Bed at 95 236

Advice to Travelers: Every Paradise Has a Lifespan 237

How I Might Have Been a Chief in Samoa 240

The Optimist 242

Best Things in the World 243

Working Off-Shore 245

Winter in the Hindu Kush 247

I Remember 251

The Truth Cannot be Killed 253

Best Things in the World 255

Queen of the Ecuadorian Prison System 257

Recovery 259

A Slum Tourist in Calcutta 263

My House 265

Worst Hitchhiking: Six Days of Bad Luck in the Sahara 269

Best Hitchhiking: La Dolce Vita in Algiers 270

Thanks, Xaxa 272

Advice to Travelers: Making it Work 274

Tokyo Skyline 276

An Affair with a 300 pound Go Go Girl 277

Election Day 279

Best Things in the World 282

Stowaway 284

Working on the Great Gate   287
Me, Dick Cheney, and the Dalai Lama   289
War Wounds   291
Best Things in the World   292
Six Paradises   294
I Remember   296
All the Good Times Aren't Over   298
Living in the Himalayas   300
Best Things in the World (which I hope to do before I die)   302
Final Advice to Travelers   303
Afterward   305
Acknowledgements   307

Foreword

ANYONE CAN BE AN adventurer. I'm a fairly average guy with no obvious gifts. I'm not the kind of man that other men automatically defer to. I don't normally make women's hearts beat faster when they see me across a crowded room.

When I set off for somewhere exotic, I'm always screwing things up. I miss my flight by a day, I pack so much that I can hardly carry my bags, my hands shake, I misplace my ticket, my shirttail is hanging out, and my fly is half unzipped. Most of the time, I probably come across as a bungling buffoon instead of the suave, swash-buckling hero I'm constantly aspiring to be. *But I Keep Going.* I don't want to sound like a sneakers ad, but the only real secret to being an adventurer is to just do it.

To be an adventurer is to be a dreamer—but not just a dreamer, an active dreamer. There's a difference. Sometimes it means giving up on other things. It takes a certain commitment to live adventurously. The old "ham and egg" joke can be drawn on to illustrate the difference between involvement and commitment: a chicken may be involved in producing your breakfast, but a pig is committed.

I respect those who stay put, take pleasure in the four seasons, and live a contented life within a circle of family and friends. I honor them, but I'm not built that way.

When I was a young man long ago in India, I once came across a small book written by a man who described himself as a traveler and adventurer. It was a modest book with no literary pretensions. I don't know its name or that of its author. Like me, he was an old man when he wrote it. I remember a couple of the stories. One was about being

1

in Moscow at the time of the revolution. I could picture myself being there, and it stirred my blood to imagine it.

I also remember a few simple bits of advice he gave for anyone who wanted to live an adventurous life. Things like "read the best books you can find about wherever you are" and "learn a trade." That small book has stayed with me through my life in a way that a lot of far grander literature has not.

Everything important I've learned in my life is here in this book. My hope is that it will inspire someone in the same way that his book inspired me. I've worked hard (and probably failed) at not making it self-serving. It's not all going to be tough sledding; along with all the pompous preachiness, I also hope to entertain with a few rattling good yarns. Some, like the dolphin story, may sound implausible, but I swear to God they're the truth.

One of several possible titles I toyed with for this book was, "Lessons and Blessings: The Life of a Traveling Man." I've come to believe that everything in life is either a lesson or a blessing. More importantly, if you learn from the lesson it also becomes a blessing. The first story in the book is in the "lesson" category. As you read through the book, it should become obvious that I've made more than my share of blunders.

Dear reader, there is a wise old Yiddish saying that states, "A smart man learns from his own mistakes, while a wise man learns from the mistakes of others." The road of excess may lead to the palace of wisdom, as William Blake once famously wrote, but that way is only one of many, and it has a lot of dead-ends where it can be easy to lose your way.

I'll give this much advice. Your life is precious. Don't waste it grinding your guts doing things you hate. Don't be drugged and hypnotized by advertising and the rest of the colossal maya-promotion industry into thinking all this material stuff is going to satisfy your soul. It's never too late. If you'd like to lead an adventurous life but feel that you're too young, too old, too poor, or too tied down with responsibilities, then read on.

Longest Night

I INSTINCTIVELY REACHED FOR my rifle when someone woke me around midnight. I remember the night as moonless, though after so many years, I wouldn't swear to it. It must have been hot like every night in the dry season. Thick dust softened my step as I walked the short distance to the perimeter of our night defense position. I was in a good mood; I loved the solitude of guard duty.

We were about a mile from the Cambodian border. North Vietnamese could cross the border at night, hit us, and be back safely in Cambodia before daylight. An entire company of ARVNs had been wiped out to the last man a couple of kilometers from us several weeks before. We drove past a large circle of their burned-out vehicles every day. It made us edgy.

Late in the afternoon we would move back to our small night defense position and circle the wagons. This particular NDP was a basic set-up with cleared land and rolls of razor barbed-wire extended concertina-style and stacked in a pyramid, forming a circle. Within this outer circle was a smaller circle of pushed-up earth, forming a berm. Facing outward on the berm were about twenty armored personnel carriers (APCs) sitting with their tracks tilted slightly upwards. Each had a machine gunner on top silently staring out into the darkness.

I have no explanation for what happened next. My friend, Frito, was atop the APC manning the gun. I called out from the ground that I was there to relieve him.

"Everything quiet tonight?" I asked.

"Yeah, real quiet, no problems," he replied.

I climbed up the ladder, directly in front of the M-60, three feet from the barrel. Frito's face and expression are lost to me, nor do I remember the impact of the bullets, but I distinctly remember the flame that shot out of the muzzle.

The first bullet missed my heart by a centimeter and lodged in my left lung, collapsing it. The second bullet entered my left shoulder, making a small entrance hole. The bullets were designed to wobble. When they hit flesh, they'd start to tumble. The exit wound tore out most of my scapula.

When I regained consciousness, I was aware of the stars above me, jewel-like and radiant. Foaming blood was boiling out of my chest with every breath. A medic was working over me with a wad of plastic, desperately trying to plug the hole.

The first person I remember talking to was our Buck Sergeant. I don't recall his name. As he looked down upon me his eyes were wide with fear.

"You took five rounds!" He paused. Then, like he knew it was something you were supposed to say, "You're gonna be alright."

Before this moment I'd never so much as broken a finger, but I knew with certainty that if I had been shot five times, I would be dead in sixty seconds. It was difficult for me to speak, but I needed to have a clear moment — no bullshit. I could barely get it out, but I told the Sergeant to go away. Then a friend of mine, a Hispanic guy who didn't speak much English, held my hand. That was a true thing.

I had been reading a Bible the chaplain had given me a few weeks before, and I knew I couldn't put it off any longer. I had to decide if I believed in God.

The answer came to me in an instant:

NO!

Nothing had been revealed to me and I wasn't going to crawl out of life pretending that it had. There were people I loved and that was as high as I could get. I could go out on that.

Just after I was shot I remember being terrified. I existed, but soon wouldn't. I had taken the miracle of being alive as if it were nothing. My actions while living seemed shallow, contemptible, driven by egotism.

As I approached death, however, all this was left behind. A peace settled on me. I could die or not die. Either was okay. The only question was — had I done what I needed to do? I don't know where it came from, but I flashed that I hadn't had a son. This was a peculiar idea as I didn't even have a girlfriend at the time. But the decision was made and that seemed to bring me back.

I remember feeling strongly that I had no reason to complain about my fate. I had made a series of decisions which had put me precisely where I was under those blazing stars. Months later, in a hospital in Japan, a fellow patient who had stepped on a mine said that he remembered thinking just after it happened, "You play with fire, you're gonna get burned." I knew what he was talking about.

Since I had a sucking chest wound, nobody wanted to give me painkillers, as that would depress my breathing. Not even an aspirin. It was a long night, and I went in and out of consciousness many times. The only way I can gauge the pain now is by remembering one thought I had. Despite being young and full of the juice of life, it hurt enough that I figured that it wouldn't be all bad if I died.

Once I regained consciousness while flying in the back of a Huey slick. I must have been on my way to a field hospital. I clearly remember the loud beat of the rotor blades and the rush of the wind through the open door. I couldn't get enough air; I needed oxygen. The bored medic absent-mindedly handed the tube to me as he gazed out the door at the lights scooting beneath us. For him, this was just another run.

The first chopper took me to a field hospital. It must have been very late at night. In true army fashion, there was paperwork to be filled out upon arrival. I must have had to tell them how to spell "Linnemeier"— I always do. Next thing I remember, I was being worked over by a very nervous doctor who must have just gotten in-country. He was assisted by an old battle-axe of a nurse. She was a bitch, but I can hardly complain; she probably saved my life.

They were trying to drain the blood and fluid out of my chest through plastic tubes sticking out of my back. The tubes kept coming out and had to be re-inserted. Each time they fiddled with them I had to be turned over. The pain was unspeakable, and every time they rolled me over I cried out, "Oh, God, Oh God!" Each time I swore, the woman admonished me. Finally, in exasperation, she asked the doctor if he could make me quit cursing. Obediently he mumbled, "Please, you're in the presence of a lady."

Sometime later during that long night they moved me to another hospital. The doctor there had seen it all and seldom talked. He may not have thought much of me one way or another, but he knew his stuff. He was competent; I could sense it and was grateful for it.

At one point someone was saying a little desperately, "If he gets worse, we'll have to operate." I remember praying to get worse; the pain was unbearable. And I did.

Next morning I woke up covered with a solid sheath of bandages from my navel to my neck, with an IV in my arm and a body pumped full of glorious painkillers.

Getting Holy in McLeod Ganj

*The world is a book and those who
don't travel read only one page.*

St. Thomas Aquinas

THIRTY YEARS AGO I was living in the amiable, cockroach-infested Mount Kailash Hotel above Dharamsala in the small town of McLeod Ganj, the exile home of the Dalai Lama. McLeod Ganj is a beautiful little place, or was, at that time anyway. It's nestled in a pine forest beneath the Himalayan Range in Northern India. The Tibetans who lived there were noble and good-natured. At the time, there were a few hundred westerners in town as well. Bearded, long-haired, patchouli-scented searchers and seekers for the most part.

The hospitable Tibetans opened their world to us. You could attend a one-hour-a-day seminar — like I did — or study for twenty years and become a monk or nun. The most bright-eyed, jovial old Lama imaginable taught the class while a sweet-faced young monk translated his lessons for us into English. It was fall and the plum tree outside our little school had turned a dark crimson. As I came into the sun-filled classroom one afternoon long ago, I was feeling particularly pleased with myself. This place was really cool; I was making all kinds of spiritual progress here and getting holier all the time. With that pleasant thought in mind, I settled into a somewhat uncomfortable half-lotus position near the back of the class on one of the large rugs that covered the floor, prepared to listen to the lecture.

The Lama began, "The first thing I have to say is that we always have to be careful of   spiritual pride."

Wow, I thought, that's interesting!

The talk rambled on. Golden shafts of afternoon sun began to stream in through a large bank of smudged windows, gently warming me. I slowly drifted off into a daydream.

Then, just barely through this gauzy mental haze I heard the Lama say, "The second main thing that I want to say today is that it's important to focus your mind and pay attention all the time."

I awoke with a start. Was this guy reading my mind?

Then, with a twinkle in his eye, the old man looked straight at me and said, "The third point I want to make today is that it is important to learn to read people's minds so you can help them." Then he burst into laughter.

Advice to Travelers:
Walk toward the Music

Say you are in a small town in Africa. You hear music in the distance. My advice is to follow that sound and find out what's going on. I can't tell you how many little adventures have resulted from doing this. I've been invited to weddings, witnessed fiery political rallies, seen colorful religious festivals, and attended some great parties in a lot of exotic places.

Speaking of Africa, an incident in Mali comes to mind. I was waiting in the dusty town of Mopti for the rains to start so the Niger River would rise. Then the rusty, old paddle wheel steamer that plied the river would be able to clear the thousands of sand bars and make it up past Timbuktu to Gao. From there I hoped to catch a sheep truck north across the Sahara.

Far away across town, I could barely make out some joyful music coming in through my open hotel window. I walked out of the seedy little building and into the dusty red dirt street in pursuit of the faint sound. It gradually grew louder and, a few minutes later, I emerged at a boisterous street party. I stood there flat-footed and feeling like a farmer come to town.

There before me was a tight circle of onlookers emitting a fetid warmth, keyed to a fever pitch and intensely alert. Within this circle, the drummers were pounding out an incessant beat with an all-consuming concentration. It felt as if something mysterious was attempting to be born.

Mali may be one of the poorest places in the world, but the women carry themselves like queens. Dressed in magnificent turbans and long flowing dresses made from incandescent textiles saturated with every hue and flecked with gold and silver, the very movement of their bodies speak of life. They radiate joy.

From time to time one of the women would move into the center and start to dance. She would begin to reveal something deep and true about herself as all eyes followed her. She allowed us to see her more naked than naked. Then, abruptly, the dancer would cover her face, suddenly embarrassed, and rush back out of the circle. Some were technically skillful, but this obviously wasn't the important thing.

As I stood there watching, someone entered the circle and the energy immediately changed. This woman was in charge. She knew who she was, and there was no fear in her. A spell was being cast. The atmosphere grew more intense, the musicians more focused. Everyone recognized that this person had *IT.* Time was suspended; all were entranced.

Then an official-looking guy in a suit rushed in and bedecked the dancer with a garland made of money. The spell ended in an explosion of celebration and the anointed one retired from the circle in triumph.

In the midst of this swirling tumult I noticed that a three-hundred-pound woman of enormous beauty had her eyes locked on me. I was a goner. I should mention here that my brother Richard can dance circles around me. Comparatively speaking, he is a real Nureyev. He is also known far and wide in our state as the second-worst dancer in Indiana. Nonetheless, the eyes of this African beauty looked deep into mine. There was no fighting it. The crowd was going insane. This poor Hoosier was in her hands. She willed me into motion.

Best Things in the World

- Jim Morrison's grave at Pere Lachaise cemetery in Paris. The graffiti and neon-colored arrows spray-painted on gravestones will guide you to the spot where he's buried. When you arrive you'll find a small group of people standing around, drinking whiskey and smoking pot. The faces change but there's always a party going on there.

- The incredible break-dancing that goes on out in front of McDonalds on Khreshchatyk Street in Kiev

- Revolutions in Bolivia.

- I arrived in Bucharest, Romania with a dozen tangerines. It was a dreary winter day. The whole city, even the people, seemed colored in shades of grey. None of the buildings were heated and no one smiled. It was a couple of months after the ouster of Ceaucescu and the end of communism. I took a cab into the city from the airport and gave one of the fruits to my taxi driver as a tip. In all that gloom the tangerine seemed to glow like the sun. He was ecstatic to get it. Later that day I met a woman who offered to surrender her virtue for one.

- The egalitarianism and rough courtesy of Australians. In the rowdiest bars out in the bush, drunken men in dusty, sweat-soaked shirts will still make a point of never showing their back to you.

- Marcia Anderson's uncanny ability to pick out four- leaf clover in a field.

- The lotus-shaped Bahai Temple in New Delhi.

- The museum at Checkpoint Charlie in Berlin. It contains displays of all the tunnels, hot air balloons, submarines, and false–bottomed automobile trunks that clever and resourceful Germans had used to escape to the west.

- I spent a week fasting in a cave in the Himalayas above Dharamsala. To add to the aura of the place, above the cave door was a metal piece representing Shiva's trident. The whole thing was sort of a lark actually. I was never lonely. Pleasant strangers dropped by to chat almost every day.

- Cycle-rickshaw rides through the streets of Saigon on balmy nights many years ago.

- Sea turtles nearly the size of VW bugs that crawl up on the shores of a beach in Malaysia to lay their eggs by the light of the full moon. It takes over an hour, and by the end of the ordeal their eyes are filled with tears.

- Coming into a strange city late at night where no one speaks your language and you've no idea where you'll lay your head. Driving through the dark streets of Prague searching for a place to stay comes to mind.

- Spicy chana masala made from chick peas. It's served up on the streets of India. You eat it with puri, a delicious bread that puffs up when you deep-fry the dough in a boiling black cauldron of hot oil. It's normally served on plates made of leaves stitched together by hand. A very upper-class young Indian girl once told me that it never tastes as good in a fancy restaurant "without the dirt."

- Hitching down the rugged coast through Big Sur on highway 1 from San Francisco to L.A.

Elephants 1

TWENTY-FIVE YEARS AGO, I was climbing Mt. Kenya with my dear old friend, Rick Owens. This magnificent mountain unexpectedly juts out of the flatlands of the great African savanna twelve miles from the Equator. The track to the peak starts on the dusty plain where giraffe graze indolently on spiny acacia trees. It ends with a steep climb through deep snow to the summit.

Early on the first day of the ascent, we were winding our way through dense bamboo thickets. The thirty-foot-tall stalks formed a corridor so thick with growth that it would have been impossible to stray from the trail. We rounded a bend and, without warning, found ourselves face-to-face with two elephants, a male and a female. For a single timeless moment the four of us froze in place, each equally shocked. The moment was abruptly ended when the male lifted his enormous trunk, trumpeting in outraged fury, and started towards us. Not to be bested, Rick instinctively picked up a stone and prepared to fire it.

I admired his pluck, but "FOR CHRIST'S SAKE, IT'S AN ELEPHANT!" I yelled hysterically. "DON'T PISS HIM OFF!"

He seemed to accede to this logic and without further discussion dropped the stone. We both did a quick reverse march and took off, assholes and elbows, down the mountain.

A hundred yards on, I looked over my shoulder: SHIT, THE SUCKER WAS RIGHT ON US! Adrenaline was squirting out of our ears as we flew down the slope. I've seen elephants crack bamboo as thick as your thigh. They can move fast, too. If he had a whim to, this creature would make short work of the two of us. At a certain point, though, the great beast became bored with me and Rick. He shuffled to a stop, paused for a moment, and then, reassured of his status, ambled nonchalantly back up the mountain.

Exhausted, we slumped to the ground. Recollecting our thoughts, we soon realized that we were now faced with a new challenge: We needed to get around these animals to reach our first night's campsite further up the mountain. A highly focused discussion ensued. Then one of us noticed a partially-concealed elephant track leading off to the right from the main path. It was dark, swampy, and— frighteningly— just one-elephant wide. If we took the trail and met an elephant coming the other way, we were dead, no questions. Still, it seemed our only option. With the greatest trepidation, we silently resumed our climb, this time through the dark green tunnel. We used a compass with the idea of circling around and hooking up with the main trail somewhere further up and beyond our elephant friends.

It was very dark and confined. I remember in particular a beautiful green snake with glittering eyes. The fetid black ooze beneath our feet threatened to suck our boots off. The air was still and dank, the undergrowth on either side thick and impenetrable. Escape would have been impossible. We spoke in whispers and stopped often, listening intently for the sound of something coming. God saw fit to preserve us for another day, and an hour later we emerged on the main track into the glaring sunshine, fifty meters above where the elephants had been.

"Rick," I said, "there's not a person on Earth I would rather have gone through that with." One brotherly embrace and we headed back up the mountain.

Elephants 2

IT WAS A GRITTY sweatbox of an afternoon. I was killing time wandering lethargically through a little broken-down zoo in Bamako, Mali. It was a sad place, reminiscent of a prison. Dusty footpaths wound their way between rusted metal pens. The cages were cramped and squalid, the inmates defeated and resentful.

Walking next to the elephant enclosure, I vaguely noted that the twenty-foot tall, heavy wire mesh fence had been beaten down to less than half that height. I didn't register any danger: It was a zoo, after all. I strolled over next to the elephant. We eyed each other with what I took to be mutual respect. He took my measure. Then, in an instant, he swept his mighty trunk through the chunk of space-time I had inhabited a second before. I hit the ground and low-crawled for dear life. A nearby cluster of Malians burst into hysterical laughter. I suspect it wasn't the first pratfall they'd seen that day.

Elephants 3

FOUR OR FIVE YEARS ago my friend and ever-faithful taxi driver, Hari, was patiently driving me back through the suffocating pollution and horrendous traffic on the outskirts of Bombay. After all the years of taking me from place to place, he knows me like the Eskimo knows the ways of the seal.

I was slumped in the front seat, dejectedly sipping bottled mineral water, tired and covered with paint, having labored for the day with my beloved Nirankari painting brothers. Hari and I were slowly making our way back to my hotel near The Gateway to India though the creeping traffic and billowing gray truck exhaust. I was looking forward to a hot shower, a short walk through the tree shaded streets of Colaba, and maybe a good meal at Bismallah's.

Amidst all the filth and industrial squalor we spotted an elephant[1] incongruously padding down the roadside with his haughty mahout perched up behind his head, holding a hook against the sensitive area at the base of the great creature's ear. I asked Hari to pull over so we could take a picture. We quickly made an agreement with the owner that ten rupees would be sufficient payment. Unfortunately, as I reached into my pocket to pay, a hundred rupee bill inadvertently fell out on the ground at my feet. The sight of it inflamed the elephant owner's greed. He lusted after that dough. From his powerful perch he looked down upon me scornfully and demanded one hundred rupees. Then

---

[1] The easiest way to tell an African elephant from an Indian one is by the shapes of their ears. African elephants have ears shaped like Africa, Indian ones, like India.

he forced the poor elephant to make threatening noises and raise its trunk menacingly.

"See, the elephant wants 100 rupees," he growled imperiously.

"Bullshit!" I yelled defiantly up at him. I hate being shaken down.

Hari sized up the situation and, using far better judgment, threw the mahout some baksheesh. He grabbed his pigheaded, idiot of a passenger by the arm, jerked me into the cab and off we sped.

Best Things in the World

- The state museum in Taipei. There's an exhibit where you can look through a magnifying glass at a peach seed carved into a toy boat with six movable oars and windows on tiny hinges. You can also view many of those ivory balls carved within balls like the layers of an onion. One I saw went down eight layers. That single piece took a family of artisans three generations to complete.

- Sitting at a table on a sunny morning at some little café in Paris with a good cup of coffee, a croissant, and a copy of *The Herald Tribune*.

- I worked for a few months as a volunteer on a kibbutz in Israel. I did various kinds of work but mainly picked fruits and vegetables. We would start early in the morning before breakfast. I'd choose the ripest avocado for my omelet and the biggest, most luscious orange for my juice.

- The goodness and decency of Swedish people. You can see it in their kind eyes.

- Chocolatte con churros, a Spanish breakfast consisting of doughnut batter extruded through a star-shaped mechanism and deep fried in hot fat. The crispy coils are then cut into finger-sized pieces and coated in cinnamon and sugar. They're eaten with a rich cup of drinking chocolate that's almost the consistency of syrup. It's hard to imagine a more delicious way to start the day, or a less healthy one.

- Camping out in a VW van at sundown on the edge of the

Sahara Desert in Morocco. Dinner was being cooked and Bach's Brandenburg concerto was playing on the tape deck. It was my first glimpse of that great expanse. I felt drawn by it. I wanted to cross it.

- Long peaceful conversations on a sultry night somewhere tropical while watching geckos scramble for insects around a porch light.

- The old student jail of Heidelberg. Every interior surface was covered with hilarious graffiti.

- Broadway musicals. My personal favorite, "The Most Happy Fella."

- Nightlife in Austin, Texas. We dropped by a little place that sells the most sybaritic chocolate ice cream I've ever tasted. There's great BBQ everywhere and a fantastic live music scene. I also remember a streaker running down the middle of the main strip. Everyone cheered him on.

- The stone-carvers of Rajasthan. They're the equal of craftsmen in any age. They could carve a '57 Chevy out of marble or duplicate the Taj Mahal.

- Abandoned rail lines that have been converted to bicycle trails. They tend to be level, since trains don't handle a grade well. Sometimes there are lots of trestles and tunnels, and often they follow streams and rivers. No automobile traffic, of course. Also no billboards.

- In Dharamsala you can still occasionally buy hand printed Tibetan money which dates from the time before the Chinese invasion.

- Getting off the plane in America after being away for a long time.

Ek Tu Hi Nirankar

Main Terri Sharon, Hun

Mainu Bakshlo

Amazing Grace (Part I)

The truth is such that it cannot be seen and not be believed.

William Blake

THIRTY-FIVE YEARS AGO, I was on a train crossing the hot, dusty plains of the Punjab on my way to the Khumba Mela. The Khumba Mela is an awe-inspiring gathering that takes place only once every fourteen years in the town of Hardwar where the Ganges first emerges from the Himalayas onto the plains of India. There's nothing like it on the face of the earth. It is said that to bathe in this holy river at any time and at any place is auspicious, but at this particular time and place, the sins of thousands of lifetimes can be atoned for. There are stories of sadhus who live alone in caves for fourteen years, walk naked across India to bathe at Hardwar at the time of the Khumba Mela, and then turn around and return to their caves. A town of fifty thousand turns into a town of forty million. With the greatest difficulty, I had gotten a place on a train bound for this holy town. My heart was bursting with anticipation. I expected great things.

Back in those days, there were no reservations for second class seats, and getting on any train in India was often a dogfight. I was lucky to have found a comfortable spot on the floor of the train car ("bogie" in Indian parlance) large enough to unroll my sleeping bag. I was looking forward to getting a good night's sleep and awakening the next morning in the foothills of the Himalayas at this incredible gathering.

But it wasn't to be.

Sometime that evening, an elderly Sikh with a full grey beard got on the train and found a seat on the floor next to me. He was dressed in a traditional turban. It and all his other clothes were white and, like all of us, somewhat dusty. There was a certain lightness to him that delighted me. (Later I came to know that "delight" was one of his favorite words. He used it often, as in, "I think you will be highly delighted...") There was a kindly glimmer in his eye and a joyful lilt in his speech. I couldn't help liking him immediately. The tight atmosphere of the entire bogie seemed to have loosened perceptibly due to his presence.

He had brought along a couple dozen hand-made badminton shuttlecocks that he hoped to sell in another town. He joked with everyone around him; then he turned his attention to me. Where was I going? What did I hope to find there? Most importantly, what were my views on God? One of the most endearing things about India is that no one shies away from this subject.

I told him that I had been studying Tibetan Buddhism but felt that all religions were pointing toward the same thing. I said that I was heading to the Khumba Mela and hoped to take some pictures there.

"Very interesting," he said. "Now let me tell you that I don't feel that we have met here by chance. If you go to the Khumba Mela, I'm sure you'll have some wonderful experiences and will take some fascinating pictures. But if you want to realize God, come with me and I'll take you to a man who can reveal God to you."

So there it was. I should mention here that when I first came to India I had vowed that I would follow every lead I came upon concerning this "God" thing. I'd had several intimations that there might be something to it. This being India, I had hopes that, along with all the smoke, there was perhaps fire here somewhere. I'd gone to see many people who claimed (or their followers claimed for them) to know about God. Some seemed ok, some gave me a bad feeling and there was one in particular that I really loved. Every single one of them was charismatic— that much was for sure. At the dead least they were all fascinating. But the point was that none of them had satisfied me.

I told the old Sikh that I'd have to think about it for five minutes. I lay back down on my sleeping bag, closed my eyes and thought. *Hard.* The whole thing just didn't fit in anywhere with my plans. Here I was, heading for one of the greatest events on earth. And it was getting very hot down here on the plains. The Himalayan foothills would be cooler. Still— I had made that vow.

I opened my eyes and, with much reluctance, said, "OK."

"Then we'll need to get down at the next station," he responded.

I rolled up my sleeping bag and stuffed it into my backpack. Fifteen minutes later, without much talk, we climbed down to the station platform and padded off together into the warm Indian night.

To be continued...

The Dogon Country

WE WERE IN MALI. I was doing a little reading and just killing time with my dear French friend, Fontaine Gerard in the dusty African city of Mopti. From here the paddlewheel steamer begins the slow trip up the river to Gao, a town situated at the northern bend of the Niger River. We were near the end of the dry season and waiting it out; the boat couldn't leave until the rains came. The river was still too shallow and we'd get stuck on sand bars.

Fontaine had read a French anthropological study of the Dogon people of Mali that described their mystical culture. From what I'd learned from him, it sounded intriguing and we set off to visit them. We hitchhiked and took ramshackle buses as far as we could. From there, it was a two-day walk through the Sahel.

We bought food in the local markets and slept under the stars. What a joy it was to be out there. Two days later the two of us arrived at the edge of a very long falaise, or cliff. It stretched in a great arc of three hundred kilometers, and was perhaps two hundred feet tall. Intermittently along this great sandstone wall were waterfalls, and at each of these, a Dogon village.

The small road we'd been traveling ended at the door of a comfortable house perched on the top of the cliff where a Lutheran missionary and his family lived. We stopped and talked to the missionary for awhile. He was friendly, but firm on one subject: we'd need a guide to continue. Otherwise, he warned, we might sit under a holy tree or next to a holy rock and get ourselves in trouble. We were poor and somehow a little opposed to this "guide" business anyway, so after he went into his house, we decided to take our chances on our own. Stealthily climbing down through a tunnel of reddish rock, we emerged five minutes later at the bottom of the falaise.

From here trails led in all directions. Fontaine had his book with him, and it contained a basic map of the villages along the falaise. The names were written phonetically, so we hoped to be able to sound them out and be understood. We oriented the map in the correct direction and then headed out along the trail that appeared to point toward the nearest village. As the two of us picked our way along the stony trail in the late afternoon, we occasionally saw a large tree or a rock that looked like it might be holy. We respectfully gave these a wide berth.

Fontaine had mentioned that first impressions were very important to the Dogon. So when a small group of bare-breasted women carrying heavy loads on their heads met us coming the other way, I quickly brought out my harmonica and launched into "Les Marseilles." At this, they broke into huge toothy smiles, dropped their loads, and began to dance. A few minutes later we parted in high spirits. It was getting late by this time and we were anxious to get to our village before nightfall so we picked up the pace. Shortly thereafter, we met a withered old man with a cane standing at a fork in our trail. With a questioning inflection in our voice we asked, "Ooma-Tooma?" A light came on in his eye. He repeated the sound, "Ooma-Tooma" definitively and pointed to one of the forks. We struck out in that direction. I stopped to talk with Fontaine a couple of minutes later, but the man at the fork hadn't moved. Though now three hundred meters from us, he shouted in a friendly manner, "Ooma-Tooma," once again pointing out the correct route.

Nighttime had descended by the time we arrived at the tiny village. There was no moon. Everyone was huddled inside their mud houses. We could sense that they were aware of our presence. The noises coming from within were not welcoming. Again, I took out my trusty harmonica, and this time struck up with "Sous Les Ponts de Paris." It lightened the mood. We began to hear titters of laughter. Soon thereafter, someone emerged from one of the houses and silently took us up a steep mud staircase to the roof where we spent a peaceful night under the great African sky, comfortably encased in our sleeping bags.

The next morning we awoke to a strange and wonderful new world. We were surrounded by a little village made of small rectangular mud huts with thatched roofs with tassels at their tip. Interspersed between the houses were curious, domed, beehive-shaped structures used for storing millet. The falaise loomed over us. Curious and unfamiliar music was playing. A corpse was being elevated on a cot raised by ropes into caves above us. According to Fontaine's book, these caves were called the "Cities of the Dead."

We cooked a simple breakfast and brewed a little tea on our portable gas stove. Soon, a man climbed up the steps and introduced himself to us. He was a visitor from a large town and the only person here who spoke French. He became our translator. Fontaine had told me that every village along the falaise had its own "homme sage" or "wise man." We were anxious to meet him. Our translator and new friend informed us that the men of the village would be meeting in a gathering spot that afternoon and that we could sit in. As we rested in the shade through the heat of the day, Fontaine explained various aspects of Dogon culture to me that he had learned from his book. Much of it was concerned with invisible, parallel worlds that the Dogon believe rest alongside the visible world. Their artwork often included parallel lines which sought to represent this.

By late afternoon it had grown a little cooler and we walked to the little assembly on the edge of town. The men of the village were sitting in a large circular building. It was open to the air and looked out across the millet fields. We shared a joint together and spoke with the "homme sage." In an attempt to be entertaining Fontaine and I took out our cameras and showed them to everyone. No one thought much of that. They'd seen similar things before. Then Fontaine thought to bring out a mirror that he happened to have with him. As it passed slowly around the circle from hand to hand, each man became transfixed by his own image. I don't believe they'd ever seen such a thing. As they passed it to the next person, they shook their heads in wonder.

C-U-P

───────────────

My son, Jacques, my first wife, Elena, and I started off working our way around the world when Jacques was one year old. We returned to America when he was seven and a half. My first trip around the world had been solo and took three and a half years— a very different proposition.

One of the most important differences was dealing with my son's education while we were on the road. Though I'm sure everything is online these days, we used a correspondence program from The Calvert School in Baltimore. It required us to travel with a crate full of books and school supplies that was very cumbersome. Many of the lessons were tedious and laborious: multiplication tables, the alphabet, etc. But there were some exciting moments as well.

Once, I was drilling Jacques on phonetic sounds while forming the letters with my fingers.

"What sound does this one make?" I said, forming the letter C.

"Kuh" he replied dejectedly, making the hard 'c' sound.

"And this one?" I said, forming a U.

"Uh" he droned.

"And this one?"

"puh," he replied blankly.

"OK, again now, all together."

"Kuh.......uh…......puh."

"Again."

"Kuh..uh..puh."

"Again."

In an instant he had it. He bolted to his feet.

"CUP!" he shouted. "It spells cup!"

Opporknockitty

OPPORKNOCKITTY SCRATCHED ON MY door forty years ago. I opened the door and she walked right in like she owned the place, wagging her tail and smelling awful. This habit of rolling in shit was her only vice, and we could never cure her of it. I lived with my girlfriend, Louise, at the time. I was a small town kid and she was a real New Yorker. She was cultured, well turned out, played the piano beautifully, and had all the social graces. She also had that big city edge and didn't take any guff from schmucks and schleppers. I can still hear her berating me in that Long Island accent of hers, "John, you're not a fighter." She taught me a lot.

Louise gave Opper a bath and then announced to me that what I needed was a dog. I need a dog like a hole in the head, I thought to myself. It would be nothing but a burden, nothing but trouble. But Louise was firm and I was wishy-washy, so I became a dog owner.

Since it was a time of fewer rules and laws, Opper could go almost anywhere with me. Some days, padding along at my side, she would accompany me on the shady brick paths across campus then sit outside a lecture hall and wait until I came out. Other times she'd grow bored and leave without me. She was actually a celebrity of sorts. As we walked together, lots of people I'd never met would happily call out to her. She'd run over to be patted then return to my side.

Oppor and I used to take long hikes in the woods with my brothers and their girlfriends. Afterwards, as we lay around laughing and talking, she'd chew the burrs out of our sweaters and lay them gently in neat little piles. She loved us. Sometimes we'd wrestle with each other for the fun of it and this would upset her greatly.

There are so many stories I could tell about this wonderful animal. She was so clever and picked everything up so quickly. In one afternoon I taught her every trick I could think of. At parties she would perform them if I asked. Something about her demeanor, though, let you know that she felt that these parlor acts were beneath her, as indeed they were. One particular stunt involved counting. She would pat my knee with her paw consecutively until I said, "Good dog!" and then she'd quit. That was really the only trick. I could ask her to give me the square root of sixteen and she would tap four times on my knee. Then, before she had a chance to tap a fifth time, I would say "Good dog" and she would stop. Everyone was amazed, and no one seemed to be able to figure out how she did it.

Opper was a very independent creature. Over time she came to feel equally at home either with my parents or at the homes of my three brothers. She'd stay for a few days with each of us, and we'd feed and take care of her. Then one day we'd let her outside to pee and she would take it into her head to go visit someone else for a while. Occasionally we would place little rolled up messages to each other in her collar. We called them Oppergrams.

She blessed us with her presence for eighteen years; but, finally her eyes grew glassy with cataracts and her body grew weak and creaky. She needed to die. My parents were divorcing and in some ways our family was disintegrating. Opporknockitty's burial was perhaps the last time we were truly together. It was her final gift to us.

It was a summer day. We stood together around her now-lifeless body in our backyard beneath the tall green trees. My brother, Richard, had cobbled together a wooden box and we laid Opper in it. We all patted her one last time. My dear sister-in-law, Christy, said, "She was a family dog." We all nodded, cried a few tears, and put her in the ground.

Advice to Travelers:
Pick Up One Piece of Trash

My dear, departed Great Aunt Helen (always known as "Honnor") taught us when we were children to pick up one piece of trash. I try to live by her advice when I remember. It's impossible to clean up everything. It might make you bitter to try. It's sort of a "light a candle instead of cursing the darkness" kind of act.

In the "developing world" once people get a little beyond the survival stage, they become (let's put the best spin on it) rather cavalier in their attitudes towards littering.

The interesting places are the exceptions. I'll give an example of one. It's a proud little country with plenty to be proud of. Its name is Eritrea. It won its independence in an epic thirty year conflict with neighboring Ethiopia, a country ten times its size with ten times its population. Ethiopia was backed by the Soviet Union with literally billions of dollars worth of cutting edge military aid, including MIG jets and T54 tanks. At times the Eritrean warriors were beaten back to the tops of a few hillsides where they stubbornly held on in hand-dug trenches. The heart and soul of this struggle were the radio broadcasts of Adey Zeineb. Her words gave people hope. The fighters tenaciously protected her position and it was never taken. She passed away not long ago, plunging the entire country into deep mourning. I never met her and I regret it. Indomitable courage is only one of the noble traits of Eritreans.

It's a poor country but spotless and safe. The people are shy but friendly. The capital, Asmara, has only one stoplight. On warm evenings people like to gather in cafes and chat with their friends. It's a small enough city so that everyone seems to know everyone else.

There is a whole sector in Asmara where skilled craftsmen using the simplest of tools turn old tires and scrap metal into a million little useful devices— Franklin stoves, crutches, crucifixes. There's a saying here that everything has its use, its re-use, and then its use again. Recycling here is a way of life.

The Trees Were Weeping

I WANT THIS BOOK to be as accurate as I can make it. The next story is slightly vague in my mind. Everything is true, but maybe a couple of things happened on separate days.

We had spent the day sweeping a small village — going from hut to hut, searching for weapons or anything else — and turning up nothing. We were on our way home. Our base camp at the time was located in the midst of the Michelin Rubber Plantation.

The late afternoon sun filtered through the dusty branches. The rubber trees formed a continuous tunnel, roofed by a near-perfect, cathedral-like arch above us that continued down the road as far as the eye could see. It was the dry season. The tracks of our A-Cavs churned up thick clouds of the red dust that covered the leaves and soon completely coated us as well. We looked like ghosts, but we didn't mind. It was fun for us to ride around in these things. We knew we could take a cold shower in an hour or so and we were used to being dirty.

Up ahead, half a dozen sad-looking ARVNs, our Vietnamese allies, were trudging beneath the thin-spun shade of the trees lining the road. Their M-16's dangled listlessly from their slumped shoulders as they slowly headed back to their encampment to bed down for the night. I'd never seen such reluctant soldiers. We stopped and told them to hop on and we'd give them a lift. Grateful, they climbed up along side us. The heat of the day had passed. We joked a little. I felt happy and content, at peace with the world, perched up behind my machine gun as we rolled along.

It was a short convoy. There were only around eight of us. Suddenly, the enemy knocked out the first track of our convoy. The drivers jerked to a stop and rotated out. We laid down a field of fire, a rainstorm of bullets that no one above ground could have survived.

The ARVNs dived to the bottom of the A-Cav and never peeked up for the duration of the firefight. Furious, I ducked inside and kicked and cursed one guy who was cowering in the corner into handing up boxes of fresh ammo to us.

Hot brass from spent cartridges was flying off everywhere, burning our hands and arms. We didn't care. The sound was beyond imagining. Forty years later, my ears still ring from it. I don't know how long it lasted, but every time we stopped firing, the crazy bastards out there in their holes popped up and took a couple of shots at us. We never once saw them. If we had, they'd have been dead.

The strangest thing was the trees. Some of them were shot all the way through. Some were toppled over. All of them were oozing thick white liquid. They seemed to weep.

Best Thing in the World

- Chinese calligraphy done by a master. Even the simplest strokes have a feel that can somehow never be faked, though occasionally you can find something similar in select little corners of children's finger-painting.

- Morel mushrooms found on a spring hike in Indiana, and fried up later with just a little butter.

- Hang gliders. Airplanes don't duplicate the feeling of being a bird - flying a hang glider does. The wind sweeps past your face, and you hear its whisper as you sail effortlessly back and forth held aloft by the updraft created by some hill or cliff that sweeps by a hundred feet beneath you. Be careful though, unlike parachute jumping, it's more dangerous than it looks.

- The town of Pokhara Nepal. It's situated on the shores of a small clear lake beneath Machapuchari, one of loveliest mountains on Earth. Considered holy by the Nepalese, it has never been climbed.

- Amnesty International.

- The solid feel of a good backpack. When I was in Dental School I kept mine packed and hung in the corner of my apartment. Occasionally, while studying late at night, I'd strap it on and stride back and forth. I found it comforting.

- The tomb of Mao Tse Tung in Tianamien Square in Beijing. It gives you the strangest feeling to experience the hushed silence of thousands of reverential Chinese as you file with them past the preserved body of *The Great Helmsman* enclosed in its large glass sarcophagus.

- Ice Cream parlors in Rome.

- Izmir, Turkey. You can sip strong Turkish coffee laced with cardamom at a waterfront café down by the harbor while puffing on a super-sized hookah with a burning ember in the bowl to keep it lit.

- The 12x12 foot plot of grass in the middle courtyard of the American Embassy in Nouakchott, Mauritania. It is probably the largest spot of green in one of the driest countries on Earth.

- French colonial architecture going to seed in the tropics. The stately old abandoned mansions in the midst of the huge Michelin Rubber Plantation in Vietnam come to mind.

- The pubs of Dublin. I once spent a long evening boozily making my way with a local guy from one establishment to another. Wherever we went, people were warm and welcoming to us. Each place had a totally different feel to it. Some had live music, while others were quiet so conversation could reign. Nowhere is talking such an art form as in Ireland. It was daunting to think of all the great novelists and poets who had raved on within those famous walls and vomited on those hallowed floors.

- Seeing the rings of Saturn through a telescope. There's immediacy to seeing it this way that no picture can duplicate. I often travel with a scope just for the pleasure of hearing people say, *wow*!

- Japanese gadgets like taxi cab doors that swing open with a push of a button from the white-gloved driver.

Stage Fright

I'M NOT GOING TO mention the country where this next story occurred. I don't want to hurt any feelings, and besides, it could just as easily have happened in any number of countries twenty-five or thirty years ago.

I was with two friends, Bob and Andrea (now Prabhati), who had driven overland in an ingenious little van that had been fully outfitted by the magazine they worked for as journalists. It had a kitchen, a bathroom, and bunk beds. In those days, even in Europe, it was a real novelty. In this poor country we were traveling through, it caused a stir wherever we stopped. As a result, one of us always had to remain with the vehicle to keep an eye on things.

One day my friends were out looking at a temple, and I had closed the curtains of the van and was about to take a nap. Lobsong, their sweet Alsatian dog, was lying on the floor beside me. The usual crowd began to form outside; I could hear them milling around. But this crowd was bigger and rowdier than most. The talking grew louder. Loud, rude jokes went through the crowd, and then rocks started to hit the roof. Lobsong started barking excitedly. When they started to violently rock the van back and forth, I knew I'd have to take some action to break the mobs momentum. I'd have to do something dramatic.

I gathered my energy for a moment, then burst though the door with as much feigned bravado as I could muster. Lobsong jumped out as well, but it soon became obvious that, though large, he was harmless as a pussycat. I felt that I had to show my utter contempt for these goings on, so I strode directly to the nearest tree, unzipped my fly, pulled out my willy, and prepared to pee. Three hundred pair of eyes were on me. Then something truly terrible happened. I just couldn't urinate. There I stood with my dong in my hand and nothing was happening. It was fifteen seconds before I heard the first titter issue out from the crowd. It started to spread.

From some deep wellspring of will, I was somehow able to force out a small stream of piss. That was good enough. I re-zipped my pants with panache and strode back to the van with maximum bluster.

Thank God, my friends showed up at that moment. We jumped in and made our getaway.

Trouble at Tilicho Pass

DESPITE THE FACT THAT all this took place thirty five years ago, every day of the two beautiful weeks I spent walking the Jomson trek has carved a path in my memory. The trek started in Pokhara, Nepal among terraced fields. On the second day, it climbed up through a dense rhododendron forest and over a vast meadow covering the saddle at Ghorapani. We heard rumors from trekkers passing back at the edge of the forest that the climbing hut near the top of the pass served chapattis and jam.

Several hundred meters of the next day's trail had been carved into the solid stone face of a sheer cliff. Later on the return trip, I napped under its shelter until a brief rainstorm passed. We ended that night at a hut next to a stream that cascaded down through series of tiered, crystal clear pools. Everyone swam in just their skin and lounged together on the rocks.

The little village of Tatopani was the next night's halt. Its name is Nepali for "hot water." Hikers soaked in the hot springs there at the end of the day's walk. As the trail approached the border beyond Mustang, barley fields replaced rice paddies and towns took on a more arid, Tibetan look.

My shoes were gradually disintegrating, but each village had a cobbler who kept me on the road. I walked with several different people over the course of the trek and everything was quite loose. Each night we ate the same rice and dhal, but each night it tasted delicious.

Nearing the end of the trek, I decided to prolong turning back for a couple days by making a side loop up to Tilicho Lake via Tilicho Pass. A German kid I had met at one of the climbing huts agreed to accompany me. The pass, though nothing special by Himalayan standards, was still three thousand feet higher than Mount Blanc, the highest mountain in Europe. Our expedition had one, almost fatal, flaw: we didn't have a tent.

The climb was different from anything we'd seen so far. Even at fairly respectable altitudes in Nepal, there are still fields and villages; but as we ascended to the pass, we left these behind. Up beyond the tree line, the trail became less defined. That day, we ran into only two people: a friendly yak herder and his wife.

We zigzagged steadily up the rocky trail, often moving along ridges. It grew colder, but naturally, we expected that. By the time we reached the top of the pass, it had started to snow. We weren't alarmed. The two of us spent a few minutes eating a little food and gazing down at the cold, dark blue lake that lay in the hollow beneath on the far side of the pass.

Only as we turned to begin our descent did our problem become apparent. The trail we had followed ascended by a series of ridges. Now we noticed that there were *many* ridges and all looked much the same. Our faint trail was being rapidly obliterated by fresh snow and the late afternoon sky that had been so clear during our ascent was beginning to cloud up. A few minutes later, we were totally socked-in by fog. We decided that the main goal was to continue going down. Following that logic, a valley should work as well as a ridge.

Progress was made until we ran into a waterfall and a three-hundred-foot drop. There was no other option: we would have to retrace our steps. At this point we admitted to each other that we had a problem. Night was starting to fall. My hands were going numb with the first signs of frostbite. With considerably more earnestness, we scratched our way on all fours through loose scree, up the steep side of the valley to the adjoining ridge, and restarted our trudge downward. We couldn't afford to make any more mistakes. By now we were fully awake to the real possibility of freezing to death.

Then all at once, miraculously, the clouds parted. We saw a spectacular golden sunset and, five hundred feet below us, the tent of the yak herders we'd met going up. There was a welcoming wisp of smoke curling up from a yak-dung fire. As I re-read this I realize that it sounds like a cliché denouement. Believe me, to us at that moment, it was no cliché; it was a gift from the Formless.

Impeccable Gentlemen

THOUGH IT'S NORMALLY UNINTENTIONAL, I often have bad manners. Gaffes, Faux Pas, inappropriate remarks, bad social timing...? Shit, I wrote the book. As a result, when I meet someone who actually has that kind of sensitivity to others that is the heart and soul of good manners, I'm always taken with them.

It was mid-summer twenty or so years ago. I was hitchhiking in Michigan when I caught a ride with a motorcycle gang (temporarily traveling together in a van). Their arms were covered in tattoos, they may have been missing some teeth, and might not have known exactly which fork to use for the salad course, but they were a kind-hearted bunch. I immediately felt completely at home with them.

We'd be cruising along and one of them might say, "Y'know this interstate is getting boring, let's get off on a local road." Everyone in the van would immediately be in total agreement.

"Yeah Man, let's get off this fuckin' road, it's all looking the same!"

"Yeah, yeah." All would concur.

Forty-five minutes later it would become obvious that they weren't making much progress and that, if they hoped to get to their destination (wherever that might have been), they'd have to get back on the main highway again. Everyone knew it, but the guy who had made the original suggestion would have to be the one to suggest that we get back on the Interstate.

As soon as he did, everybody would heartily agree, "Yeah, yeah."

"Let's make some progress here... let's get back on the Interstate!"

One thing everyone could agree on was "hitting a packy" i.e., making a stop at a package liquor store. When it came time to pay for booze or anything else, these guys were true Marxist-Leninists. It was nothing but "from each according to his abilities, to each according to his needs" for them. And man, could they put it away!

At the end of this jolly lift, I got let off in the center of a very bad section of Detroit. I soon realized this was not a small problem. After an hour of waiting for a ride, a big, rusty, trashed-out sedan stopped fifty yards past me. I jogged up to the car. The window on my side was rolled down. Three very large black men were sitting inside. In the front seat on the passenger side, a guy was shooting up. He literally had the needle in his arm. No one seemed friendly. The driver told me to stow my pack in the trunk. Alarm bells were going off like crazy in my brain. Everything smelled like trouble. As I got in the back seat, my thoughts were racing frantically.

We took off fast. Feverishly I decided that, if push came to shove, I would appeal to them to take all my money and anything else they wanted, but allow me to keep my driver's license and other documentation. Naturally, I also poured on the charm. We got to the outskirts of Detroit as night was starting to fall. The driver pulled to the side of the road by his exit. Underneath a dark purple sky we silently walked together back to the trunk. He opened it. He handed me my backpack and said, "Be cool man." A moment later I was standing there alone, and he and his two friends were off into the night.

Hard Traveling

THERE ARE FOUR ESTABLISHED North-South routes across the Sahara. (There are no East-West routes.) I've taken three of them. I may never traverse the fourth since I'm over sixty years old now, and Africa seems to be getting more difficult and dangerous every year.[2]

The most difficult of the routes originates in Gao at the northern-most bend of the Niger River and terminates at a point west of Algiers in northern Algeria. I was traveling this route with a dear French guy named Fontaine Gerard. Sadly, I've lost track of him over the years. He was a great friend and a true adventurer.

Massive trucks, loaded with sheep for the sub-Saharan markets, come down from Algeria. Returning home, they were mostly empty, leaving them room to take paying passengers. My advice to anyone crossing the Sahara is to check out your vehicle carefully before you start. We got a lemon.

It was midsummer, and it doesn't get much hotter than the Sahara in midsummer — close to 140 degrees. Our truck broke down at least once every day. One time the transmission was causing problems and the mechanic had to take it apart. I swear this is the truth. He diagnosed the problem, cut a metal piece from a tin can using a sharp knife, and placed it in the appropriate place. Then he closed the whole thing up, and we drove off.

---

[2] If you ever want a terrific geography lesson, buy the three large Michelin maps of Africa. Together they form one great map of the continent. Trust me on this. Fit them together, then step back and prepare to be shocked.

Several times a day our wheels would get lodged in the sand. The crew would dig them out and place heavy strips of perforated steel plating called "sand ladders" in front of the rear wheels. The driver would race the engine and we'd roar ahead for a hundred meters, or until we got on firm footing again. It was slow going.

Fontaine spoke only French, but he was endlessly patient with me. My French was limited and we had no dictionary; but, as we rested under the shade of the truck during breakdowns, he would draw pictures in the sand until I understood what he was trying to get across to me.

We drank tremendous quantities of liquid. Water was carried on the side of the truck in sacks made from skins of sheep. The hair was left on and all six holes (the four legs, the head, and the ass) were tied off with thin leather straps. We collected this water at the oasis waterholes where the camels shit. Its color was reminiscent of a good cup of café au lait you might be served in some snazzy place along the Champs Elysees.

One night we had exhausted our water supply and the truck was broken down again. We went to bed thirsty— desperately thirsty. I'd gone to bed hungry before, but trying to sleep while thirsty was another sensation altogether.

Sometime very early in the morning the crew spotted lights coming towards us. I woke my friends and together we were able to wave the truck down. We had to use a piece of cloth to filter the grit from the water they gave us. I don't believe anything will ever taste so sweet.

Hyperinflation:
A Lesson in Economics

Ten years ago I was in Rio for Carnival. The best place to experience carnival in Brazil is Belem, not Rio. I didn't know that at the time. Believe me though, Rio puts on a good show as well.

Brazil was suffering from hyperinflation at the time, forty to fifty percent a day! People would line up in the late afternoon at the banks to make their transactions so as not to lose value overnight. Everyone who could (in other words, the rich) dealt only in dollars.

Shortly after I got to Rio, I found myself confused by the money in my pockets. Some of the bills had large numbers on them and appeared to be worth very little. Others had small numbers on them, but you could actually buy substantial things with them. They came in various colors and differing sizes.

In bewilderment I went to the tourist office, pulled all the bills out of my pocket, and laid them on the counter. A helpful middle-aged lady who worked there segregated these confusing slips of paper into various piles.

"*This*," she said brightly, as she pointed to a group of notes, "is the old money." Indicating a second stack, she continued, "*This* pile is the new money." Then she flashed a grin and pointed to the final pile. "And *this*, is the brand-new money."

Being in Rio at the time of the carnival, the anthropologist in me naturally wanted to go to the wildest possible party, which I'd heard was put on by the local soccer club. Brazil didn't fail me that night. There were three competing bands simultaneously blaring out samba on three separate floors and the alcohol was all free. It was a total madhouse; lewd and outrageously silly behavior was going on everywhere you looked. There were drunken photographers there as well. The bigger the cameraman's lens, the lewder and sillier the pictures he got.

My fellow revelers and I actually started to begin to move as one, following the laws of some cockamammy ameba-like mob-logic. We started flowing through the whole place like a great river of hilarious, bawdy, drunken humanity. As I stumbled about helplessly, this river of nuttiness took me where it felt like taking me. Every couple of hours I'd stream past a South African bloke I knew. He'd walked here with me from the hostel where we were both staying. We'd shout something inane to each other, laugh our asses off, and then flow right on past each other like two pieces of besotted flotsam. I vow here and now that I'll never put my liver through anything like that night again.

When the sun came up on another beautiful balmy day in paradise, I found myself wearily trudging back to my hotel, totally hung-over, completely exhausted, and dead busted. As I schlepped down the street I passed a long-haired, raggedly dressed man on the sidewalk with a spoon in his hand. He was attempting to scrape what he could from an empty garbage can. He was not begging. I had no money on me whatsoever. This was too much. No one should be reduced to this. I spotted a large silver coin on the street in front of me and picked it up. I gestured to the man something to the effect of "don't know what its worth, but maybe it'll help." I handed him the coin, which as I've mentioned, was weighty and substantial. He took it, gazed at it briefly, then tossed it over his shoulder and, without reproach to me, got back to the garbage can.

Birdlife

I WAS IN GOA recovering from a relapse of Malaria. In the periods between fevers, I felt weak but tranquil. Two local dogs, Moti and Tyson, kept me company. I spent many pleasant afternoons in the feathery shade of coconut palms on the roof of my guesthouse. I read a lot, but most of my time was spent quietly observing the details of life going on around me.

For several days I had been watching a family of parrots who had made their home in the trunk of a dead palm tree in the garden. Periodically, the mother would fly off to capture insects for her young. Upon her return, the fluffy babies would poke their little heads out and squawk for attention and food.

Then one day while she was gone, two sinister looking woodpeckers, sleek as fighter jets, flew up and lit on the side of the tree trunk. Both knew exactly what they were there for. They quickly ascended the trunk, peeked into the hole, stabbed the chicks to death with their sharp beaks, and gorged themselves. It happened so quickly and unexpectedly, I didn't think to stop it. I knew it was just the balance of nature and no doubt part of the big picture, but a terrible repugnance arose within me anyway.

The woodpeckers left as swiftly as they'd come. A few minutes later, the female parrot returned and looked into the hole. I don't want to anthropomorphize, but I'll describe what I saw. After seeing what there was to see, she lit on a twig just above her home. Her whole body was motionless. No sound came from her. She just sat there. For two hours I watched her as she grieved.

When I returned a couple hours later, she was still there, still immobile, but now a few inches higher on the next branch. She remained there for the rest of the day. Next morning she was gone.

Best Things in the World

- I remember the first time I Located Orion's Nebulae through my telescope. I was in the holy city of Rishikesh. Millions of light years across space, I could see where stars were being formed from coalescing clouds of gas.

- Listening to the music of Leonard Cohen when I'm feeling down.

- The Manhattan skyline at night. To my mind it's the most awe inspiring creation of humankind.

- Putting my ear to the sand of a beach and hearing the squeaking sound of people's footsteps. Only a few beaches have this curious quality.

- Each morning in Bali the women put out beautiful, tiny baskets woven from leaves with small offerings of rice and flowers in front of their doorways. Everyone here seems to be an artist. Sometimes they don't recognize it as such though. As someone from this little island once said, "We don't have art, we just do everything as well as we can."

- Chicken swarma served hot and juicy on the streets of Damascus.

- The feeling you get when a great writer describes a feeling or experience that you have had, but couldn't find the words for. The work of Saul Bellow comes to mind. In response to a letter I once wrote him he sent me a postcard which I cherish.

- A photo in The Albanian National Museum in Tirana showing the first boat leaving the country for Italy after the fall of communism.

Every square inch of the deck was covered with refugees. The rigging was thick with more people. There were dozens more in the water, swimming to the boat; still others were making their way hand-over-hand on the line attached to the wharf. It was a testament to the human passion for freedom.

- When you're recovering from an illness and have regained enough strength to sit outside in the sun and read a book.

- The poem, "The Panther" by Rilke.

- Gaudi's masterpiece, the Cathedral of the Sacred Family in Barcelona. The interior space was like nothing I'd ever seen before. It truly felt organic, like the chambers of the human heart. The outside was adorned with curios features like carved snails the size of living room furniture.

- Setting off on my own with nothing but a pack on my back on my first trip around the world without schedules or itineraries. An open life lay before me.

- Enchanting gamelan music played at a Balinese shadow puppet show that lasted late into the evening. I wandered up front, peeked behind the curtain and watched the puppeteers' art. Children in the audience tittered and there was the smell of clove cigarettes in the air.

- I've heard it said that even those who write books on humility never fail to put their name on the cover. The little book I was given after receiving the Gyan is an exception. Simply, clearly and succinctly it lays out everything you need to know about the mission. I carry it with me always.

- Being in the delivery room when my children were born.

- Nirankaris' eyes when they are talking about the *Gyan*.

S and M in NYC

MANY YEARS AGO, I was stuck in a tiny hotel room in New York City with time on my hands. Somehow I had heard of a place called The S and M Theater. I always try to keep an open mind on all subjects, so with considerable trepidation, I resolved to go and check out this little corner of the world.

Arriving early, I slumped down in my seat and tried to keep a low profile. There were about a hundred people in the audience. By New York standards, everyone looked fairly normal. The curtain came up, and for the next hour or so we were treated to about a half dozen little skits put on by amateur actors using guns, whips, and whatnot. They dripped hot candle wax on one person and penetrated another with the barrel end of a toy pistol. But it was all for show; nobody seemed to be getting hurt.

As the final act took their bows to polite applause, an amiable Master of Ceremonies (who looked like a middle-manager in a small town bank) walked out on stage. Several members of "the community" joined him. He thanked us for coming, made a couple of jokes, then asked if anyone in the audience needed spanking. A short, middle-aged, balding fellow in a conservative brown suit bounded up to the stage. He bent over, dropped his pants, and got smacked on the bottom a couple of times by a good-looking dominatrix dressed in the classic manner— black leather, spiked heels. It takes a certain kind of courage for a guy to do something like that. We all gave him a heartfelt, solid round of applause as he walked back to his seat.

Not long afterwards, things started breaking up, though a few people seemed to be lingering. Without making much eye contact, I quietly slipped out the door and back to my hotel.

Sous Les Ponts De Paris

THE FIRST TIME MY brother Richard and I went to Europe we didn't have much money so we scrimped on a lot. At one point, we realized we'd gone a month without sleeping in a bed or under a tent. Not that I'm complaining— I've rarely been so happy.

My frugal brother (he's a millionaire now) didn't even want to waste cash on luxuries like a sleeping bag. When it came time to sleep, Richard would don every stitch of clothing he was carrying in his pack, including his three-piece suit. Then he would roll up in his military poncho and bed down for the night.

Our favorite sleeping spot in "The City of Man" was under the Pont Neuf, the ancient bridge that connects l'Isle de la Cite and the Rive Gauche. No billionaire ever had a more magnificent view. Notre Dame, one of the most beautiful things made by the hand of man, loomed above us. The lights of Paris, mirrored on the surface of the Seine, glittered before us. There were perhaps a hundred souls sharing this magnificent campsite. About half of them—decked out in love beads, tie-dyed shirts, and long hair— could have been mistaken for hippies. The other half were authentic French tramps.

A beautiful thing about that time was that every night, wherever you were, guitars and flutes would emerge and we would all sing together. Everyone knew the words to all the songs back then. People don't sing as much now. My Parisian friends tell me that these days no one is allowed to sleep under the bridges. An evening like that will never happen again.

Sometime past midnight we took the precaution of chaining our bicycles to our bodies, and then drifted off to sleep. Shortly after dawn the next morning, "les flics" gently awoke us to check our documentation. French cops of that era never questioned our right to be there.

Now It Is Clean

MANY YEARS AGO, THERE was a truck passage between Sidi Ifni, in southern Morocco, and Aiuun, the capital of what was then Spanish Sahara. It's a magnificent stretch of desert and contains all of what is most beautiful in the Sahara. I was traveling with a young American guy at the time. We caught a ride on a large, comically overloaded truck. Burlap sacks of goods were packed precariously four or five feet above the top of the truck cab and then tied down with canvas and ropes. All dozen or so passengers rode on top of this. It gave us a terrific view and was comfortable, too. Our fellow travelers were various Africans, including an elegant gentleman from Mauritania.

At the time, the Moroccan government had envisioned building a road that would pass down our route, covering it in tarmac. We could already see the surveying sticks. Our driver didn't approve. At one stop, he dug up one of the sticks and cast it down the hill saying, "Maintenant c'est propre," meaning, "now it is clean."

The images of that desert passage are still very clear in my mind's eye. I remember jumping off the tops of perfect sand dunes. I remember a salt lake twenty miles across. The air was so clear you could see for hundred miles in any direction. And not another soul was out there.

On the first day there was an open crate of groceries riding on top with us. The contents included stunted vegetables and some highly questionable pieces of meat. Everything was covered in dust. They were to be our dinner. That evening, our cook turned these unpromising ingredients into one of the tastiest tajines I've ever eaten. That night we slept out under the stars without a single man-made light to be seen.

By the second day we were getting beyond any vegetation, so in the morning, the crew gathered what little firewood they could find and strapped it on top to be used later. In the late afternoon we halted again. The sticks were thrown down and a small bonfire was built. The glowing coals from this were placed in a fire pit that had been scooped out of the sand. Then the Mauritanian gentleman took charge. He arranged small glasses around the fire in a precise circle.

We all sat silently before our glasses, watching him intently. The tea was brewed in a large metal kettle, possibly one of his few belongings. There was impeccability to this man and great refinement. His bearing was confident and noble. He wore the light blue, long, loose- fitting shirt, characteristic of Mauritanian tribesmen. On the pocket was elaborate embroidery stitched in white thread. I'm guessing that it identified him as the member of a particular tribe or family. He may have had a net worth of a hundred dollars.

A tea ceremony, though they might not call it that, is an art-form in that part of the world. Three glasses are served to each person. One very strong, one very hot, one very sweet (don't ask me in which order). In the middle of this vast, empty space, an intimacy was created. Each glass was served to the right temperature by lifting the large kettle up and down as it was being poured into each tiny vessel. Not a drop was spilt.

Early on our third day, we were about to cross over the border into what was then Spanish Sahara. Spain had a tough, no-nonsense drug policy (five years, no appeals) at the time. Just before crossing into Spanish territory, I regretfully pitched a piece of hash as big as my hand into the sand.

The border town had, at most, a hundred inhabitants. All the houses were made of packing materials. We're not talking about nice wooden crates here, these were cardboard. While the truck was going through customs, we crawled into one of the huts to get out of the sun. The only decoration inside was a small respectfully-placed picture of John Kennedy. You'll find no iconic pictures of George Bush in third-world shacks.

Advice to Travelers: Teach Me a Song

WHEN YOU MEET A foreigner who is traveling in your country, don't ask them where they are from, how long they have been in your country, or how they like your country. That's exactly what everyone asks. After a while, you can't help but be bored by the ensuing conversation.

I was once on a ship bound for Jakarta with a marvelous American woman named Dee Dekew. She short-circuited one of these conversations by asking the person we were talking with to teach us an Indonesian song. Then we taught him a song. It turned into a lovely experience, and it taught me something as well.

There are all kinds of ways of breaking out of conventional conversations when you're traveling. You can ask the person next to you to teach you a few simple words in their language: yes, no, thank you, please, beautiful, etc.

If you happen to be in a Muslim country, ask the person you're talking with to tell you a Mullah Nasrudin joke. Everybody knows a few. Supposedly, if you really get the joke, you become enlightened. I only remember one Mullah Nasrudin joke.

A man with his hands behind his back once asked the Mullah to guess what he was holding.

"Can you give me a hint?" asked the Mullah.

"Yes, I'll give you several hints," replied the man. "The object I am holding is currently liquid and has a shell. The liquid center becomes hardened when boiled. Inside the shell there is a yellowish center surrounded by clear liquid. Furthermore, it is the size of an egg, and is egg shaped. Now can you guess what it is?"

The Mullah pondered this information for a few moments. Then he answered, "Is it perhaps a small cake?"

Scattered Memories of Vietnam

I REMEMBER ONE NIGHT when we were camped out in a little firebase and were warned by Intelligence that an attack was imminent (Most of us were new in-country and we hadn't yet learned that these warnings were invariably wrong). Everyone began jabbering half-maniacally about the craziest subjects. Unconsciously, we must have been searching for something we had in common with each other, looking for some bond. I got into an intense conversation with one guy about newspaper routes (we'd both been paperboys). Somehow it seemed wonderful to remember that the Saturday paper was always small and easy to roll. Monday was slightly larger and the paper grew each succeeding day culminating in a very large Friday paper (neither of our companies published on Sundays). After our first experience of combat together we didn't need anything in particular to bind us; we got *real tight, real fast.*

Racial tensions definitely existed in Vietnam. They were much worse in the base camps, but out in the field at the platoon level, there was a feeling of brotherhood between blacks, whites, and Hispanics that I had never experienced before. It helped that we were away from the big bases— they were another world. It was sad to return to the States and see all the racial discord. Having experienced a time when race didn't matter though, we knew it was possible.

I remember the unholy sound that went up from dozens of throats when the truck full of trash that I was disposing of entered the dump outside Black Horse. A small town had grown up on the periphery of the trash heap. The residents lived in scrap houses made of dismantled cans. They existed entirely on what we discarded. When I visited

Vietnam twenty years later, there were still people near Khe Sanh whose main source of income was salvaging scrap metal from abandoned jeeps and tanks. In front of each village, rusty piles of steel were stacked alongside the road for pickup.

Our abandoned "deuce and a half" trucks had survived remarkably well. Twenty-five years later, I saw them still in service everywhere. The radiators had invariably given out, but the ever-inventive Vietnamese had rigged the trucks up with hundred-and-fifty-gallon water tanks mounted on top of the cabs. The water would slowly drip from these down through the cooling system, eventually emptying out on the road. At petrol stations trucks would fill up on both gas and water.

I first encountered incoming rounds at a base camp nicknamed "rocket city." I was awakened in the middle of the night by the sound and sight of mortar rounds exploding all around us; they were sort of like fireworks actually. I quickly scurried down a tunnel that led to an underground bomb shelter that had been dug out directly under the hooch where we'd been sleeping. I remember being surprised that the sound of incoming rounds was just like in the movies. There was the same kind of whistling sound that declined in pitch and ended with the sound of impact. Most of the guys were pretty cavalier about the whole thing. But from time to time we'd hear something coming close and that would shut everyone up for a minute. I think it's always a shock in any war to realize that there are people you don't even know who are trying to kill you. But then, we were sent there to kill people we didn't know either.

After our unit experienced combat for the first time something happened that I shouldn't lie about. Every one of us felt the most incredible exhilaration; someone who hasn't been there may find it difficult to imagine this. Let me say it as simply as I can. The problem is not that war is so terrible. If that were the case it would be easy enough to quit. The problem is that we love it too much. The best men fought the elation or maybe tried to deny it. Those with great inner fear or frustrations just let go to it. Given a chance, they did terrible things. A soldier needs to know clearly what is *not* allowed.

I remember a beautiful young girl who told us her name meant "tomorrow." I remember (or think I remember) a tennis shoe blown off by a mine with a foot still inside. Perhaps I just read it. A brilliant young man I knew went to Vietnam as a helicopter pilot. He had a lovely young wife waiting for him at home. He saw a lot of combat, and got a lot of medals. He wasn't unstable or fanatic. He died over there one night playing Russian Roulette.

I've always been fascinated with insects. The guys in my unit soon discovered my interest. Often I'd return to my tent to find some peculiar creature, rich in structures, lying on my cot. I stored my curious collection in metal ammo-boxes with tissue paper and desiccant. Then came the rainy season, and despite all of my precautions, the mildew soon reduced everything to moldy dust.

When I was there in 1969, things were still barely holding together, at least out in the field. It was different for the "base camp warriors" back in Ben Hoi and Long Binh. Insubordination was rife. I remember seeing tents with "Lifers Stay Out" signs. Blacks, whites, and Hispanics were at each others' throats. A lot of people were taking heroin. On the armed forces radio station the song, "Ruby," was played incessantly. If you don't remember the lyrics, they had to do with a GI who had lost his limbs in the war. His wife was going out on the town. In classic country and western style the singer wailed plaintively, "Oh Ruuuuuby, don't take your love to town." Somebody thought that was funny and the officer in charge apparently couldn't or wouldn't stop it.

A year or so later I heard through friends that things were falling apart out in the boonies as well. A buddy of mine told me that he would take his infantry platoon a few hundred meters outside the perimeter then settle down for a few days of smoking joints while occasionally calling in fake coordinates to the company commander. Higher officers who didn't like it stood a good chance of being fragged. The Major over my friend will never know how close he came to being off-ed. By that time almost everyone outside of Washington knew the war was lost.

Get Out

NOT TEN MINUTES AGO, there had been three of us together in human communion, sitting shoulder-to-shoulder, conversing amiably. The plane hadn't landed, but now those people weren't here. Now there was just me and my instructor. I knew why, but it was still giving me the strangest feeling.

I was in Indiana two thousand feet above the Earth sitting in the open door of a single engine Cessna with the air whipping past me at 100 mph. For some inexplicable reason, I was going through the motions I'd been taught and preparing to jump out of a perfectly good airplane. As I sat there my body was fighting against instincts which had served it well for thirty years.

Over the din of the motor I heard the instructor yell, "Get Out!" Obedient as a trained seal, I thrust my arm outside to grasp the handle mounted behind the wing... and stepped out. My body was violently flapping up and down like a rag doll in a hurricane above all that vast emptiness. I hung on desperately. I knew what was coming next. I heard the word, "Go!" I released my grip...

Yucking it up in the World's Saddest Country

TWENTY YEARS AGO I remember spicing up a long train trip in Egypt by amusing the locals on the way to Luxor with jokes from a "bag of tricks" I'd brought along with me. Inside the bag were all kinds of zany gags like squirting lapel flowers and hand buzzers— real third world ice-breakers as it turned out. I only wish I'd brought along a whoopee cushion.

Recently I heard of a book written about human happiness that claimed that, according to self-descriptive polls, the citizens of Moldova were "the saddest people in the world"[3] (Icelanders were the happiest, incidentally). It put me to thinking that it might be fun to go to Moldova with my cinematographer buddy, Matt, and shoot a video (perhaps with a band) with a suitcase full of wacky gags to see if it would cheer people up. With that idea in mind I set off for this supposedly dour land on a reconnaissance mission.

---

[3] Moldovans are apparently often searching for ways to leave the motherland. In the 2000 annual world underwater hockey championship (Trust me it exists. They have an official magazine, "Neptune," where terms like "squids" and "cuttles" are bandied about for cognoscenti of the sport) the referees began to be suspicious when the Moldovan team didn't seem to know how to put on their fins and flippers. The hapless Moldovan team then went on to be trounced, not only by the world renowned Columbian underwater hockey team (30-0), but even the less highly regarded Argentinians (23-0). The mystery was solved when it was revealed that the entire team had applied for (and eventually received) refugee status with the Australian government. As if this were not enough of a set-back to the world of Moldovan underwater hockey, a women's' team used the same ruse (again successfully) next year in Canada.

The fifteen hour overnight bus trip from Lviv to Chisinau got me into the spirit of things. The driver's non-stop, full blast, Ukrainian disco music left me sleepless. By morning my thoughts were alternatively homicidal and suicidal.

When we got to the frontier, the Moldovan border guard eyed me suspiciously. We spoke in broken French, our only shared language. Why so many stamps in my passport? Why hadn't I flown, etc.? In the end he abruptly ordered me back on the bus, which I correctly concluded meant I was in. Thank God he didn't check my baggage, as along with some beautifully hand-painted Easter eggs, it contained two surplus Soviet Army gas masks I'd bought as a joke for friends back home. That would have been proof positive that I had some nefarious scheme up my sleeve— just as he'd suspected.

When I got to Chisinau, the capital city, I checked into a big, ugly, soviet-style hotel with a red star on the roof, went up to my room, flopped on the bed, and immediately fell into a deep dreamless sleep.

Next day, bright and early, I began my search for the Moldovan soul. My plan was to find a guide, and then together we'd take a random bus out into the countryside and stop off in some little town that looked promising. We could maybe hire a horse-cart from there, hopefully driven by some grizzled old farmer with a face like a codfish— somebody who'd been beaten-down by cheap booze and had his hopes crushed by a tyrant of a wife and ruined harvests caused by locusts and potato rot. His farting, nose-picking children would be languishing at home. They probably had dreams of becoming cruel, cunning gangsters in Chisinau as soon as they got older and bigger. We'd meet them soon enough.

I'd spent the day noodling around the city, getting a feel for the place, and was sitting in a nice restaurant where I'd ordered trout with caviar sauce, when my guide Roma showed up. He was a good-looking young man, happy and full of life. He didn't seem like the type who'd be into searching out broken down horse-carts and drunken peasants. Bob's your uncle, I switched plans. Why not hit some cool dance clubs instead. That sounded *great* to him, so an hour and a half later he and his girlfriend showed up at my door. Her name was Tanya. We only shared a bit of Spanish as a mutually understood language, so communication was pretty limited, but she had a smile that would have melted the heart of Kafka or put a goofy grin on the face of Jean Paul Sartre. We hopped in their car and were off like a shot. Down the street a couple of blocks, we passed a billboard advertising gasoline. "That's Tanya," Roma shouted excitedly. Sure enough, there she was, standing next to a fuel pump and wearing some kind of gas attendant's uniform, giving us a thumbs up. "She's a singer, too," he said proudly, popping a cassette into the car stereo. I'm no connoisseur of pop music, and I don't want to sound churlish, but the song, "I Want to Hug You" probably wasn't going to be put up for a Grammy any time soon. This lovely young woman, her sweet voice and sincere delivery, deserved a better vehicle than this song.

It was a weeknight, so not too much was shaking in most of Chisinau's hot spots. But at about one o'clock, we hit on a place called "Dance Paradise" or something like that. This was the real thing with lots of thuggish doormen at the entrance shaking everybody down with metal detecting wands, making sure nobody made it into the club with heat on them. Inside, the dance-floor was thick with world-class women, all shaking their booty in micro-mini, skin-tight dresses and stiletto-heeled boots with toes so pointy you could pick your teeth with them. I was easily twice the age of the oldest person there and unlikely to be mistaken for anybody cool, but as in so many situations, being a foreigner you get cut a lot of slack. The women were amazing, but luckily the guys couldn't dance worth squat, so after putting down couple of glasses of a tasty concoction called "Sex on the Beach" I began to think I was coming off looking pretty good out there doing my own personal versions of the watussi, the mashed potato, the strut, and the funky chicken.

I made a big point of not appearing to hit on any of the women. They all had *really* big boyfriends who looked like they could hurt you. Where was all the money these guys were throwing around coming from? The answer was, you don't wanna know.

I suppose, on average, Moldavians probably are a little sad, but "on average" can sometimes be a misleading way to look at things. "On average," each person also had one ovary and one testicle.

I came to Moldova expecting to find a country of vodka drinking wife beaters and sullen babushkas, but what's the use of traveling if you've already decided what you're going to see.

Maybe I just fell in with the wrong crowd. What I saw was a country where the parks were full of passionate young lovers, and even the near-toothless old women who sold carnations on the street often seemed to have a wry sense of humor. There may have been sad people, but not *everybody* was morose. I also couldn't help noticing that the blind, old accordion player on the corner received a small coin from about every fourth person who passed him. Moldavians may be sad, but they are also kind.

Two Way Street

AT THE MEMORIAL SERVICE for Jules Hendricks, a long-time friend of his stood up and said, "In the forty years I knew Jules I never heard him say a single bad word about another person." Everyone is made of flesh and bones, and no one gets through life without making mistakes, but every once in a while, you meet someone who shows just what flesh and bones are capable of. Jules was a great intellect, though far too modest to ever put on airs. He worked for the O.S.S. in Austria after the Second World War before marrying his partner through life, Lois Armstrong. I was blessed with the chance to spend time by her bed talking to this wonderful woman as she neared the end of her life (endearingly she still enjoyed a little sip of a martini and would occasionally slip off her respirator for a moment so as to get just the tiniest whiff of a *Lucky Strike*). What a laugh she had. How I loved her.

He'd done everything in life about as well as could be done, but the final, greatest challenge for Jules was Parkinson's disease. He fought it in every possible way, but inevitably it began to overcome him. As he started to falter I once asked him how he felt about it. He smiled gently, looked off into the middle distance, and sweetly replied, "At peace." As the months passed his hands began to twitch uncontrollably and his marvelous mind began to slip away. He was losing control of his bodily functions. Eventually his behavior became erratic and dangerous to the extent that Lois reluctantly decided he would have to be moved to a retirement home where he would have round-the-clock medical support. She visited him there every day. She lovingly covered his room with photographs of friends and family.

The last time I saw Jules alive was in that room. When I entered, he didn't seem to recognize me. I had brought along some recent pictures of my children and as I showed them to him, I described what they showed and what the kids were doing. His eyes had a glazed far away look. His head jerked back and forth uncontrollably. He uttered incoherent sounds. "Baaaaaaa, Gaaaaaaaaaa." This went on for about twenty minutes, and then it was time for me to leave.

With tears running down my face I choked out, "Jules, I just want to tell you that knowing you has been one of the great experiences of my life."

He turned his head toward me and said, "GaaaaaaaaaBaaaWaaGaa two way street."

I Remember

I REMEMBER MY GRANDFATHER had an immense pile of lumber at his farm which he had salvaged from a barn he had torn down. Over the course of his life, he was always working on some carpentry project (a bobsled, a swing set, a feeding stall) and he gradually used the lumber for these projects. He once told me that he expected the pile to last his lifetime. I was out of the country when he died. Shortly after I returned I drove down to the farm and walked the land which was filled with so many happy childhood memories. I walked down to the once mighty pile of lumber. Only half-a-dozen boards remained.

I remember watching Rick Owens catch a four-pound fish in the Nile using a string and a safety pin baited with a bread crumb.

I remember talking one afternoon to Dr. Gabor, a music professor and a friend. A noisy lawn mower was running down the street. I told him that I'd heard that most lawn mowers run at B flat. He perked up his ears, listened for a moment then quickly replied, "No, C sharp." With that he pulled me into the living room of his house where a piano sat. He hit C sharp and damned if he wasn't right.

I remember visiting a beautiful little island a mile or two off of Dakar in the country of Senegal. There was a fortress there where slaves had been kept while awaiting transport to the New World. A local man standing outside the prison offered to serve as my guide. He took me from one dark room to the next explaining in great detail what had happened in each of them. It was unspeakable. Those who died were chucked out the back into the sea for the tides to carry away.

I remember trying to convince the Australian cops that I was Canadian rather than American. They were evacuating Darwin as quickly as possible after Cyclone Tracy and had gotten wind that I had been working illegally. For the two years previous to this, I hadn't told a single lie. In the next thirty minutes, I had to tell about fifty in rapid succession. I stashed my passport and other documentation in my crotch— the one place they didn't pat me down— and told them I had left it in Canberra at the Japanese Embassy. I tried to dredge up all the information about Canada I could remember, including what province Winnipeg (supposedly my hometown) was in. Almost all communication was down due to the cyclone. I was gambling on the fact that they wouldn't be able to get through to the embassy to check my story. I squeaked through and caught my plane to Sydney.

I remember sitting on the edge of a high cliff in India staring off into the bright haze that lay above the great flat plain below. When the wind shifted and I could barely make out the sound of the mighty city just beyond the horizon. It throbbed and beat like a human heart.

The Tower of Gao

IT WAS EARLY SUMMER. I was in Gao, a river town in the country of
Mali just south of the Sahara. Anne Marie and I were splitting up. She
was French Canadian. We'd traveled together for a couple of weeks.
My French buddy, Fontaine, and I were heading north from here across
the desert. We'd already bargained for our passage with a truck driver
and were due to set out early the next morning. Anne Marie had
another agenda, so our ways were parting. I wouldn't hear from her
again for three years. I was in dental school when I received a nice poem
from her about Africa. At least I think it was nice. Her handwriting
was sort of artistically creative, you might say. Also, my French wasn't
too hot, so I never quite got it translated, but it had the refrain, "Oh
Africa." Or at least I think that's what those two scribbled lines meant.
Anyway, it looked cool on my bulletin board for one of the two years I
spent beavering away, futilely trying to learn a trade.

We'd heard stories about the great tower at Gao, hundreds of years
old and fashioned from clay, with palm wood beams protruding out
from it. It was far and away the highest thing in the city, many stories
tall, and shaped like a great cylinder, tapering gradually at the top.
There is an outside spiral staircase that leads up from the base. Seen
from directly above, it must look like a giant seashell. It's an amazing
sight.

It was early evening when we arrived. A small crowd of local people
was milling about the bottom. We talked with them for a while.
Everyone seemed to think that it was a bad idea to climb the tower after
dark, with the bad spirits and all. I wasn't put off. With a bit of forced

bravado, I declared that I didn't believe in this stuff and was going up anyway. A little reluctantly, Anne Marie agreed to go with me.

At this, one of the young fellows in the crowd said he'd come too. By the time we actually started, several more had decided to come along. The higher we got, the more people joined in. It began to take on the feel of a party. We started to run. We reached the top of the tower, laughing and out of breath. Looking to the north, we could see across the scattered lights of this African city, and in the distance beyond that, the vast darkness of the Sahara.

Cyclone Tracy

IT WAS CHRISTMAS EVE and I'd caught a ride up to Darwin from a mine in the Northern Territories of Australia where I was working. I had some friends who were living communally in a big old house there, and I was looking forward to spending the holidays with them.

It was early evening when I arrived. Everyone welcomed me in. A stiff wind was blowing outside, but inside, all was cozy and secure. There were cyclone warnings on the radio, but we didn't give them too much credence. Two weeks before, there had been warnings as well and nothing much had come of it. Just before I settled down to sleep, in addition to the wind, I heard the sound of metal garbage cans tumbling down the street.

Around two in the morning, I was shocked into wakefulness by the large double doors of the living room crashing open. The fantastic pounding of the storm that had been outside was now inside as well. We all leapt out of bed and ran downstairs in varying degrees of disarray. There were about twenty of us, including one beautifully naked young lady.

Luckily, there was a technically-minded German among us and he took charge. We managed to get the doors shut, and soon heavy boards were braced across the door and hammered into place. As the storm grew stronger, our barricade began to look insufficient. We had to brace the door with our bodies against the tremendous onslaught of the wind. The house was built on heavy steel poles and elevated two feet above the ground; but despite the heavy steel girders, it swayed with each renewed gust. Several times as we strained against it, the door pushed us back, bowing like something in a cartoon windstorm.

70

And it kept getting worse. Next thing the radio station went out; the transmission towers were blown away.

As we struggled with the door, I looked at the German guy and, over the sound of the howling wind, shouted a stupid question: "What's going to happen?"

Reasonably enough he yelled back, "I don't know."

Eventually, almost imperceptibly at first, the storm started to abate. A few minutes more, we figured, and we could quit leaning against the door. The eye of the storm passed, and then the second side hit, but with a softer blow. At one point, I peeked out through a keyhole and saw the trees outside bent parallel to the ground, quivering.

Next morning, the sun rose in a clear blue sky and we awoke to an unbelievable landscape. It had been the worst cyclone in the history of Australia. A city of fifty thousand people had been blown away. But Aussies are a hardy lot. Though many had lost almost everything they owned, they were cheerful. Joking and swapping stories. Just happy to be alive.

Walking the rubble-filled streets that morning, I don't remember seeing a single house in town more intact then ours. Bless the carpenter who built it. Most of the houses had been flimsy prefabs of one type or another. "Scattered like a deck of cards" was the simile that kept coming to mind. As I walked further into the city, I distinctly remember seeing someone's refrigerator sitting on top the water tower.

The Worst Thing I Ever Did

WHEN I STARTED TO write this book, I made up my mind to be as truthful as I was capable of. Being truthful isn't the same thing as saying everything. I'm not going to tell what the worst thing I ever did was because it's none of your business and it wouldn't do you, or me, or anyone else any good. Nonetheless, I know it, one other soul knows it, and obviously God is not mocked. I went for about fifteen years with the burden of it. I couldn't let it go and I couldn't forgive myself. "By chance" I ran into the person I'd harmed and told them how badly I felt about what I'd done.

"Oh," they replied, "I never held it against you; I always understood the situation you were in. That's why you did it."

Best Things in the World

- Driving across the Bonneville Salt Flats in a rented car at high speed with my eyes closed.

- The annual "joke night" on the radio program, "A Prairie Home Companion."

- Hyrax. Rick Owens and I found these furry, little burrowing creatures resembling small ground hogs living in the grassy meadows above the tree line on Mt. Kenya. We learned later that their nearest surviving relatives are elephants.

- Shaherazaad, the beautiful little dark-eyed Kashmiri girl who accompanied my six-year-old son on a fishing trip in her canoe. They were about the same age. Jacques was squeamish about baiting his hook, so she sweetly did it for him. When a light drizzle started to come down, she plucked a lily pad from the lake and placed it on her head for a rain hat.

- The early novels of Saul Bellow, especially "The Adventures of Augie March."

- Australian drinking songs. "The Good Ship Venus" is my favorite.

- The Villacambamba Valley in Ecuador. It has rich soil, a near perfect climate, sensual rolling hills, and the sweetest water I've ever tasted. It's slightly too expensive to make my list of $500 paradises, but if you've got $700/ month, I'd recommend it.

- Isfahan, Iran from the air. From the plane I could see the magnificent central square entirely framed by mosques. I was checking it out on *Google earth* a couple of months ago when I came across something quite intriguing. Outside the city, near the airport, is a very large circular configuration. My first thought was that it might be some sort of nuclear installation. Check it out yourself and see what you think. Type in "Natranz Iran" and the program will zoom in to the nuclear facility there. You can make out piles of earth brought up from tunnels that have been excavated.

- Tools and brushes that feel good in your hand.

- Sundays in Tiananmen Square in Beijing. On a bright and windy spring day you'll see people flying every conceivable kind of kite. There are hundred-foot-long dragon kites and kites that flutter like swallows. You can see grandparents assembling simple little kites for their grandchildren and Americans wearing spandex, flying space-age kites that rip back and forth across the square at 300 mph.

- The sweet lychee drinks they sell in Vietnam in cheap plastic bottles.

- Patagonian clouds. The wind is always blowing down there. It whips clouds into configurations (corkscrews for example) that I'd never seen before.

- The Temple of the Tooth in Kandy, Sri Lanka where what is purported to be the Buddha's tooth is kept. You can't see the actual tooth, only a gold casket said to contain a series of smaller and smaller caskets and finally the tooth itself. It is said to have been smuggled into Sri Lanka in the fourth century in the hair of a princess. Two of my brothers are dentists, so naturally they got postcards from this holy spot.

- Monkeys who steal your bananas when you're not looking. I can never be angry with them.

Amazing Grace (Part II)

A SHORT TIME AFTER leaving the train, my new Sikh friend, Wassu, and I came to a large well-lit house. It was filled to overflowing with joyful Nirankaris. The appellation "Nirankari," as I later learned, is Punjabi for "Formless," one of the many names for God. Everyone was in a very elevated state. There was an air of spiritual intoxication. They warmly welcomed me and excitedly spoke of God Realization. All seemed confident that I would meet "Baba-ji" tomorrow and have God revealed to me as well. I remember seeing a picture on the wall that particularly struck me. It showed a Moslem, a Sikh, a Christian and a Hindu all dressed in their normal garb and all sitting at the feet of a kindly-looking gentleman who appeared to be explaining something to them.

Next morning after breakfast and in high spirits, we all piled into a giant Tata truck and drove to a medium-sized city somewhere in the Punjab, singing all the way. I can't remember the name of the town. A sort of festival was going on. There was a parade as well.

When we arrived, Wassu asked if I'd like "a holy glimpse of The Master." We walked by a large white float where I first saw Baba Gurbachen Singh, my dear beloved Guru (I'm sorry that there is no real English equivalent of the word Guru, so I hope that any negative associations a reader might have with this term will be excused).

He was seated on a couch that was covered with white cloth. He looked friendly, even jolly. Surprisingly to me, beside him were his wife and children. He was a family man.

After this, my friend and I joined in the joyful parade. Like most people there, sometimes we were in it, and sometimes we sat by the roadside and watched it go by. A single-engine plane flew over and dropped confetti on the happy throng. Once there was a group just in front of us, singing and dancing ecstatically. I asked Wassu to translate and he said, "God is in front of us, God is behind us, God is above us, below us, and within us."

An hour later we reached the fairgrounds where perhaps fifty thousand souls had already gathered. Not a single westerner was among them. Baba-ji was already there and seated at the front of the tent. The longest line I'd ever seen stretched back from the stage. When devotees finally reached the front, they put their head to the Gurus feet and received his blessing. The two of us entered the huge line. As we slowly made our way forward, my mind was in tremendous turmoil. For one thing, I didn't want to put my head on his foot. It seemed to violate something in me.

As we approached Baba-ji, my friend looked at me straight on. I can still see that dear man's face as I write this. "It will be wonderful to receive his blessing— wonderful. But if you are serious about God realization, ask him for it."

When I reached the front, I stood to the side. One after another, people were placing their heads on his feet and he was silently blessing them with his hand.

Finally, I sucked up my courage and said, "Pardon me sir, but will you reveal God to me?"

Sometimes a moment can change the entire trajectory of your life. He looked deep into my eyes and a beam of light actually shot out from his eye and entered mine. My head jerked backwards. A tremendous smile lit up his face. "Yes, I will."

To be continued…

Little Old Ladies in Tennis Shoes
Who Know How to Live

WHENEVER I'M IN BOMBAY, at least once I try to get up early in the morning and walk down to the small, neatly trimmed park just behind the massive arch of the Gateway to India. If you ever go there about an hour after dawn when the mist from the harbor is just burning off, you'll find a group of about twenty ordinary looking, middle-class Indian folks milling about. At seven o'clock sharp an old gal with a very serious expression invites everyone to form a circle.

With a bit of severity in her voice, she announces, "First we will begin with the vowels." Then, totally unexpectedly, she throws her head back and cries out, "Ha-ha-ha. Ho-ho-ho. He-he-he."

From there she leads us through cell-phone laughing, machine gun laughing, Australian laughing, tiger laughing, kangaroo laughing… the laughter, real or imagined, of every animal, mineral, or vegetable we can think of. I'm saying to myself, this is nuts, but somehow I'm laughing anyway. We're all laughing uproariously. All those faces that had seemed so boring have been transformed by joy. The tired-looking old man across from me is now vital, animated, and very lovable. This hilarity goes on for about thirty minutes. Then we recite a little poem that includes the phrase "East or West, laugh is best." Then we wish each other a happy day and go our own ways.

I wrote this piece last year. I'm sorry to report that the "small, neatly trimmed park" is in the process of being "beautified" according to the ugly little billboard put up next to what used to be a little oasis of tranquility. The new project answers Bombay's crying need for less green-space and more pavement. Undeterred, and in spite of the rubble, the little old ladies are still out there in the same spot every morning, still laughing.

Advice to Travelers:
Try Every New Fruit

ONE THING I'VE GOTTEN into the habit of doing soon after arriving in a new country is checking out the local fruit stands. It gives you a lot of opportunity for serendipity.

There are few of life's little pleasures that are quite as delightful to me as discovering a tasty new fruit in a faraway land. Southeast Asia is loaded with possibilities. Mangosteen, jackfruit, and the infamous durian come to mind.

How to describe a durian? First, the smell: it's something akin to a particularly poorly-cleaned latrine or, some people say, smelly socks. Most hotels outright ban them on that premise alone, and signs with a red slash through a picture of a durian are common. They're big, too. A good-sized one weighs about fifteen pounds. The taste is nearly impossible to describe. It has a kind of creamy, custardy, slightly astringent taste, but not quite that. Nothing is comparable. Due to the odor, they're never exported. To taste one you'll have to fly to Kuala Lumpur.

Every serious traveler has a favorite locale for mangos. For me, it's Northern Australia. When the fruit starts to ripen there, the locals go a little crazy. It's called "Mango Madness." There is no comparison between these big beautiful babies and the supermarket variety, shipped green from Mexico, that we get at home. Even these, however, can be quite good compared with lesser fruits. You've detected my prejudice perhaps.

In India you can always get a lively debate over where the tastiest mangoes grow, though the Alphonso Mango is often mentioned. The story goes that one Maharaja required that all his concubines have breasts shaped like luscious, sweet Alphonsos.

I have a friend in America who is the dearest man and the purest soul— a Mahatma if there ever was one— Professor Puri. Once we were talking about the religious concept of ego detachment and the need for it. "Yes, Professor, but what about mangos?" I said. He smiled broadly and a faraway look came into his eyes. That passion perhaps remained with him.

I have to confess that after visiting a hundred countries I was beginning to feel jaded, fruit-wise. I felt like I'd tried them all. Been there, tasted that. That changed a couple of years ago when I found myself in Manaus, the gateway to The Amazon. There were juice bars there like I'd never seen before. Fruits like Inga, abiu, marimari, pitanga, acerola, taperaba, sorva, pitamba, uxi, pupunha, seriguela, bacuri and jambo. Amazing stuff! What an adventure it was exploring them.

Sometimes unpromising-looking fruits can surprise you. Fontaine Gerard and I were several days out on a trek in Mali. One day we were shopping for food in a local market. There were pretty slim pickings. Every slab of meat was completely black and undulating from the solid layer of flies swarming it. Lying on a filthy blanket, I noticed some severely withered-up little orange-colored fruits. They looked vaguely reminiscent of rotten tangerines you might come across in a compost pile. As they were the best things on offer, we bought a few.

A few hours walk down the piste, my friend Fontaine and I halted under a tree and took a break. I opened one of the sad little fruits with my Swiss Army knife and discovered stringy looking flesh with many large seeds inside. It was all we had, so I popped it into my mouth. I actually think a small tear came to my eye. It was so delicious.

Friendly Fire

I DIDN'T WANT TO go to Vietnam. I could have gone to Canada... or prison. I knew it was a bad war. I've got no excuses. I'd been a failure as an inner-city school teacher which would have given me a deferment.

When my draft letter arrived, I didn't tell my friends I was going into the army. I'd made up my mind to go and didn't want to argue with them about it and spoil the last few days before I went in. On the appointed day, I just went to the induction center. I like to think I'd do it differently now. When I came home, back to "the world," I lied about how I got injured — initially, anyway. A lot of us lied about one thing or another. Then I just got tired of lying.

Probably half the Americans injured or killed in Vietnam were casualties of "friendly fire" like I was. At least, that's according to a very unofficial survey I did in the hospital in Japan where I was recovering. We were straight with each other there. For every bullet the VC and NVA expended I bet we expended 50,000. There was lots of friendly fire around. So it was easy for some of us "friendlies" to get in front of some of it by mistake. The point was, if you were hit by friendly fire, somebody would have to get in trouble and nobody wanted that. Besides, it would create a lot of paperwork.

One day a sincere looking Lieutenant came into the hospital to present me with my medal. "Look, I don't want to give you a long, flowery speech but let me just say that your country is proud of you." With that, he handed me the medal. That was fair enough.

A week later the same serious young Lieutenant came to see me again. He apparently didn't recognize me. His paperwork must have been screwed up. Again he looked me squarely in the eye and with great sincerity said, "Look, I don't want to give you a long, flowery speech but let me just say that your country is proud of you." Then he handed me a second one.

It Is Forbidden

MANY YEARS AGO, MY old friend Rick Owens had just finished up his internship and residency. Having spent most of his life up until then in school, he felt like he deserved a break. Sitting around a campfire on a summer night in Brown County, we had agreed to meet in Cairo and see the great pyramid by the full moon. I came overland; Rick flew directly to Egypt. I think we missed the full moon by a few days. I didn't mind. It was just great to see him again.

The city was a madhouse, an anthill. Commuters hung precariously to the top and sides of the buses as they lurched through the teeming streets and camels walked through the center of town. It was great.

We stayed at the youth hostel near the Nile, which in those days cost a little less than fifty cents a night. Among the travelers, there was a fellow who had hatched the idea of coming to Egypt to spend the night in the king's chamber of the great pyramid of Cheops. He said he'd lost his nerve and wasn't going to attempt it. For my part, I thought it was a capital idea and Rick was willing to put up with me, so the two of us resolved to try it ourselves the next day.

It was about dusk when our taxi got to the site. No matter how many pictures you may have seen of the pyramid, it's still a shock. At first sight, you get more of a "mountain" feel than a "built by man" feel from it.

Skirting along one side, we found the passageway in the face that led down to the chamber. It was closed for the night. The guards were 100% into picking up some baksheesh for allowing us to spend the night. The problem was that the fellow with the key was off somewhere. He couldn't be found. One of the guards suggested the next night as a possibility, but we had already booked a train up the Nile for the next day so it wasn't going to happen.

Disappointed, we walked around the pyramid and discussed other options. We could still climb to the top. That might be fun. We were about a hundred meters up when someone spied us and sounded the alarm. The guards began yelling, "It is forbidden! It is forbidden!" I don't know if it was the right thing to do, but we didn't stop; we just climbed faster. The guards scrambled up after us. We redoubled our speed. They probably could have caught us if they'd really wanted to, but after a few minutes' effort they gave up the chase and went back to their post.

We arrived at the top just in time for the Son et Lumiere show. At one point the whole pyramid was lit in red and the voice of Richard Burton boomed out, "Life fears time, but time fears the pyramids." I can't stand Son et Lumiere.

An hour later everyone had gone and we were left alone to contemplate the lights of Cairo on one side and the deep inky darkness of the empty desert on the other.

Best Things in the World

- Nutella.

- The artwork in the cemetery of the small limestone quarrying town of Bedford, Indiana. Many of the old stone carvers were immigrants from Italy. The most moving piece is a depiction in stone of a workbench covered in tools that belonged to one of the men. It's just as it looked on the day when he died.

- All over India there are temples where, for a rupee, you can be blessed by the tip of an elephant's trunk on your head. It's a startling experience and perhaps the best two cents you'll ever spend.

- Surfers who roam the Earth from South Africa to Bali to Hawaii searching for the perfect wave.

- Lamu Island, Kenya. There is only one car on the island and only fifty meters of road to drive it on. Everyone got around on donkeys except for one government official who every morning drove the 50 meters to his office in a Land Rover. People were friendly, the weather was perfect, and lobster dinners cost three dollars.

- My favorite juice bar in Manaus, Brazil. Every morning I'd have the woman there make me a banana milkshake with a little scoop of Guar Ana powder added. It tastes great and kicks you in the ass like espresso on steroids.

- The giant obelisk in Jakarta that Indonesians jokingly refer to as "Sukarno's last erection".

- Learning to scuba dive in the clear tropical waters off the south they'll coast of Sri Lanka. We glided amongst jewel-like fish in a surreal underwater landscape composed of piles of house-sized boulders.

- The Vatican. After I'd visited innumerable castles and palaces throughout Europe there was still nothing to compare to the grandeur of its sumptuous interiors.

- There's a suspension bridge over the Ganges in Rishikesh where the children will sell you dough balls to toss into the river below. Large carp rise up from the murky bottom and devour them.

- The evening Stephen Colbert stood ten feet from President Bush and satirized him in front of the entire Washington Press Corps. I've never seen a better example of speaking truth to power. As Jon Stewart remarked the next evening, "Stephen, you were ballacious!"

- The beautifully carved Charles Bridge over the Vitava River in Prague.

- The square in front of the Medici Palace in Florence. On a hot summer day I once ordered a Coca Cola in a café there. The perfect snooty waiter took immense pleasure in referring to it as "American champagne;" you had to love the guy for that. I think 20 years ago in Rome, or maybe it was Paris, some poor Yank misunderstood the plumbing situation and shit in the bidet. Word spread, and Europeans have been tough on us ever since.

- Chewing ghat in the late afternoon with a sweet old man who turned out to be the head of the Yemeni secret police.

- A magnificent splaying of wavelengths: the double rainbow I once saw over the city of San Francisco. It may have been the day before I left for the war.

Beanheads Eating Smack-Sized Bites

BEFORE I STARTED O.C.S. (Officers Candidate School) at Ft. Belvoir Virginia, I had no idea how many "privileges" I'd been enjoying previously. Things like "hair privileges." When we entered the program, our heads were totally shaved. We were now "beanheads" or just plain "beans." Then there were things like sandwich privileges, sidewalk privileges, even eyeball privileges (any side to side eye movement) as in, "ARE YOU EYEBALLING ME, BEAN?"

For infractions, like eyeballing, our Tactical Officer would yell for us to "DROP!" at which point we had to hit the ground, hands first, and start knocking out pushups until we were told to quit. Then we had to immediately return to an accentuated pose of attention called a "brace." "SUCK THAT CHIN IN, CANDIDATE, I WANT TO SEE A DOUBLE CHIN... TRIPLE CHIN!"

Sometimes Tactical Officers, or upperclassmen, would stand one inch from our noses and scream at us full-out. For some reason this never bothered me. I just stared at their foreheads and zenned out while they yelled themselves hoarse.

My first sentence when addressing a Tac Officer was always one of only a few options. First, "Sir, candidate Linnemeier..." then, "yes sir," "no sir," "no excuse sir," "reports with a statement sir" or, "reports with a question sir." All movement when we weren't marching was done at double-time.

One of the few pleasures we were allowed was singing while we marched in formation. I was the company song leader. On grey winter days those guys could pour a lot of soul into "California Dreamin'" or "The Prettiest Girl I ever Saw was Sipping Bourbon through a Straw."

Mealtimes were always especially difficult. There was an upperclassman at every table to keep an eye on us, making sure no one "eyeballed' or took "gross bites." Only "smack-sized bites" were allowed. A smack-sized bite could stretch across two tines of a fork, but no further. Anything more was a gross bite. If you were caught taking one of these you were told to "Sit Up!" (stop eating) or "Take A Fix!" (stop eating and look up at the ceiling). For every meal you had to have both an "interesting fact" (e.g., the surprisingly large number of square miles of some city in Maine) and a "gross interesting fact" (e.g., the ejaculate of an average boar is almost a quart) for the entertainment of the upperclassman at your table. If your facts weren't interesting or gross enough, or if— God help you— someone cracked a smile (Do You Think This Program Is A Joke, Candidate? blah, blah, blah, Sit Up!) you were in for it.

As a result, no one got enough to eat. The solution was "pogie bait runs." After lights out, someone would sneak off the post and arrange to have pizzas, sandwiches or some other form of "pogie bait" surreptitiously delivered. Nighttime was also when we needed to put the barracks in impeccable order and accomplish other chores, like spit shining our boots. When we were done polishing them, the toe could be used as a shaving mirror. I'm not exaggerating. After dark was the only time these things could happen; everybody knew this. Nonetheless, a lookout was always on duty to watch for the "night officer." If we were caught in violation of "lights out" there'd be hell to pay. Maybe it meant a three-hour forced march in the middle of the night. Maybe the night officer would just scuff up the floor (which we'd just buffed to perfection) with his boot heels as he paced back and forth while sonorously lecturing us on the need to get sufficient sleep. Maybe he'd have us go through the manual of arms using our footlockers instead of a rifle. Those perfectly arranged footlockers took us hours to arrange. The socks were rolled up super-tight and packed in the corner, just so. Shirts and underwear were folded perfectly. The belt buckle was Brasso-ed until it glowed and the belt itself wound as tight as humanly possible, etc. After going through the manual of arms a few times, the contents were in shambles. The footlockers would then somehow need to be redone later that night so they would be perfect again for inspection in the morning.

All this led to our second big problem: insufficient sleep. We averaged about three hours of sleep a night; we were always dead tired. But, if we looked too sleepy, or if someone dozed off, the instructors would write us up. And of course that was trouble.

The instructors were mostly civilians and were judged by how well we performed on the tests. They all had gimmicks. Some told lots of god-awful jokes, e.g., Q: What do you do in case of fallout? A: Reinsert and take shorter strokes. Another guy had a huge gong he brought to the classroom. Whenever he rang it and wrote something on the blackboard, we would dutifully write it down as this meant we would see it again on the test. He also had "good-to-know information." In other words, *forget it*. A third instructor had a long bamboo pole with a cocked mousetrap attached to the end. If he caught someone dozing off, he'd just keep talking as he slowly tiptoed over to the side of the room, picked up the pole, and extended it back through the classroom and carefully over the ear of the sleeping Candidate. Then Snap!

Two months into the program, we had a chance to take a bus trip out to the rifle range. It was a nice little break and something we'd looked forward to for weeks. Before boarding the bus, our Tac Officer warned us that we would be expected to maintain perfect posture while we were driven across the base and that there would be No Eyeballing. "There are going to be enlisted men out there and when they see you, I want them to think that you are supermen!"

All this would have been preposterous if it weren't for the fact that there was a war going on and most of us, after graduation, would be shipped straight to Vietnam where we'd be responsible for the lives of the men under our command. If we were going to break, better now than then.

I guess I wasn't superman material because, six months into the eleven-month program, I dropped out. They'd made the mistake of giving us two weeks off for Christmas. I went to a rock festival in Miami. All those pretty girls and the two weeks of unrestricted eyeball privileges were enough for me. Having enlisted people address me as "sir" and the better pay wasn't worth the extra year of service I'd have owed the Army as a result of taking a commission. I dropped out the day I returned from leave.

A month later, I found myself demoted to the rank of Spec-4 and onboard a chartered Boeing 707 on my way to The Republic of Vietnam.

The White Rose

I WAS IN VIENTIANE, Laos back in the early seventies, "going to seed in the tropics" with a vengeance. I lived in a small dark room in a three-story wooden rectangle of a place with peeling lead-based paint outside and bare wooden walls inside. It was more brothel than hotel but served as both. No pictures adorned the walls and there were no windows; this place was pure business. While I was residing there, a lovely and innocent looking young woman gave me a dose of what someone with a bent for poetry has called Bullhead Clap.

There was an anarchic feel to Laos back then. The CIA was flying planeloads of heroin out of the country on Air America flights, and the Pathet Lao were fighting with the Royalists not far outside of town. For enough money *anything* was for sale. If you'd ever wanted to sleep with three women, fire off an AK47 in the air, or smoke opium until you had the vitality of a bedbug, this was the town for you.

There was a totally un-quaint restaurant downtown that nonetheless served great French food. I'd just polished off a delicious Sicilian steak there when I fell into conversation with an Australian guy at the next table. He mentioned that he was going over to a place called *The White Rose* after dinner and would I like to tag along. I'd already heard stories that the girls danced naked with the customers there and that pretty much sold me on the idea.

I'm trying to remember how the place looked, but no picture comes to mind. We walked in, sat down at a booth, looked around a bit, and were surprised to find ourselves the only patrons. Two attractive young women joined us and we ordered beer all around. The owner was a sultry, middle-aged Chinese woman in a black silk skirt slit to the waist. She welcomed us and made polite conversation while we sipped our drinks and the girls played with us beneath the table. Everything seemed to be going swimmingly in this little corner of the world so far from the banks of the Wabash.

After a few minutes, an athletic-looking young woman walked up to our table and asked if we'd like to see the floorshow. I believe she said it would cost a couple of dollars. That sounded reasonable, so my new friend and I each kicked in a dollar. There are limits to the information that I'm putting into this book, and what went on out there on the dance floor exceeds that limit. Suffice it to say that it was naughtier than anything this Hoosier had ever seen. At any rate, after the show was over, the woman came over to our table, looked straight at me and said, "Now we go upstairs and I do everything." It was too much for me. I chickened out. I left her an outrageous tip, walked out the door, and never looked back.

Advice to Travelers: Dig Deeper

Never give up on a country until it reveals its beauty to you. I've been fortunate enough to have traveled to over a hundred countries and one thing I've learned is that every one of them has its own characteristic beauty. Some are straightforward, like the cathedrals of France or the Himalayas of Nepal. In other places you have to dig deeper.

I won't name this country since I have no desire to malign it. Similar things could just as easily have happened in a lot of other places. As soon as I got to the capital, a clever pickpocket "bumped into me" and I almost lost my glasses and a bit of money. When I brought it to his attention, he quickly returned them. The city was full of thieves. Even when I sat on the city buses next to a random person, someone would occasionally try to nick things from my rucksack.

People were deathly afraid of drafts. Even when the temperature was a hundred degrees, no slit in the windows of buses was allowed. Most people wore heavy clothing when traveling. One day I was on an especially long ride. Fortunately, I had a window seat and was able to break the rules just slightly. By pushing the window back half an inch and pressing my nose to the gap, I could get a little fresh air.[4]

I was never on a long distance bus ride where a fistfight didn't break out at some point. On one particular ride, a con man (after years of

---

[4] This turned out to be not as crazy as I'd originally thought. Many diseases in this country are endemic. People are almost always sick with something. As antibiotics and drugs in general are too costly for most people, sweating it out, the equivalent of having a fever is the best available treatment. Conversely, when you're sick, drafts can be deadly.

traveling I've learned to spot them) with a mouthful of ghat made a point of sitting next to me. He was with a bunch of his buddies, and from time to time, they would lower their voices and talk conspiratorially in the local language. His eyes would occasionally shift towards and away from me, avoiding direct contact. I knew the set-up. When we stopped for the night, they would attempt to rob me— violently if necessary. I was perplexed and there was no one to turn to. I decided that the only way to throw off their plans was to unexpectedly get off the bus with my backpack in the middle of nowhere. With this in mind, I abruptly jumped to my feet, told the driver to stop, and quickly dragged my backpack off with me. Everyone on the bus was shocked. No one got down with me.

I was all alone out there. It was late afternoon and darkly overcast. The countryside consisted of undulating hills of lush, green grassland. There wasn't a tree anywhere. It looked primeval. Identical, small villages of simple mud dwellings were scattered equidistantly about a mile and a half from each other across the vast landscape. Gaunt, parasite-infested cattle grazed indolently between them. I hoisted my pack to my shoulders and struck out toward the nearest cluster of huts. On the outskirts of the tiny village a cadaverous old woman dressed in colorful rags greeted me with a quizzical expression. What possible reason might I have for being here? I might just as easily have descended from Alpha Centauri.

Within five minutes, half of the village was gathered around me. I made gestures asking if it might be okay for me to pitch my small tent just outside the village. No one seemed to object, so I quickly nailed in the stakes and set it up. A couple of young ladies asked if they might join me inside, which might have been jolly but I gracefully demurred. A tremendous rainstorm hit soon afterwards, but within my little, water-proof, nylon shelter, it was dry and cozy. I had a few sardines, a chocolate bar, some water, a candle, and even a book to read. I fell asleep, grateful to be within this tiny enclosed world.

Next morning I fixed breakfast inside the tent on a small propane stove and was prepared to face the challenge of the new day. I emerged to find a fresh, clear sky overhead. A crowd gathered to watch me take down the tent. Everyone seemed amiable enough, though one canny fellow hatched the bright idea of charging me for the campsite. I was content to pay and happy to be on my way.

The hard-packed, red clay road stretched out invitingly across the deep green of the soft, sensual hills. I only had to wait for thirty minutes before a friendly guy driving an enormous olive drab Russian-made truck stopped and gave me a lift. He was traveling with his girlfriend. They were a lot of fun. That ride took me all the way to a game park as large as the state of Rhode Island where, for a couple of days, I was the only foreign visitor.

This story could go on interminably, but for our purposes let's cut it off now. I should mention that during my stay in this country, I contracted malaria and typhoid fever. I took treatments for both. I was in my fifties and this country damn near killed me. I never gave up on it though, and in the end, it showed me beauty— transcendent beauty. I'll never forget it. That's my point. Never give up on a country until it reveals its beauty to you.

Everything You've Heard About the Sixties is (Mostly) True

PEOPLE WERE DOING DRUGS— a lot. It was the psychedelic revolution. LSD is broken down by the body after about 8 hours. At that time a person comes down from their trip. There is another psychedelic called STP which resists this breakdown and takes much longer to metabolize. People can be up for 3 days and nights on it. Back in the 60's in my hometown two people I knew had been tripping for a couple of days when they suddenly realized that it was Sunday. Being in such an elevated state, they thought it might be fun to go to church. They chose the local Episcopal Church (where the WASP elite traditionally worship). They burst through the great doors and walked down the aisles, shouting joyously, kissing babies, doing God knows what. It turned out that this church was no place to have a religious experience though. The police were called and they were taken away.

Hitchhiking in America was better in the 60s. The cops were always friendly to us. If you spotted a VW bus with a hand-painted peace symbol coming down the road you could pick up your pack: you were definitely getting a ride. We knew it was over when long-hairs started passing without stopping. My brother Phil (sporting shoulder-length hair) would yell at them to "Get a haircut!"

There were no "hippies" but there were travelers, freaks, artists, and truth seekers. ("Hippie" was a media word, used only by the Establishment, the Outsiders. We used it only ironically or facetiously.) Not long ago, I met one of the original Merry Pranksters who was living with his young wife and child in Ecuador. They were hiding out from the law. He told me stories of traveling across America on the bus with Ken Kesey and Neal Cassidy, turning people on to LSD. He'd been there for the original Kool Aid Acid Tests.

It's impossible to separate the sixties from its politics. In my opinion, the political climate was shaped by two conflicting points of view: one used a flower and one used a fist. One was the way of Gandhi and Martin Luther King. It was inclusive. It was an attempt to awaken people to live up to what was best in them. There was an opposing point of view. It viewed the world as a struggle for power, a feeling that it was us versus them. In the end, the latter prevailed.

Eventually, the media grew tired of all this boring peace and love stuff; the drama of conflict sells newspapers. Aggressive people on both sides were able to grab the spotlight. It's far more complex than that, of course. But if I had to simplify what happened that's what I'd say. Besides, as George Harrison wrote at the end of the era, "all things must change."

Twenty years after "The Summer of Love," I visited "The Farm" in Tennessee. They had kept the spirit alive after it seemed to have died out everywhere else. When I was there, it reminded me of how things used to be, how things used to feel. It wasn't something that had been imagined after the fact; people really *had* been kinder to each other back then. Everything felt differently.

Fire in the Hole

I HAVEN'T LEARNED THAT many skills in my life, but two of the best were acquired while working in an isolated iron ore mine named Frances Creek up in the Northern Territories of Australia. The first skill was how to drill holes with an air track drilling machine. I learned on a beat-up old Atlas Copco drill powered by an air compressor that shook like fury and produced a tremendous racket. It was intimidating at first, but practice makes better. Eventually, I grew to love the work. When I was drilling, the sounds of grinding and hammering completely engulfed me. I was shut off from the rest of the world, in the midst of a non-stop boiling cloud of debris. The blinding dust continuously shot in my face. That, plus the oil spit out by the machine, coated my protective glasses, making it very hard to see (Despite being so close to the Equator, I never got a tan. I was too covered in dirt and oil for the sun to penetrate). In order to make this monster drill a hole, I had to detach myself from all the apparent chaos. I had to focus.

First the track needed to be moved into position and the boom swung into place at the correct angle of attack. That was the easy part. Then there were the four controls that needed to be gently manipulated: the up/down lever, the rotation lever, the jackhammer lever, and the air pressure lever. The trick was to get all four of them working together harmoniously. It's easy to screw-up, but there were times when the dust was shooting out of the hole just right and the bit was steadily hammering and grinding away through the ore that I felt a certain Zen-like detachment. For a time, at least, I was content with my place in the universe.

When I first arrived at the mine, they put me to work as a powder monkey. This is a job almost any guy (and probably a fair number of women) can relate to. Lots of people seem to enjoy setting off a good explosion. I call it harmless, and I call it fun. Most of the explosive power in a shot normally comes from ANFO (Ammonium Nitrate/Fuel Oil), a mixture of fertilizer and some type of petroleum product like kerosene or diesel oil. It's economical, yet still packs plenty of wallop. In order to set the mixture off, however, you need dynamite. And in order to set off the dynamite, you need a blasting cap.

In our mine, shots were set off electrically (though it can also be done by burning a det-cord). The explosives were put into the recently drilled holes with the electric lines coming out over the edges. We connected these up in a line, then joined them and ran them to the next series of holes directly in front of them. The holes were staggered. Usually, there would be three parallel lines, and we placed small delays between them. That way the line of holes closest to the face of the cut would explode first, followed a split second later by the second line and yet another split second later, the third. All this took place faster than the eye could detect, but it allowed for the succeeding explosions to blow freer since preceding ones had loosened the rock in front of them.

When everything was in readiness, the crew moved back a couple hundred meters from the blast site and hunkered down behind our vehicle. The blaster would sing out, "Fire in the hole! Fire in the hole! Fire in the hole!"

Then that beautiful moment when he'd smack the plunger down and *set her off.*

The Mayor of Fifth Street

My FATHER WAS A good man, cultured, and a bit corny as well. Sometimes in the middle of telling a joke at the dinner table, he'd load up his pipe and nonchalantly stroll out of the room with God knows what on his mind. He'd go take a leak or gaze out at the weather for a minute, then walk back into the room and deliver the punch line. He was a man at peace with himself. He loved tall trees, well tailored suits, the books of Thoreau (especially *Walden Pond),* and the music of Bach. He was far from being a genius, but he was steady and had a kind look in his eye. People knew instinctively that they could trust him.

He always looked sharp. In his youth he was handsome as a movie star. One year he was named one of the ten best dressed men in Indiana. Back in his salad days, he drove a series of expensive sports cars and was a bit of a ladies man. He played golf and the piano, both with great enthusiasm but mediocre results.

He was a good citizen, involved in the United Fund, The Boys Club, The Varsity Club, The Bloomington Redevelopment Board, the local dental society, and lots of other things as well. Regardless of the organization, almost invariably within a year or so, he'd be elected president. He was that kind of guy.

I picture him most clearly striding confidently down Fifth Street from his dental office to the bank on Washington Street with his fat wallet filled with endorsed checks to be deposited into his account (he had a terrific practice). As I'd stride along in his wake, he'd be filling me in on business gossip, note approvingly some newly planted trees, and maybe bitch a little about any litter we encountered. He came to be known as, "The Mayor of Fifth Street."

He could be cantankerous, especially about politics. He paid a lot of taxes and didn't much like how it was being spent. That was the government though. He wasn't a tight ass. On a personal level, he was generous to all who knew him, even slightly. Over the years he helped out a lot of people without expecting anything back. Working his way through college during the depression, he'd occasionally known hunger. He worked hard, and money was a big deal to him.

I don't want to make Pop out to be a saint. He wasn't— not by a long shot. On balance though, his faults were only human and easy enough to forgive.

I'm afraid he often saw his eldest son as a bit of a ne'er-do- well. You could see his point. I'd de-pledged my fraternity, dropped out of dental school to work my way around the world, and eventually become an amiable, but rather disheveled housepainter. There were times when he seemed to show a bit of approval for his wayward son though. Once when I had written him a letter about working on an oil platform in the Persian Gulf, he sent me a return letter that included the words, "Sounds like you're living an interesting life." While I was off traveling to the ends of the earth, people had started to ask him where I was these days and what crazy thing was I up to. Eventually, I think he began to enjoy saying that his boy was living on a Pacific island or crossing the Sahara on a sheep truck. His three other sons were all in the professions and doing fine; maybe it was alright to have one black sheep in the family.

As he got into his late eighties, much fell away of course. He spent most of each day sitting in his favorite brown leather chair by the great windows of the living room that looked out on his beloved trees, the creek that bordered his property, and the meadow beyond that. The classical music station was left on low in the background, and he would sit and watch the birds at the feeder, reading a bit then dozing off. Friends and family would drop by to chat, but his circle of activity was gradually contracting.

His wife Maggie kept him neat, spruced-up, and well fed. She gave parties from time to time, which gave Pop a chance to socialize a bit without having to leave the house. He was thirty years her senior, so she was out and about more than he was. They'd have tiffs about money from time to time, but they loved each other deeply. She was a good wife. She looked after him and cared about him. He was fortunate to be with her and he knew it.

My father was cogent until his last few hours. We all had a chance to say good bye. Sincerely, we all told him we loved him, and sincerely he told us that he loved us. Maggie had placed his hospital bed in their bedroom beneath the tall windows with a southern exposure. There was rain, but also occasional sunshine that shown down on him through the tree branches for his last day. By that afternoon he was no longer able to take care of his own bodily functions and I had to help him. He was a proud man and I know he abhorred this. He died that night.

My daughter and I sat side by side at his bed as he slept. His breathing was ragged and uneven. His mouth was formed in an "O" shape which Mike Sullivan once told me is a sign that life is nearing the end. Thea and I talked together, and every few minutes we swabbed his lips and tongue to keep them from drying.

Maggie and her two children, Susanna, Anita, along with Anita's partner Emily, decided we'd stay the night. We agreed to take turns sitting up with my dad that night. We didn't want him to die alone. After my time was up at about one o'clock in the morning, I awoke Maggie, and then I lied down and fell asleep there in the room. At about three she awoke me and said, "He has stopped breathing, I think he may be dead, can you check his pulse?"

There was no pulse. We hugged each other and cried a few tears.

"He was a good man," she said.

"Yes," I agreed, "he was."

Homesick Down Under

I was living in a small commune in Auckland. Not a far-out kind of commune. Just a "share the cooking, dishwashing and house cleaning" kind of place. It was a very pleasant set-up, but only a short-term proposition for me. There was an extraordinarily beautiful young lady living there, too. She was a seamstress and a "magic lady," like the one in the song "Suzanne" who "feeds you tea and oranges that come all the way from China." No romance, but ah, she was lovely.

Back in those days, New Zealand had zero unemployment. You could just walk down the street, make a few inquiries, and you'd come up with a job. On my first day in the country I had gotten hooked up with a job at a construction site for a sky scraper (only 3 or 4 stories high at that point). Most of my fellow workers were Maoris, terrific guys, and very agile. They kept me out of trouble and saved my ass a couple of times. My plan here in this miniature metropolis was to only work long enough to make a little traveling money.

New Zealand should be on anyone's "top ten most beautiful countries list," especially the South Island with its fjords, mountains and sensual farmland. That's what they say anyway. I didn't get that far.

After a couple of weeks work, I was ready to move on. I gave a perfect seashell to the magic lady and hit the road heading south. I stayed in some nice youth hostels and the scenery was beautiful, beautiful, all very beautiful, but something wasn't right. I'd probably made a mistake by seeing the film *American Graffiti* in Auckland. I had been traveling for three and a half years and hadn't regretted a moment of it. But seeing that movie had planted a seed in my mind. For the first time since leaving Indiana, I missed my homeland. No beautiful mountains could fill the need to see home again. I was standing on the side of the road with my thumb out when that realization came to me. I thought about it for a minute, then crossed the road and stuck my thumb out going the opposite direction. Three weeks later, with an enormous grin on my face, I found myself knocking at my parents' door on Ballantine Road.

The Man in the Culvert

THE DEFENSES THAT SURROUNDED a typical American base camp in Vietnam seemed impenetrable. First, a strip a half-mile wide around the periphery of the base was cleared of all vegetation by bulldozers. Beyond this area, sensors were placed that could detect the sound of padding human feet. Within the cleared strip were three rows of razor-sharp barbed wire. Called concertina wire, it came in big rolls which could be extended, connected with other rolls, and piled pyramid fashion to form barriers. There were three concentric circles of these barriers spaced a few hundred meters apart. In the late afternoon we attached flares out in the wire which could be tripped by the slightest motion. If we saw one ignite after dark, we knew where to fire.

Tanks, A-Cavs, and bunkers were situated at the innermost part of the perimeter at thirty meter intervals. Guard duty was constant at each position throughout the night, and every active guard was accompanied by two sleeping comrades who could be awakened in a moment. We had sniper scopes to see in the dark and every man was heavily armed.

Each position also had crescent-shaped, Claymore mines placed in front of it. They could be detonated electrically by the push of a button, spraying a hailstorm of shrapnel pellets outward. That alone should kill anyone in front of you. If a tank was knocked-out by the enemy, there were others in reserve that could move in quickly and block the hole. The back-up crews in these were on constant alert as well. There were Huey gunships fueled and ready at the airfield inside the base camp; they could be in the air within two minutes. Each was armed with miniguns which could, in three seconds, spray enough bullets to put a round in every square foot of a football field. Additionally, there was a slow-moving plane nicknamed "Spooky" that had three of these miniguns. If that was insufficient, we could call in artillery or an air strike.

Once an hour during the night, at a time that was not announced beforehand, the officer in charge would tell us to open fire with everything we had. I saw a photo of this deadly procedure taken from a plane flying overhead. Every tenth bullet had a tracer that let you know where you were shooting. Like everything, bullets are pulled to the ground by gravity. This makes each one's path describe a parabola. Seen at night from the air, a base under attack looks like a beautiful, giant, and very deadly flower.

It sounds impossible, but NVA sapper teams would sometimes penetrate all these defenses and get inside the base.[5] A week before I got to this particular base camp, one of them got in and hid himself in a culvert that ran beneath a road that circled the inner perimeter. Next morning, someone discovered he was there. They got a translator with a bullhorn to try to convince him to surrender.

The pentagon had devised what was called the "Chu Hoi" program. In Vietnamese the term means "Open Arms." The idea was that any NVA or VC who put down their weapon would be pardoned and given a small farm, replete with ducks and pigs. They offered this to the man in the culvert. They tried to convince him for twenty minutes. When he refused all this, they tossed in a grenade. A few days later, bits of flesh and shreds of a uniform were all that remained of this brave man.

This was a war we were never going to win.

---

[5] Later in the book I'll tell how 35 years later in Hanoi I met some of these sappers and learned how they did it.

Best Things in the World

- Hearing the Indianapolis 500 start with the words, "Gentlemen, and for the first time in the history of the Indianapolis 500, lady, start your engines."

- The one hundred foot tall Buddha carved into a cliff in Bamian, Afghanistan. One beautiful afternoon in 1972, I sat up on the roof of a hotel with my brother and Christene, an English girl I was traveling with, smoking a joint and gazing at this remarkable carving looming over our heads. Thirty years later, fundamentalists dynamited the statue into rubble.

- Cappadocia in Turkey. It's a valley of bizarre rock formations honeycombed with houses and churches. They were used by the ancient Hittites and later by early Christian communities. At one time some of the tunnels dug beneath the structures penetrated ten stories beneath ground and connected to other cities. 20,000 people once lived here.

- Latvian names like Epp, Toivo, and Allo. How peculiar our names must sound to them.

- The first time I actually heard a French girl say, "Ou La La."

- There is a very popular restaurant in Rishikesh that has a eunuch who sits on a platform in front and presides over the establishment. He wears a lot of makeup and his hair has been oiled so it comes to a single, spiked point. He's called the "Choti Wallah Man." His bizarre presence seemed to draw people in, so the restaurant next door finally decided to put in a Choti Wallah look-alike in front of their restaurant. That worked equally well. Today, they sit amicably and thirty feet apart on a little pedestrian walkway of this small town in the foothills of the Himalayas where the Beatles once stayed at the ashram of The Maharishi. There's no apparent rivalry between them. They both love to shake hands and both love to have their picture taken with you.

- Marcia Anderson's pesto on penne. The basil and cherry tomatoes come fresh from her garden.

- The books of Vikram Seth.

- Buenos Aires, a sophisticated city with art museums, magnificent parks, beautifully dressed women, and great little restaurants and cafes. Just as much fun as Paris, but everything costs a fifth as much.

- Sitting quietly on the massive rugs under the vault of the great Blue Mosque of Istanbul. It felt peaceful to listen to the soft murmuring of prayers while the sun filtered down on us from above.

- The great pink expanses of flamingos over the blue water of Lake Nakuru. Forty percent of the world's flamingos live in two lakes in Kenya. It's a nice, tight little ecological cycle. The flamingos poop in the lakes causing algae to flourish which the flamingos then eat.

- Pi. Eric Isaacson, a mathematician friend of mine, can recite the first hundred digits by heart.

- Evening feasts in Kabul, Afghanistan during Ramadan. I remember the roasted meat and the fat yellow melons.

- "Snuggletown" at Burning Man.

Amazing Grace (Part III)

The glory of Him who moves all things penetrates the universe and shines in one part more and in another less. I was in the heaven that most receives His light and I saw things that most receives His light and I saw things that which he that descends from it has not the knowledge or the power to tell again; for our intellect, drawing near to its desire, sinks so deep that memory cannot follow it

The Paradiso Dante

DESCENDING FROM THE STAGE, he made his way through the crowd and took my hand saying, "Baba-ji has told me that I am to reveal God to you." After thirty-three years I have no clear memory of how this man looked or of any of his mannerisms. His name I do recall: Mr. Mehta. I have never seen him since.

We found a vacant room, and he shooed the little children out of the windows and pulled the curtains shut so we could have some privacy. He told me first that what he was about to convey was not attached to him personally. He was no one special other than the fact that Baba-ji had allowed him to convey this sacred *Gyan* (Punjabi for knowledge).

"In order for God to be revealed to you, you must make five pledges which can serve as guidelines for the remainder of your life. It is very important that you thoroughly understand them, have no reservations about them, and accept them. I will take as long as is required to explain all five of them. Does that sound okay?" It sounded reasonable to me.

"The first pledge is based on the fact that everything has been given to you by God. For example, your body, mind, and wealth are gifts entrusted to you. It is for you to use them wisely."

Ok, I had some questions there. Abject poverty is common in India. Thirty-three years ago it was *more* common and *more* abject. You couldn't ignore it. The problems seemed almost endless— an ocean of them. Coming from the west, I'd felt overwhelmed by them; lots of people are. It had seemed to me that if I wished to make any spiritual progress, I was going to have to give everything away first. I explained this to Mr. Mehta. He countered that by giving away everything I owned, I might help people materially but would do nothing to alleviate their spiritual suffering. We went back and forth with this for quite a while.

Finally, he said, "Look, there's nothing in the *Gyan* that says that you can't give away everything you own, if that's how you feel."

"OK," I said, "I guess I have to accept that."

The second pledge was easier, at least in principle. I was not to be prejudiced against anyone due to their race, color, caste, religion, sex, or social class. This seemed to me right and eminently reasonable. Living up to it has turned out to be harder than I expected, but of course, the idea is right.

The third pledge flowed naturally from the second. One is allowed to eat as one likes, clothe and house oneself as one likes, but you are to remain entirely tolerant of others' choices in these areas. Unity is the important thing. Any kind of uniformity is not exactly discouraged, it's just thought of as rather boring. Nirankaris enjoy each others' differences.

The fourth pledge was the other one I had to knock back and forth a bit. Essentially, it states that after receiving the *Gyan,* one is not to retreat from the world by living in a solitary hut in the jungle or alone in a cave in the mountains. Furthermore, one has to earn his/her livelihood and not live from handouts.

"Look," I protested, "I enjoy being off by myself from time to time. That would be hard to give up."

"No, No" he remonstrated. "Continue to do this, just don't live there permanently. Fulfill all of your family responsibilities, your social responsibilities, and all other reasonable responsibilities. Whatever you do, just do it with God consciousness. If you're a doctor, or a father, or a street sweeper, just do it with God consciousness."

"OK," I agreed, "that sounds ok, too."

The fifth principle is quite simple. You are not permitted to reveal God to anyone until given permission by Baba-ji. I readily agreed to this. A few things were explained to me that I'm honestly not sure if I'm at leave to tell or not. Let me defer those.

Then a prayer was issued up, at which point Mr. Mehta said, "OK that's it." A sudden wave of embarrassment swept over me. I already knew this stuff. Nothing seemed to have been added. He had spent all this time explaining things to me, but they were things I'd already known. I tried to cover my embarrassment by making small talk.

"Mehta... I think I read a book by a man named Ved Mehta. Are you two related?"

"Oh yes, yes" he said. Then he smiled and gave me a big hug. The next moment was the most astounding of my life. I got it! God really was everywhere! All those things that had been written in holy books were true, *really* true! Everything was there and always had been there, I just hadn't the eyes to see it. God truly permeated everything!

I could hardly stand up. My life up to this point was seen for what it truly was: nothing but an elaborate attempt to fulfill my ego. I was utterly undeserving of this.

My beloved friend Wassu rushed up to me. His eyes were wide. He could see what had happened. I saw everything in the depths of those beautiful eyes. Along with the awe, I could see that in one tiny little corner of his mind he thought he might be more respected now that he had brought me into the mission. I saw all that and everything else, but it was alright. Compared to the warehouse of hubris, endless schemes, and bullshit I'd been carrying around with me, this was *nothing*. I loved him so completely. I felt compassion for all my fellow beings. It seemed impossible. It had happened. I was enlightened.

Someone excitedly grabbed me by the hand and said, "We'll take him to see Baba-ji."

I was totally lost as they pulled me up and down stairs and through hallways. Then suddenly, he was there in front of me with those same twinkling eyes.

"Now you understand?" he asked. I fell to my knees and put my forehead on his feet. I felt as if I could rest there forever. He patted me on the head and said, "That's ok, go and have something to eat."

Didn't You Learn Anything?

I DON'T MEAN TO be sanctimonious about this next story. So long as you're a meat-eater, you're a party to whatever it takes to put that slab of bacon into its nice, clean, plastic wrapper.

Shortly after I was released from the army, I enrolled in graduate school again. The Veterans Administration paid for my books, tuition and supplies, plus a stipend. On top of this, I had my disability pay. I was a veritable student prince with no money worries whatsoever. I didn't even have to feel beholden to my parents. Nonetheless, I worked from time to time— more as a diversion than anything else.

An old friend of mine had a job working in a slaughterhouse. He invited me to visit. It was night work. From the time the place closed in the evening until two or three in the morning, he and his crew toiled away in that dark factory, cleaning up the mess left behind. It was ghastly work and probably unhealthy as well, but the members of the crew seemed to take a certain curious pleasure in all that.

There were many terrible tasks (washing out machines for de-bristling hogs, wiping down shears that had been used to cut through bones and snouts... that kind of stuff), but perhaps the worst job was cleaning up the "killing floor." Hundreds of animals had been killed there during the day. The floor was deep in blood. Somebody had to wade in with hip-high boots and unplug a stopper, allowing the blood to drain off into a large tank below. The dried blood was re-used as a basis for fertilizer.

I got the complete tour and then it was time for a break and a late night snack. Meat sandwiches appeared in a whole new light when eaten here. We talked for a while. Then my friend asked me if I wanted to join the crew.

There was a voice in me that wanted to take this job and have this dark experience. Another voice said, "Didn't you learn anything?" I hesitated for a moment, then politely declined.

Advice to Travelers:
Trekking In the Himalayas

I ALWAYS RESIST TREKKING since it can be hard work. But, like planting a tree, I've found you never regret doing it. There have been years in my life that have had fewer memorable moments than the ten days that I spent on the Jomson Trek in Nepal over thirty years ago.

Walking in the Himalayas is different from walking in the mountains at home. Logistics are easier. There are people living up in these mountains. That means the trails are much better maintained and basic food and lodging can be found almost everywhere except the highest passes. You can get up a lot higher, too. Even a middling pass is at least a couple of thousand feet higher than the highest peak in the Alps.

As a general rule when trekking in the third world, the closer you get to the trailhead, the cheaper it will be to arrange things. For example, I recently completed a trek to the Pindari Glacier in Uttaranchal. If I had booked this seven-day trek in America it would have cost at least $2000. If I'd arranged everything in Delhi, it might have been $400. I put a package together in Almora where it cost $250. At the actual trailhead, if I were hiring a porter and paying for food and accommodation as I needed it, the total cost would have been less than $100.

The Chicago Marathon

ABOUT TWENTY-FIVE YEARS AGO, I attempted to run the Chicago Marathon. I didn't quite finish. I "hit the wall," as they say. Somewhere around the twenty-second mile, my liver ran out of glucose. It wasn't like being exhausted. I felt like a car that had run out of gas. I simply wasn't going any further.

It's exhilarating on a clear fall morning to experience a great city gone strangely quiet, with no automobile traffic. There were some ten thousand of us, all decked out in our athletic gear, pumped up and ready to run. As a courtesy to the serious runners, we were segregated into groups according to speed. That way, the fastest people didn't have to waste time at the start of the race moving through the mass of slower runners. I was well toward the back of the horde, along with my eight-minute-mile sisters and brothers.

The signal was given to start, but there was no movement for five minutes because we were so far to the back— a human traffic jam. Then finally we were off... slowly at first. The crowd applauded as we passed; we were all grinning.

Picking up speed a bit, we wound our way through "The Loop," across the river, then out onto Chicago's pride: the magnificent sweep of Lakeshore Drive. The course was flat and fast, laid out so that it ran south along the lake to the Museum of Science and Industry where it crossed the median to start the return trip north.

It was quiet out there along Lake Michigan. The crowd had thinned to an occasional spectator. My fellow eight-minute milers and I were clumping along about three miles before the switchback when a sound of voices like I've never heard before or since started rippling back toward us through the river of runners. I exchanged perplexed looks with the people running beside me. What was going on?

Then we saw him. Moving perfectly. Like a god. His stride so graceful and powerful— it was the front-runner. He was all alone. He had crossed the median miles ahead and now was coming back towards us on the parallel road. Every person running out there knew how difficult the beauty he had was to attain. A tremendous cheer came up from every heart: Go... Do It Man, Do It!

Bleak Moscow

Thirty years ago, I had a day stopover in Moscow on an Aeroflot flight from Nairobi to Frankfurt. The sky was a clear sapphire blue as I stepped out of the tropical warmth of the lobby of my ornate old hotel into the hard cold immensity of Red Square. I strolled past the architectural confection of St. Basils Cathedral, admiring this perfect little multi-faceted jewel from a more frivolous age. Stalin was of a different mind. Everything built during his regime was to be monumental in size, immovable, heavy, soulless, and the world's largest if possible.

I walked across the square and into the mammoth G.U.M. department store— architecture at its most Soviet-licious. Seven thousand surly clerks grudgingly toiled within these grey walls. Dowdy looking clothes and shoddy merchandise of all description were on display in the dark halls. The vending machines sold shots of vodka in paper cups. Beer was vended into the same tired looking glass used by the last patron.

Out on the street again, I wandered into a gargantuan, subway station with massive murals and sculptures of muscular, determined-looking proletarians protecting the motherland and doing all kinds of heroic work. From there I descended by the longest escalator I've ever seen into the catacombs below, where trains rumbled in and out through dark tunnels. I took one at random and got off at a random stop. Endless rows of grey, apartment buildings— grimy and much in need of paint— greeted me as I climbed the stairs and rose to the air. I'd seen enough. I hailed a cab and was back in my stuffy, warm hotel half an hour later. The dour concierge at the end of my floor eyed me suspiciously as I exited the elevator. I plopped onto my fluffy over-sized bed and stared up at the ceiling. I felt comfortable to be back in my room with its plush, brown, over-stuffed furniture and discretely hidden microphones.

I Remember

I REMEMBER THE EXCITEMENT of being a boy lying out on the grass and looking up at the night sky to watch Sputnik, the first satellite, pass overhead.

I remember camping with Rick Owens in the highlands of Kenya just outside of Aberdaire National Park. We had no vehicle and there was no way the rangers would allow us into the game-park without one. The animals weren't pedestrian-friendly. Early next morning, we stealthily circled around the park entrance gate on foot. It wasn't the only rule we broke there. I don't think you were even supposed to get out of your car to pee except in enclosed areas. Once we found fresh lion pug marks. I know it sounds stupid, but somehow they were bigger and more daunting than I would have expected. That night we set up camp within sight of a long thin waterfall that fell from the edge of a lush, green escarpment about a mile in the distance. In the morning I was shocked to discover the distinct tracks of a rhino leading straight to the edge of my tent. You could see how he had nearly bumped into it before taking a careful detour around it and blithely continuing on his way. At some point that night his massive horn must have been about eighteen inches from my skull.

I remember making my way through customs at the sleek, ultra modern Hong Kong airport three or four years ago. A very serious woman in a very official looking green uniform strode directly up to me, pointed something that looked like a Buck Rogers space-aged pistol at my forehead, and fired. A red light came out of the barrel. Without a word she turned on her heel, walked away quickly, and was gone.

I remember how, back in the 70's in Goa, the outdoor privies had holes in the back to allow pigs to enter. It was more than a little disconcerting the first time I encountered a huge hog, with mouth agape, a foot beneath my naked rump.

I remember making the acquaintance of a young man in Samoa who was born in Flushing, New York. He was married to an exquisitely beautiful, honey-skinned young woman with hair down to her calves. She had been born into a royal family on some tiny Indonesian island, which made this American guy, Prince something-or–other. His business card referred to him as such. He was an elegant guy and made his living as a professional backgammon player.

I remember an acupuncture treatment I was given in Holland by a fellow I knew there. His set-up was slightly different than the traditional one. An electronic sensor allowed him to locate acupuncture points by sound. When he was on the right place, it emitted a sort of buzz. Then he'd give me a small hit of electricity. At one point he came to a spot that he claimed was important for happiness. "Great," I said, "Crank up the juice on that one." He did, and I found myself laughing uproariously. He started laughing as well. It was great. I just wish I could remember where that spot was.

Friendliest Country in the World

THIS IS A TOUGH call. It could be Turkey, or maybe Yemen, but one thing is for sure, it would definitely be a Muslim country. There's a Kurdish saying that goes, "a guest is a gift from God."

I think of the tents I approached in the Sahara. It was always the same. I was welcomed inside, placed on the best carpet, and served tea. Everything was done in the most gracious manner. They may have had few belongings but they were magnificent hosts— veritable kings. I always felt at home.

I'm going to be a little arbitrary and pick Syria as the friendliest place. I once spent an hour on a street corner in Damascus and was invited to dinner twenty times. I finally accepted an invitation and it was great, of course. I love France and I love England. This is nothing against the French and the English, but don't expect to be invited to dinner twenty times in an hour while standing on a street corner in Paris or London.

Ikebana in Tegucigalpa

I WAS DRIVING BACK to America from Costa Rica in "Brownie," my old, battered pickup truck. Everything in my life was falling apart. Elena had written me that she was filing for divorce and taking my two beloved children with her. I felt deeply disheartened. Driving through Honduras, the transmission started to make a terrible racket. I made my way slowly into the capitol, Tegucigalpa. I crept through the little streets and into a local garage with the truck making fearful clanking noises. Surprisingly, I learned it was only a minor problem (the universal joint had given up the ghost). They told me my truck would be ready in the morning. That was a relief.

I had an unexpected twenty-four hours on my hands. These days, practically every little capital city seems to have a new-age-style vegetarian restaurant with nice music, just as every capital has always had a Chinese restaurant. That's a good thing to remember if the local food tastes like mildewed cadavers, slightly warmed.

Chomping into my tofu, I noticed that on the bulletin board of this little restaurant there was an announcement that an Ikebana Master from Japan was giving a demonstration that day for the edification of the local women's club. So, improbably that afternoon, I found myself sitting in one of the plush red velvet seats of a small auditorium in the midst of seventy-five elegantly turned out Honduran ladies; they were the cream of society in this tiny country with its musically named capital. On the stage were arranged twenty or thirty colorful vases of various shapes and sizes. Also, there was an immense array of gorgeous tropical flowers, palm fronds, and various cut plants.

An impeccable old Japanese gentleman, small but perfectly formed, was introduced to the club members by the chairlady. He smiled politely, then crossed the stage and quickly fell upon the assembled vegetation with a quick-fingered vengeance. He worked intuitively. There wasn't the slightest wasted motion. Extraneous stems and leaves showered to the floor as he skillfully clipped, cut, and arranged at furious speed. The materials at hand were beautiful in and of themselves, but the mans genius was most clearly seen when even dried-out leaves with insect holes were occasionally placed by him so as to reveal their previously unseen beauty. For an hour my burden was lifted, fascinated as I was by this totally unexpected happening.

But finally, all the vases were filled. The diminutive gentleman was given a rousing round of applause. The chairlady thanked him profusely (addressing him as maestro) and presented him with a small painted picture.

I believe it was Pascal who once said that life was like a prison from which every day, fellow prisoners are taken away to be executed. It's a perfectly valid, if dreary, way of looking at our condition, but it just doesn't lend itself to interesting developments. There are a jillion little coin tosses of fate (or maybe an unspeakably complex design) that can put you in unexpected situations. There are all kinds of ways to see things (I'm trying to avoid the word "paradigm" which for some reason I dislike) but one is to think of life as an adventure. It's one of the primary themes of this book. Adventures don't always require you to buy a ticket to Raratonga, but they *do* always require you to push your comfort zone.

In the little vignette I just described, a serendipitous occurrence just happened, and all I had to do was jump on it. But of course you don't always have to wait for interesting little adventures, you can search them out. If you are planning on going to the ballet next week, why not go to a monster truck rally instead (or vice versa). If you normally watch Fox News, try The Colbert Report (or vice versa). If you are about to read something that further confirms what you already believe, then consider reading something that takes an opposing point of view instead. If your friends all drive Volvos and Subarus, get to know some Cadillac drivers and try to strike up a friendship. Go to some new church. Order something on the menu you've never eaten before. Push it.

A Tour of Duty in Vietnam

THIS NEXT STORY IS fragmented. I find it impossible to put all the pieces of memory together into chronological order. My aim is to give a feeling for what it was like.

Shortly after arriving in country, I was assigned to the Eleventh Armored Cavalry Regiment. They told me at in-processing that it was a "cap-busting outfit." That was true enough. All these years later, my ears still ring from the thousands of rounds of ammunition we fired off. Our regimental commander was Colonel George S. Patton Jr., the son of the famous WWII general. Most of the men liked him. He wore a peace symbol, as did a majority of soldiers there. But he also carried around with him the skull of a Viet Cong soldier with a bullet-hole through its forehead. One Christmas he sent out cards with photos of dead VC stacked like cordwood with the inscription "Peace on Earth."

I was deployed to Black Horse Base Camp, a relatively secure spot, and the headquarters of the Eleventh ACR. The first job they put me on was working with a team that swept the five miles of unpaved road between our base camp and Xuan Loc, the nearest town. Early every morning, we left base camp and slowly made our way up that little dirt road to town swinging metal detectors back and forth a few inches above the clay. The trick was to pick up a telltale bleep in the headphones, indicating that buried below the dusty red soil were the small touch-plates of a mine, often the only metal in the apparatus. If you missed them and stepped on the touch-plate, the two pieces of metal would touch, completing the circuit and detonating the mine.

When something was detected, we would fall back and allow the most experienced person to probe the area with a knife. If he located a mine, he would make the decision whether to put a hook around it and pull it out or blow it in place with some C-4 explosive. We tried not to explode mines too often as doing so left sizeable holes in the road. Ironically, the touch-plates were invariably made from metal clipped from our discarded c-ration cans. There was lots of other metal lying around; they could have used anything. Obviously, the VC found it amusing to blow us up with our own stuff.

Midway along the road to Xuan Loc was a prominence called Banana Hill. Here we had a permanent observation point with night-vision equipment that could see everything along the five-mile stretch except for a one-hundred-meter-long dip in the road just short of town. That's where "Charlie" would usually bury the mines. It was a nightmare trying to detect small bits of metal here. Over the course of three or four years, lots of things got blown up in the dip and metal pieces were scattered everywhere. Innocent Vietnamese civilians were far more vulnerable than we were. Just before I arrived at the base camp, fourteen civilians were killed when their flimsy little motorbike/bus hit a mine.

Minesweeping wasn't the most dangerous duty in Vietnam, but it wasn't without its risks either. One day not long after I got to Black Horse, I was assigned to another duty when a man I knew only slightly stepped on a mine and bought the farm. He was about my size, and no one else wanted them, so I inherited a dead man's clothes.

Best Things in the World

- A fighter jock at Ramstein Airbase who took off in a jet one day and, for no apparent reason, seemed to go crazy. Far above us, he was burning up his F-14 with loops, dives and impossible ascents. For a few minutes traffic stopped and all the offices emptied out as we forgot our daily routines, stared up at the sky and cheered this madman on. There'd be Hell to pay once he landed, but for now…

- I was standing by the road south of Darwin waiting for a ride when the first kangaroo I'd ever seen in the wild hopped across the pavement. Somehow, it's always a shock to see "zoo animals" in their natural habitat jumping around like they own the place.

- The street corner snake charmers of India who will let you try your hand at coaxing a cobra out of a basket with a wooden flute.

- Lying in a hammock watching the dark green jungle go by as we drifted down an obscure river in the Bolivian jungle on an oil barge.

- My friend Rick Owens is a superb stone-skipper—perhaps the best. I once challenged him to skip a 10-pound cinder block across the surface of a pond. It didn't work, but he came close.

- The CD, "Urban Zulu" by Busi Mhlongo. I bought it at a little record store in Cape Town along Long Street.

- The Archeological Museum in Mexico City. From the outside, the cable-supported roof looks unappealing, but there's a delightful visual jolt when you come through the small doorway and into this grand, cavernous space. You feel the awe of suddenly discovering a vast, hidden world.

- Majnu Ka Tilla, a magical Tibetan enclave in the midst of Delhi. In the narrow streets monks in red and saffron-colored robes mix freely with beautiful young Tibetan girls.

- First view of the Grand Canyon.

- The shopkeepers in the ancient city of Fez, Morocco. Sally, an American woman who I was in love with, and I spent a beautiful day lost in the medina drinking mint tea and smoking keef with these wonderfully hospitable men.

- The ruins of Tha Phrom adjoining Angkor Wat. Unlike Angkor Wat, these ruins were never restored or cleared of jungle cover. It's very evocative. A lot of movies have been shot there.

- There are over twenty species of hummingbird in Central America. You see their iridescent little bodies everywhere, hanging in mid-air then quickly darting away.

- The clove toothpaste you can buy in any Indian market.

- Getting waylaid in Munich for Oktoberfest. In the huge beer tents, thousands of people linked arms and gently swayed back and forth to the music. Outside, normally staid Germans were running about whooping it up, clobbering each other with foam rubber sledge hammers. This was no time to be a spectator. After putting down a few liters of some very fine brew, I was as pie-eyed and slap-happy as the next guy.

Up the Niger Beyond Timbuktu

There is no moment of delight in any pilgrimage like the beginning of it.

Charles Dudley Warner

THE RAINS FINALLY CAME to Mali. Children ran around deliriously, splashing in the puddles. Then the river began to rise. For us it meant that the down-at-the-heels, rust-bucket of a steamboat that traveled the Niger could now make it up river to Gao without getting stuck too often. Tied to the dock, she may have looked a little past her prime, but she had a classic design reminiscent of riverboats on the Mississippi before the Civil War, driven by a giant paddlewheel in the stern. She was a rugged old dowager, a survivor.

The Niger River forms a great muddy brown loop as it flows through Mali. It divides the country in other ways as well. On the outer bank is the edge of the Sahara. It's dry, and the people are, for the most part, Arab Muslims. The inner bank is greener, and most of the people are black and either Christian or Animist.

My friend Fontaine and I were, as usual, traveling as cheaply as possible: deck class. I had a Quebecois girlfriend at the time named Anne Marie. She spoke no English, nor did Fontaine.

We spent a wonderful few days on that old boat. I remember in particular a conversation I had with a wise old Malian gentleman. It was late afternoon. Everyone had crowded up at the stern to watch the trickiest part of the journey. For a half-mile stretch the captain would have to guide us through a formidable obstacle course of boulders as the current rapidly picked up speed at this narrow bend. Everything went well; we slalomed right past those great smooth rocks looming up out of the water not thirty feet from our fragile-skinned hull.

Soon afterwards, most people had drifted back to the rear but the old gentleman and I lingered on for awhile. We spoke about the Vietnam War. He asked me who I thought was responsible for it. I'm still not sure that I can answer that question. Partly me, of course.

Next day we anchored on the muddy banks at the outskirts of Timbuktu. Everyone wanted to go into town, just to say that they'd been there. I was concerned that the boat would leave without me, so I only saw the suburbs. It was dusty and desolate. There really wasn't much to see, but let's not forget the fun of being able to say that you've been to Timbuktu.

Anne Marie was in First Class, which on this tub was only a tiny fetid little cabin. Every evening, filled with lust, our hero would climb up the rigging on the outside of the boat to her stuffy little room on the top deck. The second night we were apprehended and taken down to the Captain for "trial." I'm sure he couldn't have cared less, and in fact, initially seemed rather amused by it all. But then Anne Marie flew into a tirade. About two minutes of listening to this shrilling banshee and his amiable forbearance was at an end; he was fed-up. He said he'd have to put us off at the next stop. A smile crossed Anne Marie's face. This development pleased her to no end. For some reason she had a secret agenda to turn this whole thing into some crazy, romantic adventure.

No Road... Middle of Nowhere... Probable Sickness... Nothing to Eat But Slugs, Grubs, and Millet... There's such a thing as *Too Much Adventure,* and this was crossing that line for me. I'm afraid I wasn't very gallant. I did my best to shush Anne Marie up and apologized profusely to the Captain. I saw his point, we'd mend our ways, we'd never do it again, blah, blah, blah. Of course, that was good enough. He only wanted for us to show a little deference to his position, nothing more. He had no desire to kick us off in some God forsaken spot.

At most of the stops we made along the river, the villagers hadn't seen anyone from the outside world for a full six months. As soon as we arrived, dozens of tiny canoes would shoot out into the brown, silt-laden river and surround us. Everyone would gesticulate madly. All seemed desperate to try to sell us something, or even just to get a look at us.

The next stop was a different, lonelier outpost. There were only a hand-full of people there. Among them was a magnificent aristocratic looking Bedouin with a white headdress that streamed behind him in the late afternoon breeze. He was sitting proudly astride the most beautiful Arabian horse I've ever seen.

Seeing this, my lady friend and I looked at each other. We might have gotten to know this guy.

Saved by Dolphins

INDIA HAS ALWAYS BEEN a refuge to me. Being halfway around the world from America helps me think more clearly. Almost twenty years ago I went through a hellish, contentious divorce. I eventually lost everything— house, wife, children and all my money. I won't go into all the details; I did everything wrong. It was a total disaster. That year was as painful to me as being shot in the chest and shoulder— just slower.

If you're ever going through a bad divorce, go the extra mile. If that doesn't work, get yourself a competent attorney who likes you. Then let it go. Those three sentences were learned the hard way over many difficult years.

If you just keep plugging along, though, life will usually, slowly, almost imperceptibly at first, start turning around. In my case, a year later things were beginning to go a lot better. I was living on the beach in Goa and in love with a very sweet, young Japanese woman named Tokiko. One day, though, I picked up my mail at the tiny local post office and got news that made me realize that ten thousand miles of space was not going to be enough this time.

It has always been my habit while in Goa to go for a long swim in the late afternoon in the warm, green water of the Indian Ocean. Swimming alone through the waves and under that great blue sky has always been a kind of prayer for me. This time I didn't stop. I kept thinking over and over, "Oh, God, this is more than I can bear... More than I can bear." That was my only thought. I just kept swimming. I was far beyond where I had ever gone before. I had no desire to turn back.

Then something like a miracle occurred. I became aware that a tight circle of dolphins now surrounded me. Shocked, I came to a quick halt and began treading water. I was transfixed. I could clearly see their eyes, like wet jewels, but they never met my gaze. I felt their presence deeply. Once, as its slick, grey, muscular body breached the surface, I heard one of those dear creatures clear his/her blowhole…"Puuuuch!" For twenty minutes they continued to circle me. I was lost in them. Then, just as suddenly as they'd come, they were gone.

I turned to the shore. It was only a thin line on the horizon now, but I knew I could make it. Nothing had changed except I knew I could bear it.

Life in the White Cocoon

ONE CLEAR SUMMER DAY a friend of a friend named TJ was showing us his hometown, Johannesburg, South Africa, a crazy place and one of the most dangerous cities in the world. It's located in Gauteng Province (All the license plates include the letters "GP" and some say this stands for "gangster's paradise"). Many South Africans exist full time within well guarded enclaves and secure shopping centers. It's referred to as living in the "white cocoon."

Driving into the center of the city, we skirted the edge of Hillborough, a tough area the police rarely enter. Right on schedule, an ugly looking fist fight broke out between two taxi drivers in the middle of the intersection just in front of us. They stood toe to toe slugging it out, bare fists smashing into grimacing faces, with no man giving an inch. We drove around them. TJ remarked nonchalantly that we were lucky they didn't have guns.

Five minutes later we were cruising through the quiet, tree-lined streets of an area that might have been mistaken for Beverly Hills if it weren't for the huge walls and the ubiquitous "Armed Response" security signs.

Practically all of the more expensive houses in South African cities have "Panic Buttons." You hit them when you're being robbed. It notifies a car full of armed guards stationed nearby who will normally respond within 3-4 minutes. Many people have armored doors to their bedrooms where they can hide while the rest of the house is being ransacked. I heard more than one story about how terrifying it is to be locked alone in your room while desperate men with firearms smash through your belongings just beyond those doors.

Crime is in the back of everyone's mind when you're in Jo'burg. I asked TJ how often they'd been burglarized. He thought for a moment.

"On average, one time a year. Once, me and my parents had to hide under a big table while a gang of thugs ransacked the place. They never steal the art though."

We dropped by TJ's house and he went for a quick swim while Marcia and the rest of us walked through the lovely terraced garden that climbed up the hill behind his home. TJ's father was an architect and the house was a joy. Outside, it incorporated simple materials with bright colors and interesting forms. Inside intimate spaces were broken up somewhat eccentrically. There was a wonderful use of natural light and a jungle of fascinating African art. It struck me that the same amount of brick, glass, and stone could have built a soulless box of a house. The place inspired me, made me want to try my hand at building something myself again.

It was lunchtime now so we hopped back into the car. With jack rabbit starts and squealing tires TJ drove through the winding shady streets like a mad man and ten minutes later we arrived at an African-style sidewalk restaurant. Our waiter there owned a snowy white cockatoo that he'd raised from an egg; the two went everywhere together. The bird was sitting in a tree beside our table, but when Marcia mentioned that she'd kept cockatoos herself, the waiter brought the lovely little creature down on his hand and rested him on her chair. We all chatted amiably over our drinks sitting beneath the trees that shaded us from a bright blue African sky.

After glancing through the menu I sucked up my courage and ordered mopani worms. A plateful of deep-fried, lightly spiced caterpillars in tomato sauce soon arrived. Thank God they weren't mushy inside. The exoskeleton of the head crunched a little as I chewed. I wouldn't order them again.

We hit the road again. This time to an African market— dozens of little stores chock-a-block with this and that. Plenty of dreck made strictly for tourists, but also some wonderful stuff. I bought a small, mysterious-looking mask that came from the Lenga tribe who live dead in the center of the Congo.

There was only an hour left, so we spent it at the *Apartheid Museum*. At the door they arbitrarily issued us black or white tickets that determined which entrance we took. Marcia and I were separated in the process, and it was a little confusing when we might get back together, which of course was the whole point. Inside was lots of information, beautifully presented about the struggle for freedom that went on here. Near the end were pictures of voting lines, blocks long.

South Africans of all races love their country passionately. On the way home I asked TJ if part of the appeal of Jo'burg to him was the danger. He denied it.

Advice to Travelers: Bargaining

FIRST AND FOREMOST, MAKE sure you actually want what they're trying to sell you. A common method is to nonchalantly get you to make an offer on a item "just for laughs," then you become so involved in the bargaining process that, before you know it, you're purchasing something you had no intention to even offer for in the first place.

Once you've decided that this is something that, on your own, you've actually intended to buy, you can begin the great process of haggling, which is a relatively lost art here in America. Here's a bargaining ploy I've found useful over the years: Once the guy gives you his first offer and you give your counter offer, don't just work to meet in the middle. Instead say, "I really like it, let me think about it and come back later."

When he protests say, "I'll take it right now for (some fairly low price) or I can come back later and we can agree on a price then."

This often works, but you have to stick to your guns and be ready to walk if you don't get your price— they can smell a bluff. Of course, if you feel you want to subsidize the business, just pay full price. Always be friendly. Ham it up if you feel like it; stagger backwards like you're utterly shocked by his first offer, etc. Have fun.

The Art of War

THE MOST EXTRAORDINARY AND unexpected sight I have ever seen in my life took place on the day Neal Armstrong first stepped onto the moon. It was the middle of the dry season, dusty, cloudless, and hot as blazes. We were constructing a helicopter landing strip. It was backbreaking work. Early in the day, some Major cruising by in his chopper spotted us down below him laboring and sweating without our heavy steel helmets on. The miserable bastard actually swooped down, hovered thirty feet above our heads, and shouted through a bullhorn that we'd either put those pods on or he'd land and "start kicking ass and taking names." God, how we cursed that asshole!

The landing-pad we were constructing consisted of a few thousand, hundred-pound, interlocking sheets of PSP (Perforated Steel Planking). When locked together, the pieces formed a single solid surface approximately sixty meters long by thirty meters wide. We had been told that an ARVN unit had been assigned to the same job the day before. When a helicopter had attempted to land, the draft from the choppers' rotors had picked up the heavy PSP, scattering it like deadly fallen leaves that had been sent aloft by a sudden gust of wind. Two South Vietnamese soldiers were killed.

It was late afternoon. We had almost completed the last phase of the work, anchoring the final side of the helipad to the ground, when a giant double-bladed Chinook helicopter suddenly thundered overhead. We desperately tried to wave him off, but the pilot didn't seem to understand. I can still see the tail end of the chopper swinging back and forth as it hung there above our heads in the pale afternoon sky. I clearly remember thinking that it looked like an immense, stupid insect trying to make sense of what lay below it.

Then the pilot did the worst possible thing. He detoured around the edge of the helipad to the unsecured side. There was nothing for us to do but run like hell. Just before I dived into the relative safety beneath our A-CAV, I turned my head to see an utterly unexpected sight. Without any of the pieces detaching, an entire wall of metal was effortlessly rising up just behind me.

When we emerged a couple of minutes later, standing before us was a perfectly sculpted ocean wave of steel over twice the height of a man... frozen.

Why I Love Holland

THE NETHERLANDS IS THE most civilized place I've ever visited. I feel at home when I'm there. The land itself is spectacularly featureless and overcrowded, but the people are friendly. They laugh a lot. I feel relaxed in their company. Anything a peaceful, questing, exuberant soul might want to do to explore life is allowed in this little nation. You won't be imprisoned for it. They look after people. Fairness is always an issue with them.

Of course, if you talk to a typical citizen about this they'll immediately deny it all. Then they'll tell you about some new issue that proves an exception to what I've just said. They're never satisfied with how things are, but are always tinkering with things a bit, always debating. It actually feels like a democracy. That's part of the beauty of the place and its citizens.

The first time I visited Europe I was out bicycling by the Zeider Zee with my brother Richard under a warm clear sky. We'd cycled all day and the highest elevation we'd encountered was the slight hump in the road crossing a canal.

We had stopped for a lunch of bread, cheese and fruit. There were farmers harvesting tulip bulbs near the road and we offered to help. By the end of the afternoon, we had become friends. They offered us dinner and a place to stay the night. The main course was a hearty soup and we, as guests, were given an up-scaled version: theirs contained hamburger meatballs while ours had hunks of steak. After dinner I was talking with the farmer and, this being Holland, asked if he smoked hashish.

"No, no, no, certainly not," he chuckled.

"Then what do you think of the hippies on the Damrak in Amsterdam, lying around, smoking hash all day?"

A strange look of incomprehension crept across his weathered features. He answered slowly, "This is a free country; what possible difference would it make to me?"

Many years later I found myself in Amsterdam with only two Guilders left in my pocket. With one of them I bought french fries ("pommes frites") and mayonnaise, which I ate with great relish, and with the other, several flowers, which I gave away. No worries.

Flash forward twenty years. I was in Amsterdam again. This time I was well scrubbed and accompanied by a nice looking wife and a beautiful child. I was driving a shiny new car. We looked like the kind of people any country would be happy to allow within their borders.

I happened to see a Dutch policeman and went up to him and said, "You know, I was here twenty years ago without a Guilder in my pocket. Back then the Dutch cops treated me with the greatest courtesy. I thought they were the best in the world."

With a face that was both stern yet not unkind, he looked me straight in the eye: "Yes, and we still are."

Why I Love India

I FEEL MORE AT peace with myself and the world when I'm in India, like I'm closer to who I really am.   I love the feeling of freedom.   I don't smoke anymore, but India is the kind of place where you could probably light up a cigarette in a hospital ward.   You get the feeling that all things are possible here.   If you've always wanted to be a doctor or an engineer or an architect, you could get away with doing it in India.   If you can dream up a house you want to have built, or a sculpture carved, or a piece of furniture constructed, there are skilled craftsmen here who can turn your dream into a reality.   It won't cost much either.   If you see someone sick or injured and you know what their problem is, you can go to the pharmacy, buy whatever medicine you need and treat them.   This makes my American doctor friends cringe.   In my defense, I try to keep it to simple stuff.

Sometimes India seems a little chaotic, but with the exception of traffic, it's one of the safest places I've ever been.   Planes and trains have the same safety record as in Europe and there's practically no violent crime.   It's disconcerting when you first get to Bombay to walk past people sitting on the sidewalk cooking up "brown sugar" in a spoon and shooting it up with rusty needles.   It looks like a dangerous place, but it isn't.   I'm not saying that even the smack dealers here are like the Care Bears, but I am saying that they will not harm you.   Even if they tried, bystanders would intervene on your behalf, and the cops don't put up with any shenanigans.

In India I always feel like I never have to do anything I don't want to do.   Say one of the lenses falls out of my glasses, or I need a rubber tip on my walking stick.   Instead of fiddling around with it like I would in America, I can pay one of the workers at my hotel fifty rupees and it *will* happen. Someone will be delighted to make a little extra money and do it for me. They're hard workers. I can spend my time doing what I enjoy.

Outside of the cities you don't get the sensory overload that is so common in the west. You can concentrate on one thing at a time. It's easier to find the time to focus and observe an ant, listen to a bird, or read a difficult book. For that matter, it's a wonderful environment to write a book. Lots of great literature has been produced here. Most countries are fortunate to have one great book written about them. India has had dozens.

Anything can happen the next moment. You might be walking down the road and a man riding an elephant offers you a ride into town. But not just regular things: sometimes miraculous things happen.

It's a country of tremendous diversity. The differences between a Ladhaki, a Goan, and a Bombayite are far greater than the differences between a Swede, a German, and a Londoner. Indians speak well over four hundred languages (just like the Swiss, practically every Indian speaks three or four). There are dozens of distinctive cultures, each with its own dress, cuisine, music and architecture. In ten miles of travel you can find yourself in another world.

You meet some really villainous people here, but also some truly sublime ones. Things are often very extreme. A city like Benares can be both incredibly beautiful and incredibly ugly at the same time. You can legally buy black tarry-looking blocks of hashish here in government run stores close by the Ganges.

I remember one evening sitting quietly in a small boat at twilight gazing at the steps of one of the great ghats that lead down to the dirty brown river lugubriously making its way to the sea. The soft clouds overhead were tinted deep purple. Hundreds of people were bathing, temple bells were tinkling, and dark black smoke was rising from the burning funeral pyres of the recently departed.

There's nothing boring about India. There is a man in this wonderful country who has remained standing up for thirty years; I talked to his cab driver who described how difficult it was to drive him around town in that position. There are people here who live their lives naked, or "sky clad" as they say, or you might turn a corner and encounter someone buried up to their nose in the dirt.

India has far more faces than that though. A few years ago I visited a two-hundred acre oasis of green in the midst of the scrubby wasteland outside Hyderabad. It was home to a computer software company. Inside the compound was an eighteen-hole golf course, swimming pools, tennis courts, even a zoo. Strangely though, no one was playing golf or viewing the giraffes. The action was elsewhere. At the epicenter of this Garden of Eden was a formidable-looking building referred to as the "core area." Inside, I got a glimpse of the new India. I spoke to an impeccably dressed young man hurriedly walking down a well polished hallway about what kind of hours he was putting in.

"Normally about eighty," he replied, "unless there is some kind of push going on. Then we just lose track." His movements were bird-like: quick and precise. There was a fire in his eye. He was proud of himself, proud of his company, and proud of how he was re-making his country. India is much more than naked sadhus.

One of the most diverse and curious tribes in India are the western travelers. Lots of searchers and seekers have been drawn here, lots of unique people, and some a bit daffy I'll admit. Over the years I've met a guy who has made his living (a very good living) for twenty-five years by painting rectangles, another one who was writing a book that will revolutionize everything, another who was starring in a new TV series, another who supported himself by putting on live sex shows in Japan. I could go on and on.

There's an incredible physical diversity to India as well. It has every kind of environment, and every kind of climate. Throughout the whole year, it's always comfortable somewhere. Long-term visas are easily obtained and, outside the cities, everything is dirt cheap except for a few things you don't really need anyway. Two of my $500/month paradises are found here.

Indians love complexity. Almost everyone seems to be able to do difficult sums in their heads. In addition to crossword puzzles, local newspapers occasionally include geometrical theorems for their readers to work on. Indians don't trust anything simple. I once saw a book of matches with a corny Dutch landscape complete with a windmill and a girl in wooden shoes on the front flap. On the back was an elaborate diagram for deciphering the day of the week for any date until 2020.

In a thousand lifetimes you could never discover every facet of this wondrous jewel of a country. I love it as I love my own homeland, America.

Best Things in the World

- Many years ago I arrived in Istanbul on the deck of a boat. It was very early in the morning. I awoke with a thin coating of dew on the outside of my sleeping bag. But inside that little fleece lined cocoon I was snug and dry. The ship was quietly cutting through the dark water of the Bosporus. Through the gray mist I could barely make out the shapes of the great mosques as they glided past me along the shore.

- Itinerant magicians of India. For a few rupees extra, they'll give you a private showing revealing all their secrets.

- Walking the Otter Trail along the coast of South Africa.

- Swimming with stingrays in the shallow clear water of Caye Caulker off the coast of Belize. As they swam around us, they cast beautiful undulating shadows on the white sand beneath them.

- The "Chimera Building" in Kiev with its jungle of fantastical animal heads, and gargoyles peering down from the roof and above all the doorways. It's the work of an eccentric genius named Vladislav Gorodetski who made it his home at the turn of the 20th Century.

- I once lived for a few days in a tree house in Ecuador. One evening at dinner I let it slip that it was my 50th birthday. At about 8 o'clock while sitting on my balcony reading a book I was surprised when a small group of travelers quietly gathered around the base of my tree and broke into "Happy Birthday to You." I loved that little place. Once I remember waking up to a bird landing on my windowsill.

- One of the high points on the hippy trail to India in the 70's was Chicken Street in Kabul where shopkeepers sold juicy fresh pies to hungry travelers.

- The small medieval university town of Tubingen in the midst of the lovely Black Forest in Germany.

- There is a castle near Heidelberg that sits atop a long steep-sided valley covered in vineyards that encloses both sides of the Neckar River. The castle houses a remarkable private aviary that contains, along with other raptors, Andean Condors with twelve-foot wingspans. (The cover of this book shows a picture I took of the silhouette of one of these great birds and its handler.) When released into the air, the giant birds utilized thermal updrafts and swept majestically back and forth along the valley. Sometimes in response to their handlers signal, the condors were made to fly only a foot above our heads. As the great shadow swept over us, it seemed more like the shadow of a plane than that of a living creature. You could hear the soft sound of air parting as the huge bird passed just above us.

- The temple-town of Pushkar, India on the edge of the Rajasthani desert. The small city encircles a sacred lake surrounded by temples and bathing ghats. During the evening of Diwali, tiny paper boats with candles are floated on its surface.

- The first day of summer vacation when you're ten years old.

- Discovering that medications in India cost roughly 4% of what they do in America.

Driving a Cab

My FIRST JOB AFTER getting discharged from the army was driving a taxi. The cab companies were always hiring. It was only a short term proposition as I had already been accepted into Dental school for the fall. The pay was lousy but I enjoyed the work so long as I didn't have to drive over forty hours/week. As with most jobs, anything beyond that and it began to feel like a grind. I had short hair, which was very unfashionable. At the time, hip young people of my generation felt they were beyond fashion. How little insight we had.[6]

My short hair left me free to redefine myself with every new ride. Sometimes I'd put on a hillbilly accent to see what effect it elicited from my fares. I never said anything foolish, I never acted like a fool, but whatever I said was said in a country accent. What a revelation! I'd never understood why country folk so often seemed resentful of city slickers. Now I got it.

College students were especially contemptuous of me. As we drove along, they often sat slouched in the backseat as they made snide remarks to their pretty girlfriends. They knew I could overhear, but they didn't care. I was a lesser being to them. Sometimes I felt like climbing over the seat and throttling the little bastards. I had a short fuse back then; these days people often ask me if I just woke up.

My brother Richard once said that everyone has a story to tell and that a taxi ride might be just the time for it. As soon as someone would

---

[6] Back then some GI's, in an attempt to be acceptable enough to get laid, would affect a sort of "pirate look" using a bandana around their heads.

get into my cab I looked for what they had to teach me. There was always something. Sometimes people who knew we'd never see each other again never said to anyone else. Sometimes I did the same.

Fishing in Goa

THE TWO DOGS FROM my hotel accompanied me to the beach where I met up with Arun and Anand. It was four in the morning with no moon and quite dark. We placed dry clothes under the seats of their twenty-foot long, open boat, and then the three of us pushed the craft down toward the dark sea. I was on the outrigger side at the point where it attached to the hull. My friends put grooved wooden blocks lubricated with cashew nut oil under the hull to help us move the boat forward. It had been positioned barely above the high tide-line. The men knew just how high the water would come. It varied from night to night. They calculated it in their heads from the relative positions of the sun and the moon.

I've had little experience with ocean-going boats having grown up in landlocked Indiana. So as soon as the boat was in the water, I scrambled in over the gunwale and let Anand and Arun push it out beyond the breaking waves. Left alone on the beach, the dogs howled for a while but soon gave up and returned home. We paddled hard, straight into the surf. About a mile out, we made a turn and the two men began to lay out the nets. Arun was having some difficulty trying to steer from the rear and let out the nets at the same time. I realized that I might be helpful. I asked if I might steer, so he could give full attention to putting out the nets. He pointed out a star to keep my bearings by. I used the same paddling technique my grandfather had called the "lazy J." It involves a slight correcting movement of the oar away from the boat at the end of each stroke. For some reason I was surprised that it worked on the sea just as it had on rivers back in Indiana. I could keep us on a straight line.[7]

Fifteen minutes later the net was out. Everything had been accomplished for the time being. We chatted for a while in my laughably inadequate Hindi. Then the two of them curled up in blankets and went to sleep. They encouraged me to do the same, but I was so entranced by the scene around us that I only wished to listen to the water gently lapping against the hull and lie out under the stars and the great dark sky. From time to time, Arun would wake with a start at curious knocking sounds and barely audible grunts, and say, "Dolphin." To my uneducated ear they would only have seemed like the random noises of the ocean. I hadn't seen a dolphin this year. I had thought that perhaps the area had been over-fished and they had left.

As the sun lightened the sky to the East, however, I sighted a big healthy dolphin cresting over the waves quite near our boat. As the sun rose over the land, I began to see many more in the distance.

Now it was time to bring in the catch. Arun again gave me instructions for the proper line to follow, and I guided the boat slowly forward as the two of them brought in the net. It was a poor haul: a few prawns, some small kingfish, crabs, sand shark, and the occasional starfish. A poisonous sea snake had become entangled in the net as well. Arun cautioned me to leave it alone.

We pointed our little boat toward the coast and pulled hard for the shore. The sun was well up by this time and the seagulls were crying and flying to and fro as we pushed our little craft ashore.

---

[7] A peculiar realization came to me: I wasn't seasick. Prior to this, even if the boat I was on was merely sitting in the dock, swaying to the waves, I would become nauseous. When I mentioned this to a friend who had his own sailing boat, he was not at all surprised. He said of course I wasn't seasick; I was guiding the boat, I was at one with it. No one ever gets carsick when they're driving the car themselves.

Drugs

I DON'T SMOKE CIGARETTES or do drugs. I only occasionally drink alcohol. It wasn't always so. I was a two-pack-a-day smoker and, back in the 60's and 70's, I took a lot of mood modifying substances of one type or another.

My last real "trip" was in Australia, in the lush virginal rainforest of northern Queensland. I was traveling with a woman named Pandora (a name you'd never forget) at the time. We'd hooked-up at a commune in Sydney and had hitched up the east coast together. We stopped off for a few days at a tranquil little farm owned by a friend of hers. Small brown and white-headed Psilocybin mushrooms grew there in the cow patties. The tender flesh of these little fungi turned blue when bruised. The first morning after we arrived, we ate a couple of handfuls.

It was a glorious day; many wonderful things happened. I could never describe it. But everything comes to an end. The sun was going down. The two of us were gazing in awe at the enormous pink and salmon colored clouds gliding by above us. We were starting to come down. It's only when you start to "come on" to a trip that you remember what tripping *is* and it's only when you're coming down from a trip that you realize you've been tripping. The revelations granted to us were starting to recede, and we were gradually drifting down into everyday consciousness. Totally unbidden, a thought came to me. *Life by itself is a trip*. It's so easy to forget that it's a deep and wonderful miracle that we are here. It came to me that I'd learned what I could learn from psychedelics and this should be my last time.

I am definitely not recommending that anyone take drugs. Nobody gets to heaven on LSD. Opiates are addictive and turn you into a terrible lay. Cocaine improves only one thing, your perception of how cool you are. Maybe I personally needed to take consciousness-expanding substances like mushrooms and LSD to get an inkling of certain things. I'm a little pig-headed sometimes. All that talk about "expanded consciousness," "the one-ness of being," "nirvana," etc sounded intriguing to me, but also a little wooly-headed.

These experiences were my experiences and I've tried to be truthful about them. I salute those souls who, without the use of chemicals, simply trust the intimations of the divine that come their way and follow those intimations.

For some reason, perhaps only known to The US Drug Enforcement Agency, LSD, psilocybin mushrooms, and peyote buttons are put in the same category as opium, heroin and morphine. They are *not* related other than the fact that they are opposites. One may open the doors of perception. The other is an escape from life and pain. One group is addictive and the other isn't. I'm not a gifted enough writer to describe the experience of psychedelics, but maybe I can give an idea of what opiates are like.

We were in Peshawar near the Khyber Pass. One night, mostly out of curiosity, I asked our cycle rickshaw driver to take us to an opium den. We knew we were getting close when we started seeing signs on every ramshackle wooden building saying, "Off Limits to all Ranks." Those in power didn't mind getting paid off for letting the places operate, but they didn't want the troops to get addicted.

We got to the rattiest section of this very tough border town. I remember climbing some dark, rickety stairs to a bare upstairs room. We smoked some opium and the next thing I knew, I was laying face-up on the floor examining the ceiling. William Burroughs once wrote about spending an entire day on smack looking at the end of his boot.

Sometime that evening soldiers came in carrying guns. They laughed at us lying there so helplessly. I distinctly remember thinking, "I don't care if they shoot me, just so they don't make me stand up."

Years later I was in Luang Prabang in Laos. I'd gotten there by way of a muddy jungle road, traveling in a beat-up old bus that had slowly made its way up there from the capitol. The day before I left Vientiane, this same bus had been stopped and robbed. The week after, it happened again, but this time they killed everyone on board except an Australian who survived by playing dead while the thieves (probably moonlighting soldiers) picked through the corpses searching for money and jewelry.

With belated good sense, the bus service from Vientiane to Luang Prabang was canceled. The only way out of town was now a forty-year-old DC-3, which was immediately fully booked for several weeks.

I had time on my hands and this town had only two forms of diversion. There were the ladies of easy virtue and there was the opium den. I chose opium, which put me out of service as far as women were concerned.

Every night I went to the same little house. Inside, it was dimly lit by smoky oil lamps. The customers (I can't remember what anyone looked like) lay in a circle, our heads resting on bricks covered in burlap. The floor was filthy, vermin-ridden and covered in straw. We were beyond caring. As we lay there on our sides, directly in front of each of us was another brick where we could put a coin to pay for the next hit. A cadaverous looking old man moved slowly around the circle with a pipe fashioned from a gourd. He pocketed my coin and put a dab of black tarry opium on a spot on the side of the gourd. Next to the spot was a pinhole-sized hole. He lit the stuff for me. I sucked the open end of the pipe and the sickeningly sweet smoke curled up through the tiny hole through the gourd and into my lungs. I felt nauseous. When only a bit remained, he made a gesture that came from his body not his eyes: could he have the last portion as a tip? I nodded. He took it neat. I looked into his eyes. I felt as if I was looking down into the eyes of a tortoise or a dark well. It was terrifying; absolutely nothing was going on there— *Nothing.*

I was sliding helplessly and irresistibly into a terrible addiction that I'm certain I never could have prevailed against. But luck (or God) hadn't deserted me. The drug had a curious effect on my body. It paralyzed my bladder muscles so I couldn't pee. When that happened I had to quit. I suppose that's another time when I almost died.

Advice to Travelers:
Don't Give Out Sweets

I KNOW IT SEEMS innocent enough, but I have come to understand that it is a bad idea to hand out sweets to children in developing countries. The same goes for things like pens and pencils. I've walked through tiny villages in the Himalayas where instead of waving, every child I passed asked me for a pen. If you want to be helpful give a couple of dozen pens and pencils directly to the teacher. They'll distribute them to the children.

Kids are always grateful to accept anything you give them. The problem is only seen by the next traveler. Perfectly normal children will have been turned into beggars.

End of lecture.

The Jericho Bar House

UNDENIABLY, THE WORST HOTEL I've ever stayed in was the Jericho Bar House. Again, I won't mention the country where this took place, since I don't want to besmirch its reputation. It has so many other delightful aspects.

Rick Owens and I must have known— should have known— that we were in for trouble. When we walked into this place to get a room, the patrons at the bar were drinking homebrew beer out of discarded motor oil cans and casting threatening looks in our direction. Our "room," as we discovered, was little more than a fetid space cordoned off with chicken wire. The floor was packed-down earth with a ratty, little, no color rug covering a section of it. I don't recall any furniture; maybe there were a couple of cots. Nonetheless, it was the only place in town, so we unrolled our sleeping bags and decided to make the best of it.

Within five minutes we were itching and scratching from mites, bugs, and fleas. Locally, biting pests like these are collectively referred to as "doudous." (I finally got rid of these critters two days later by dusting everything I owned with a toxic looking flea powder called "Doom"). All this was taking Rick and me close to our limits of tolerance. The limit was reached when a concerned good samaritan came back and told us that the guys at the bar planned to get tanked up this afternoon then rob us of all our stuff at nightfall. We cleared out *pronto*.

Racing At Sweet Owen Speedway

THIS LITTLE ADVENTURE TOOK place in Owen County Indiana about thirty miles from my hometown. During his undergraduate days, my brother Philip had gotten to know a young fellow at work who owned a "street-stocker," the lowest class of stockcar. The rules stated that in this classification the engine couldn't be modified, but the car might be lightened and stripped to the bare essentials.

As soon as Phil told me about this car and how his friend might be persuaded to let us drive it in a race, I was on fire to see the thing. Next day I got the chance.

It was definitely not cherry and it'd seen trouble in its time; the dents, holes and rusted-through panels spoke to that. There was a sizable hole in the floorboard through which you could see the pavement beneath. To get inside, you had to wiggle your way in through the drivers-side window. The interior was gutted except for one small seat. There was not an ounce of fat on the thing. All the window glass had been replaced with chicken wire. There was no muffler, of course; that was just dead weight.

But the thing had a hell of an engine. Turn the key and that beast rattled to life and made a tremendous noise. It got my heart pumping just sitting in that baby listening to the motor. I sat there, revving it up a little from time to time, and it was very responsive. I was going to take this car and make it my bitch!

Phil's friend knew just the place for us to get started, the racetrack with the loosest rules in southern Indiana: "Sweet Owen Speedway."

Arriving early, we checked out the scene. The set-up was basic: nothing but bleachers and a slightly banked quarter-mile oval dirt track nestled amidst the cornfields. A few disinterested looking spectators were up in the stands, but most of the fans seemed to be congregated in the pits. This was where all the action was taking place. Off-duty mechanics and country folks milled about curiously, checking out the cars, cracking jokes, sipping Mountain Dew, and slyly sizing up the competition while munching on corndogs and tenderloins. Drinking amongst the drivers, if done at all, was done discreetly. There were some tough looking customers; they looked like guys who could hold their liquor. I found that reassuring (sort of).

This was a gentleman's sport. Instead of the fastest qualifying car being put in the pole position, it was put in the rear. Since we were the slowest qualifiers, we were going to be starting right up front.

They announced our race over the tinny sounding PA system. I was ready. I fired up the engine. What a racket it made! My confidence soared at the sound of it, proud to be at the wheel of this powerful machine. I rumbled out onto the track under the stark white lights. To tell the truth, at this point, I was starting to get a little scared. I eased the car up the line and into position in the front row on the inside. The exhaust fumes stung my eyes. Everyone was aggressively revving their engines, itching to get off. My heart was pumping like crazy. What a scene! My ears rang from it. I was primed and ready for this test of manhood… or kind of ready. I tried to focus. Be still oh my hormones and remain in your glands lest your master do something unworthy!

The white flag dropped. I slammed the pedal to the metal. We were off! The chaos that ensued was indescribable. All that folksy camaraderie had come to an end. These guys weren't messing around; their jaw muscles were locked and every man out there was aiming to win. This was no time for halfway measures. You define the moment or it defines you. On the straightaway I mashed the pedal to the floor. Coming into the turns, I braced my body and recklessly threw the vehicle into gut wrenching, balls-out, four-wheel drifts.

Inexplicably, despite all my heroic, manly effort, five minutes into the race every single car had somehow passed me. It grew strangely quiet back there.

Then, far up ahead, one of the drivers spun out on a curve. Hope stirred anew in my flinty breast; some honor might be salvaged. I might not finish dead last.

His engine had quit; he was dead in the water. In a triumphant surge I blew right past him. Humility was a thing of the past. I was now securely in the second-to-last position. Then a chill ran through me. In my rearview mirror, I could see that my rival had restarted his engine and was back on the track— *headed for me.*

I screwed up my courage and redoubled my efforts. Hell-bent, this enraged hillbilly caught me on the straightaway. A moment later we were neck-and-neck going into the turn. I was on the outside and this wild country boy was on the inside. Big clods of dirt came raining through the window striking me on the side of my helmet. CLUMP CLUMP CLUMP. It was man against man.

Once more the Sturm und Drang abated. Once more I found myself serenely in last place. It was just another of life's bitter pills. I was not to be a famous stockcar driver.

I've slowly come to the realization that I simply may not have any great talents. I'll never be one of those people who can memorize the Koran, or sit naked on a block of ice and show signs of fever. I'm not smart enough to count cards in blackjack and beat the house in Vegas or steady-handed enough to draw the Taj Mahal on a grain of rice. You play life as best you can with the cards that are dealt to you.

Recently I've taken to the habit of putting a small rosebud in the hatband of my fedora which I then cock just so. As I walk down the street here in the Ukrainian city of Lviv, there's a spring in my step as I pass beneath the arches of these fine old medieval buildings. I may not be anything out of the ordinary, but I'm just glad to be here in a new city, a new country. God made me a traveler; it's who I am. As the tip of my walking stick clicks against the cobblestones, I feel like an aging Boulevardier, making my way through the world, keeping an eye out for some little unexpected bit of loveliness.

Best Things in the World

- I was walking through an empty space in the desert at The Burning Man Festival when I saw a phone booth with the sign, "Talk to God." As I was passing, the phone rang. I picked it up and someone said, "This is God, may I help you?" It was nice that the guy at the other end took his job seriously and tried to give wise advice.

- Hearing the call to prayer from dozens of mosques in the midst of the ancient city of Saana, while sitting in the mafraj on the top floor of a hotel at sunset.

- Flan served in a coconut shell in Vietnam.

- Traveling with an introductory college astronomy textbook, I discovered that what it described was as bizarre and unlikely as anything I had ever read.

- Passionate tango dancers dressed formally in black are often seen busking on the streets of Buenos Aires. The onlookers are discriminating connoisseurs of the art. They treat the performances with deep respect.

- Exploring a flower with the macro lens of a camera. Getting lost in it.

- In southern Africa there's a species of bird called the sociable-weaver bird. A couple of hundred of these finch-like birds will build a communal home as big as a small haystack in some tree. Colonies can be a hundred years old.

- The wooden ship building town of Mandvi in Gujarat. All along the river you can see boats in different stages of construction with crews of workmen cobbling them together using the simplest of tools. Not small ships, either, but huge Noah-sized arks as much as 200 feet long. The worksites are open and the carpenters friendly. You can climb up on ladders into the bellies of these great beasts of the sea and chat with them.

- Kayaking the Sorrona River in Patagonia. Sometimes we barely made headway paddling into gusty headwinds. First night we camped in a sheltered, wooded spot where the ground was covered with orchids. Next night we arrived and pitched our tents near a glacier that calved small blue-tinted icebergs into the lake below.

- Arab hospitality.

- A big, brightly-colored, indoor *Schwimmbad* with waterfalls, waterslides, saunas, restaurants, and lots of pools of all sizes (each with different water temperatures). It's the perfect place to spend a gloomy, rainy winter day in Germany.

- The desert at Wadi Rum in Jordan. Marcia Anderson and I camped here once, along with a couple of other travelers. It's the place where Peter O'Toole first meets Omar Sharif in the film "Lawrence of Arabia." The air was crystalline. We lay in the sand and watched satellites trace across the sky.

- Entering the pig-calling contest at The Indiana State Fair and belting out my grandfathers pig call, "IP DIMINITY ONKTY SONKTY SONKTY ONKTY YAHOO!"

- Compost piles.

- Thai islands where the water is so clear that boats look like they're floating in air.

Fear and Greed:
Playing the Stock Market

ONE REASON I FEEL a little disjointed from time to time is that there seems to be a bit of everything in me. Maybe everyone feels that way. All I know is that it makes it hard to act like I'd like to act: with the clean decisiveness of some wise old Kung Fu master. But screw it, I'm not like that. There's part of me that couldn't care less about material stuff, but another part that just likes making money. Kept under control, I like to think it's a harmless vice.

Nine years ago I was in Bombay with my second wife and dear friend, Marcia Anderson. Currencies all over South East Asia had collapsed[8] and local stock markets were in freefall. All over the area, stock prices of perfectly good companies making perfectly good profits were in a vicious nosedive. Some of this was rational; some was not.

Stocks have a certain underlying value based mostly on the profits, or potential profits, of the companies they represent. There is a little jiggery pokery as you might expect, but on the whole the SEC keeps the market fairly honest. Profits can be calculated and potential profits guessed at. Then there are the emotions of fear and greed. Sometimes the market is greedy, at other times fearful. This is a huge factor and

---

[8] At one point you could buy a Big Mac sandwich for $.79 in Indonesia. I still find it helpful and interesting to check "The Big Mac Index" on The Economist magazine's web site. There, you can find out the current price of the famous sandwich in over two hundred countries. It's a good, though incomplete, way to compare currencies.

is essentially irrational. There are lots of other factors of course, most of which nobody understands. By its very nature, you can never fully understand or predict the market.

The real point I want to make here is that it seemed to me, at the time, that markets throughout South East Asia were consumed by fear. The fear was, to a certain extent, irrational but that didn't stop it from being self-fulfilling. I felt strongly that stock prices were too low and therefore it was the right time to buy. The problem was that I didn't have any extra money. I phoned my bank and essentially they said, "No soap."

Marcia, bless her, said, "If you believe in it so strongly, I'll loan you $2000." So I became a stock speculator. I bought shares in a Philippine phone company, or maybe it was an Indonesian one. Someone once said that in the short term the market is a voting machine, but in the long term it's a weighing machine. Anyway, I thought this company was a sound company in the long term that was now vastly undervalued.

Within two weeks it had dropped another 1/3. There were ups and downs from there on, but more ups than downs and a couple of months later I sold for a nice profit. That got me started. My good fortune after that still astounds me. In the worst of the next three years, my stocks went up over 400%. Everything I bought went up like a rocket. Three and a half years after that first investment, my portfolio was worth $125,000.

All I needed were three more "doubles" and I'd be worth $1 million in equities. I figured that would be enough. I wish I could report that I took this humbly. I didn't. I remember telling someone, "In order to do well in the market you have to understand the world." In other words, I was in the grip of insufferable hubris.

Then things started to turn on me. Every buy decision I had made previously was right. Now they were all wrong. My Midas touch had turned to shit. I couldn't understand what was going on. One thing is for sure though: you can't argue with the market; there's no use clinging to some attitude about where it ought to go. It's like the ocean; it doesn't care. When my pile had shrunk back to $50,000 I threw in the towel and sold everything.

I wish I could report that I've now acquired a Zen-like detachment to how my stocks perform. It wouldn't be true. It still gives me a jolt of adrenaline when they go up and, at best, a feeling of philosophical resignation when they go down.

It's a game and the money is how you keep score. It's not the big game, but it's an interesting game.

Jacques playing with young monks in Ladakh.

Jacques watering our camels in a small village in Rajasthan.

Guard duty, Black Horse Base Camp, Vietnam 1969.

Painting the great gate at the Bombay Smagam.

Thea and my father.

Trekking on the outskirts, Aberdaire National Park in Kenya, 1971.

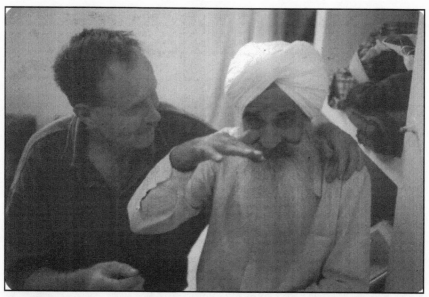

Wasu Singh, man who took me to meet Baba Gurbachan Singh.

Blessed by an elephant in Sri Lanka

Baba Hardev Singh, his mother Raj Mata-ji and his wife Pooja Mata-ji on the stage at the annual Smagam."

Pushing our safari truck out of the mud.

I'm an Angel

I WAS ONCE A dental student. My father was a dentist, but considering the fact that I have shaky hands, it was a poor career choice for me. Anyone who has ever had a toothache will appreciate what a blessing of civilization good dentistry is, but it was a mistake for me, and I was truly miserable trying to make a go of it.

At the time I was living in Indianapolis in a subsidized housing project called *The River House*. My roommate, a fellow dental student, and I were the only white folks living in this high-rise apartment complex except for two women in an adjoining tower who we rarely saw.

Our next-door neighbors were Tommy, Anita, and their six-year-old son, "the dude." Tommy was a heroin dealer and Anita was a prostitute. Together they had a $500/day smack habit. Every day they had to come up with living expenses, plus that $500. Somehow they always did. As Anita once said, "Tommy is an expert at everything illegal." He was a formidable looking guy— definitely over two hundred fifty pounds— and he kept himself well-armed. In his business you needed to be. Improbably, we became friends.

Tommy did business out of another locale, as did Anita, for the most part. Shortly after we met, I ran into Tommy in the corridor. I was shocked to see him with a thick bandage wrapped around his massive neck.

"What happened to you?" I gulped.

"When a man needs a fix man, sometimes he really needs a fix," he replied.

Apparently, he'd been jumped from behind and had a knife put to his throat. Tommy didn't seem resentful though; that's just the way it was.

One evening, I was hanging out with my three neighbors in their apartment after a long day of classes. Tommy had just shot up some smack and Anita was showing me a book she'd bought about making fondue at home. The dude was buzzing around the living room with his arms spread, saying, "I'm an angel, I'm an angel." We all kind of chuckled. It's just one of those thin slices of life you carry around with you. I remember for his sixth birthday Tommy gave his son a hundred dollar bill.

One weekend my brother, Richard, had hitched over from a little college town in Ohio where he was going to school. We stayed up late talking before finally turning in. Sometime that night, we were awakened by a tremendous pounding on the door:

"Let me in, let me in, I'm a friend of Tommy's!" Out of shock or hospitality or some combination of the two, I opened the door. In crashed a humongous black guy I'd never met, carrying four or five guns, needles, syringes, and a couple of dozen packages of smack. Two minutes later Tommy himself was beating on the door with more of the same kind of stuff. I let him in too.

"The Rollers are here," he excitedly explained, "We got the word." A minute later through the thick wooden door we heard a commotion in the hall. They both crouched, drew their guns, and got ready for trouble... Luckily, it was only another resident walking down the hall. The cops were on another floor busting someone else that night.

I don't want to go on and on, but let me tell two more quick incidents. All these things occurred in the six-month span that I knew their little family. They lived an intense life. Again I ran into Tommy in the hall outside his "crib." This time he was wearing a plaster back-cast. I asked him what the deal was. Apparently, the cops had been busting down the door where he'd been dealing. The place was on the second or third floor, I don't remember which. Anyway, Tommy had done hard time before and didn't want to repeat it. Rather than getting busted, he'd jumped out the window, picked himself up, and scrambled off into the night.

The last time I saw Tommy, he and a friend were surveying the thick yellow tape stretched across his doorway that read, "Homicide Scene, Do Not Enter." Tommy explained that Anita had been "making it" with an elderly white man when the poor bastard had had a coronary attack. She didn't want him dying on the premises, so she dragged him out of their place. That was their story anyway. It sounded like bullshit to me. At any rate, Tommy cut through the tape, went in, and fetched the fancy shotgun he was looking for. That was the last I ever saw of them.

Cultural Adjustments

MY FIRST ENCOUNTER WITH the Third World took place in Ceuta, Spanish Morocco. It was a hot, dry day in this unpleasant little border town. My brother Richard and I were traveling with two terrific young American women who had hitched with us down the east coast of Spain. To make life easier we were in the habit of designating one person to do the hassling while everyone else relaxed. When it was time to buy the bus tickets across the border to what used to be referred to as "French Morocco," it was my turn to stand in line and deal with it.

Things were going fine until one young man cut directly in front of me. In broken French and Spanish, I explained as politely as I could, that I had been there first, and would he please step to the end of the line. This appeared to work, as he nodded his head in agreement and left.

It seemed a little excessive, but after this incident, I thought I'd take the added precaution of extending my right leg out to the side to guard my place in line from further encroachment. But two minutes later, a second fellow stepped right over my leg-barrier and barged in directly ahead of me. Again I patiently explained that I had been there first. But this guy wasn't buying it. This pissed me off. I grabbed him by the arm and started pulling him backwards. He deftly grabbed the metal grid of the ticket window with his free arm, and held on like a demon. Not to be bested, I braced my legs to the wall and yanked for everything I was worth. Suddenly the ticket window collapsed and the two of us found ourselves covered in glass in an angry heap on the hard floor.

Luckily, before things escalated, the cops arrived and broke things up. "My God," I thought, "is this what I am going to have to do every time I have to do something as simple as buy a ticket? What kind of place have I come to?"

As an experiment, next time I was in a "line" (which looked more like a mob to me), I changed my tactics. I elbowed, pushed, shoved and jockeyed for the best position just like everyone else. I was amazed to discover that nobody got angry and nobody felt like I was doing anything amiss. No problems.

A second adjustment I had to make in Africa had to do with my concept of timeliness. In three months, starting in Morocco, traveling down through the Sahara to Senegal, across to Mali, then north through Algeria, I traveled by boat, train, plane, truck and bus – dozens of rides. Rarely did a trip start on time, and *absolutely never* did it arrive on time. The only question: would we be an hour late, a day late, or a week late? Occasionally it was more than a week, but that was the exception.

Best Things in the World

- We were trekking in the austere, treeless landscape of Ladakh under the immense cloudless sky. Along one of the trails, we encountered a wall of stones three feet tall and a half mile long. On every stone was engraved the prayer, "Om Mani Padme Om." Twenty years later I learned these were carved by criminals. It was thought that by carving this invocation over and over they would become better men.

- Ubud, Bali, the artistic soul of Indonesia.

- Hearing Toccata and Fugue emerge from a mighty organ and echo through the cavernous space of Notre Dame Cathedral in Paris.

- The bizarre looking Jantar Mantar in Jaipur, India. It was constructed by the Maharaja Jai Singh in 1728. The grounds are filled with a multitude of giant pink structures that were ingeniously designed to serve as sundials, predict eclipses, and follow the course of dozens of heavenly bodies.

- Gigantic, twenty- thousand foot tall cumulus clouds you can see at the beginning or end of the monsoons in Southeast Asia.

- The beautiful central square in Krakow, Poland. The weather was biting cold and the wind whipped tiny flecks of snow in my face as I walked across it. It was at the time of *Glasnost*. That afternoon I met some young college students at a little bar. I mentioned that it must be exciting to be young and living in such a tumultuous and important time. One replied that, "No, it just felt normal."

- Dancing in Africa… you *know* you're in the big leagues.

- Porch swings in small Indiana towns.

- A massage in the steam filled marble chambers of some ancient Turkish bath (hamam) in Istanbul.

- The two comfortable but modest homes in Fort Myers, Florida where neighbors Thomas Edison and Henry Ford over-wintered. The houses are surrounded by a botanical garden of plants Edison felt might have some practical application. There's a magnificent banyan tree out front. Fords house next door contains a major historical site: the first swimming pool in Florida.

- Learning from a man in Syria how to cut the skin of an orange in the shape of a flower. He told me that once when he was in the army he'd handed a French soldier a cigarette and the man had spit and thrown it to the ground.

- Kas, Turkey, a little village on the clear, dark-green water of the Adriatic. It was here that I ate the most delicious tomato, the most delicious grape and the most delicious pear of my life.

- The Vietnam War Memorial in Washington, D.C. It's meant a lot to those of us who were there.

- *The Deutsche Museum* in Munich. In a country that revels in technology, this is the temple.

- Farmers' markets in the shadows of giant cathedrals in Germany. Many of them have been going on every Saturday for over a thousand years.

- The poetry of Yeats.

- The Paradores of Portugal— palaces converted to hotels.

Advice to Travelers: Get Off the Rabbit Run

MOST TOURISTS HAVE A strong tendency to follow well-defined patterns. I was once in the Aran Islands off the coast of Ireland. In the summer they receive a flood of visitors. I was there in November, which is definitely the off-season. On a cold, rainy afternoon I was having a conversation with one of the locals when I asked what it was like in the short three-month period when so many tourists come to the island.

He surprised me when he said, "You know, actually, it's not too bad. There are three things that tourists want to see here: one is an old castle at the end of a spit of land, the second is a beach located outside town, and the third is a museum along the landing wharf. Everyone travels on a triangle between these three sights. If you get fifty yards outside this triangle, you never see anyone but your neighbors."

A similar thing happens in Bombay. There are two or three blocks along the causeway there where you'll run into more drug dealers, pimps, rug salesmen, and destitute children than anyplace else in India, or maybe the world. It wears you out. Last year I discovered that by simply going to the other side of the street where there aren't any tourist attractions, I could walk largely unmolested. By going up a few side alleys away from the oceanfront, you can begin to encounter the Bombay where people actually live. You'll know you're off the trail and have discovered a tiny facet of the real India when no one lets you pay for anything and you're treated as an honored guest. As a corollary to this phenomenon, most of the best places in the world take a little effort to get to.

Ram Rahim Nagar

A FEW YEARS AGO a fury was set loose in India. In the city of Ayodhya, an ancient mosque that had been built on the foundation of an even more ancient Hindu temple was razed by fundamentalists. They were egged-on by politicians who hoped to gain from the conflict.

A few days later a train-load of boisterous Hindu pilgrims returning from Ayodhya were stopped at a station somewhere in Gujarat when a mob of incensed Muslims fell upon them. They bolted the trains doors shut, soaked the cars with gasoline, and set fire to them. Fifty eight men, women, and children screaming and clamoring at the barred windows were immolated.

The blow was passed on. Riots broke out all over Gujarat. The epicenter of the violence was the immense, grimy industrial city of Ahmeddabad. Mobs (Hindus this time) of merciless men surged through the streets, not to loot, but to murder. Men with a passion to see blood running on their hands, to smash flesh with bricks, and feel bones breaking, to rape, to have their skin hot from burning buildings, to kill.

There was a quiet village of working people in the midst of the city. Untouchables and impoverished Muslims for the most part. It was once a separate town but had over time been engulfed by the growth of Ahmeddabad. Even so, it retained a separate identity. As a symbol of what the founders wished it to be, the village was centered on a peaceful public square with a modest Hindu temple facing the tomb of a Muslim holy man. It was hoped that the town would be a place where Hindu and Muslim could live harmoniously. Its name was Ram Rahim Nagar.

Nagar means town. Ram is the Hindu name for God. Rahim is an Arabic term most often translated as "The Compassionate."

On February 28th of 2002 word began to spread that riots had broken out in the city. Terrible things were happening everywhere and word had it that the police had been given instructions by the local head of state that they were not to interfere. Women were being raped then burned alive to dispose of the evidence. Everyone in the tiny village was terrified, but they knew what they had to do. Three gates led into the village. Hindu and Muslim standing shoulder to shoulder, armed only with sticks took up their posts at those gates. The seething mobs poured out of the mighty city and descended upon them. The young men stood their ground. They defended their town. They were not moved.

Not long ago, my friend Matt Bockelman and I spent an extremely hectic week in Ram Rahim Nagar, speaking with the local leaders, interviewing teachers, attending religious gatherings, and in general getting to know the place. We were trying to learn what makes it so different. We shot around fifteen hours of film that Matt will try to edit down to twenty minutes. We hope to get the necessary funding to go back and shoot a full length documentary.

Three Warnings

More than one of my friends has told me that they've never come so close to dying in so many ways in such a short period of time as when they've been traveling with me. I'm not sure this is a compliment.

Rick Owens and I were camped for the night with about twenty other people from our safari truck somewhere on the vast plains of East Africa. It was beginning to get dark when we heard a deep rumbling coming from somewhere down a nearby gully. We decided to investigate.

As the two of us started down the sandy ravine, we heard a second, much louder roar. We both agreed that it might be wise to take along some kind of protection. A collapsible aluminum tent pole should take care of that. Better safe than sorry.

We stealthily made our way toward some bushes at the bottom of the ravine. This time we heard a truly tremendous roar that would have rattled a car window. That is, if we'd been in a car. Rick turned to me and I to him. Our eyes met and the identical brilliant thought simultaneously came unbidden to both of us: *What the hell are we doing here?* We turned and walked quickly back to camp, never to know what lay behind those bushes.

Best Things in the World

- German flower shops. You don't just find the daises, roses and baby's breath available in America. In Germany you can buy flowers once a week over the course of a year and never buy the same kind twice.

- Collecting little bags of soil samples from around the world for Eli Lilly. It was a dream job for a traveler. I did it for over twenty years. The scientists at the fermentation lab cultured the contents to see if they contained previously unknown bacteria that might be useful in the manufacturing of new antibiotics. Their favorite sample was from a spot in New Delhi where people were in the habit of spitting betel juice. They found all kinds of amazing new organisms in that one. With the advent of genetic engineering, the lab was no longer cost effective. When it was shut down, I lost a great little job.

- Breakfast at the Taj Mahal Hotel in Bombay. The Beatles always stayed here when they were in town.

- Swimming beneath giant ceiba trees in the sky blue pools of Agua Azul in Mexico.

- Adbuster Magazine. I often disagree with it, but I always find it provocative. It's changed my mind about issues more than once. I find it useful to read it and The Economist consecutively.

- Sunset at Sandakphu. We saw the full frontal wall of the Himalayas, including four of the world's five highest peaks. The view stretched in front of us from horizon to horizon, pink and purple as far as our eyes could see.

- *Bloomington Paint and Wallpaper.* Best damn paint store in the world.

- The Cosmos, a club in Amsterdam that was subsidized by the city. The sign next to the bar read "No dealing on the premises" which really meant that smoking hash or marijuana was ok there. It had a library, restaurant, sauna… everything. Once I heard some intriguingly beautiful music being played in one of the rooms. Avant-garde and unlike anything I'd ever heard before. I wandered in to find the room full of instruments and a couple dozen people (mostly "non-musicians") tooting, strumming, and clanging away. I picked something up and joined the band.

- The songs Ladakhis sing while they're threshing grain.

- Evenings on the burning Ghats of Benares along the banks of the sacred Ganges. Devout Hindus believe that to die and be cremated in this holy city ensures liberation. Despite the terrible pollution, I saw fresh water dolphin breaching the surface of the dark brown river here.

- Climbing up through Yankee Basin in Colorado with my son and my brothers. The wildflowers were in full bloom up the whole side of the mountain. Every rock and flower looked as if a Zen master had placed it there.

- The resourceful street children outside the Calcutta Museum who put on circus acts to earn money. I've seen two kids bend steel rebar between them by running towards each other. There was a boy who danced for twenty minutes with his head buried in gravel.

- Salads with flowers.

Professor J.S. Puri

I HAVE YET TO meet anyone who didn't like him. Most of us are hopelessly in love with this marvelous man. In his early days he was a freedom fighter in India and a close companion of both Nehru and Gandhi. He lived for some time on Gandhi's farm in Gujarat. He was also, in his own words, "a jailbird." The British imprisoned him on several occasions. He always recalls these times fondly. He was allowed writing materials and full access to mail and books. His personal servant was permitted to stay with him as well. After India became independent, he was briefly involved in politics until he received the *Gyan*. Ever since he has been a brilliant star in the galaxy of the Nirankari Mission.

Thirty-two years ago, the Guru of the time, Baba Gurbachen Singh sent him to Chicago where he was told to spread the mission throughout North America. When I returned to America, I found him in a humble little apartment in Cicero, one of the poorer sections of Chicago. At that time the entire North American Nirankari Mission could comfortably hold a satsang on a rug in his home— and it wasn't a large rug. Today there are thousands of American Nirankaris.

Where would I be were it not for this Mahatma? I hate to think of it. Through my two divorces and innumerable shenanigans, he has remained my mentor and friend. From someone who was raised in a traditional Indian manner, accepting me has required a tremendous amount of tolerance.

His conversation is brilliant and thoroughly unpredictable. Let me give you a couple of examples. One day, in the midst of a conversation we were having, I used a sentence with the word, "perfect." Suddenly, this normally deeply gentle soul seemed fiercely upset. "Perfect! I despise this word! John, if you ever expect perfect in this world, you will never be happy— never."

Another time, he was speaking with my dear former wife when he remarked, "Marcia, you should always try to be good, but not too good." I should add that his own idea of "not too good" is most people's idea of pretty doggone good.

Once we were discussing the Guru. Presently, this is Baba Hardev Singh-ji. I should say at this point that Nirankaris consider the Guru to be God's presence in the world in human form. It is not the human form, however, to which we give our devotion; it is to the presence of God. "John," Professor Puri said kindly, "there are many things in this world that you can understand, but you will never understand the Guru."

Professor Puri is now in his eighties. His body is a near total wreck; practically every system is falling apart. I always try to sit directly in front of him, since I know that inclining his head even slightly to the left or right causes him dizziness and grave discomfort. Despite this, this king among men always tries to touch my feet when I first see him, as this the Nirankari custom (It is also a custom when greeting other devotees to say, "Dhan Nirankar" which is Punjabi for "Glory to the Formless"). These gestures symbolize the recognition of God within all of us, as well as the inherent equality of souls.

His body is suspended in life by the slenderest of threads. He is often in pain and often exhausted. But get him talking about the Formless and enthusiasm (the root of which, after all, is "God within") suffuses every cell in his body. His eyes sparkle. His voice steadies and strength comes into his every gesture. The phrase, "servant of God" comes to my mind. Perhaps coincidentally, this is the Hindi translation of the name of the next saint I wish to speak of, "Dev Das." It is said that if the digits of a hand were all the same, the hand would be less useful. Each finger has its own use. The same is true of individuals.

Dev Das

THERE ARE SO MANY wonderful Nirankari saints. They'd be a whole book in themselves. I don't know why it is, but when I try to picture the quintessential saint, my dear old friend Dev Das often comes to mind. He's rather short. I only notice this when I see a picture of him. He's about fifty years old with a bit of gray in his hair. But his manner is vigorous, surefooted and solid.

He lives behind the Nirankari Bhavan in Bombay. It's a single room with considerably less square footage than a kitchen in the home of an average American physician. Possessions are simple and neatly in place. Pictures of Baba-ji and Mata-ji smile down from every wall. The room always has a fresh coat of light blue paint and everything is spotlessly clean. He lives here with his wife and two daughters. Whenever I arrive, always unannounced, he jumps up to hug me and shouts "Dhan Nirankar!" *Sotto Voce,* he dispatches someone to run across the road and buy me a coke, since he knows that's my drink of choice. His English is limited and my Hindi far more so, but he knows me well and we communicate easily. I've spent hours there, sitting on the edge of his bed surrounded by smiling faces, when I've laughed more and harder than I have in some years of my life. When I'm with him so many things seem funny.

He reminds me of no one so much as Hanuman, the much-loved Hindu monkey God who specializes in service. Hanuman was always doing humble service for the royal pair, Sita and Ram. He's often pictured carrying a mountain to them. Recently, I gave Dev Das, or Deva as he's also called, a card with Hanumans picture on it. He put it lovingly under his shirt, laughed like crazy, then joyfully ran off to sweep a room or clean a toilet.

No job is too humble for this great man. Sometimes, however, he will be asked to sit in front of a small Satsang. At that time his clothes will be spotless and he will bear himself with the greatest dignity. This bearing and dignity is not for him but for what he represents at that moment. When Baba-ji is in Bombay and Deva has done every possible thing that needs to be done, I have occasionally seen him far in the rear of the congregation, his hands folded, his head bowed, and his mouth repeating the prayer:

"Ek Tu Hi Nirankar.
Main Terri Sharon, Hun
Mainu Bakshlo"

"Oh Formless God, I surrender to thee. Kindly forgive my sins."

Slipshod Manor

MANY YEARS AGO I was taking a National Outdoor Leadership School Course. We spent 40 days up in the Wind River Range of Wyoming, hardly encountering another human. Our instructor was a guy named Kim Fadiman. He was a Harvard grad and the best teacher I've ever had. A recurring theme with Kim was the concept of impeccability. It was his belief that a person should strive for it in all endeavors. I admired him like crazy.

For a week or so I did my level best to attempt this impeccable thing. Every task I did, I tried to do it as well as I could. One very small aspect of impeccability that Kim taught us was to always have the straps of your backpack tucked-in, not swaying in the breeze.

One day I was walking along a very steep ridge with a huge drop off. I tripped and started bouncing end-over-end down the incline. Things were looking bad. I was gaining speed. Suddenly, I slammed to a stop. One of my dangling straps had lodged in a cleft between 2 rocks, arresting my fall. I took it as a sign. The noble path of impeccability wasn't to be my way.

When I moved into a house 20 years later, I put up a brass plaque by the front door that read, "Slipshod Manor."

I Remember

I REMEMBER A WINTER evening at the ballet in Moscow. I believe *Turandot* was being danced. It was a magnificent performance. At intermission thousands of small plates of ice cream with blueberries were served to us balletomanes in a vast room upstairs.

I remember resting up in a tiny oasis in the Mauritanian desert after a long haul over packed sand roads in the back of an overcrowded, open truck. I was traveling with two Dutch women at the time. They were terrific— always laughing, never complaining. We were between two legs of a journey. It was hotter than hell, but at least there was water. One of the women had collapsed with heat exhaustion the day before. We needed a break. Most of our day was spent lying lifelessly in our room on our sagging beds. Someone hatched the clever idea of sneaking up behind unsuspecting people and pouring a bucket of cool water from the well all over them as they napped. Now *that* was a shock to your consciousness. It caused no mess since thirty minutes later everything in the room would be bone dry again.

I remember a place I was told about that wasn't on any road or trail. It took me several hikes to find it. I was walking up a steep valley when I saw a tiny house farther up the slope. The door was unlocked and there was a sign that said, "Welcome, come on in." Inside was a simple room with a small bed, a stove and a desk. I opened the desk drawer and found an article from *The Christian Science Monitor* that was written about this house. It said that it was open to all, but that often people who seem to need it have discovered it. There was a pen and a guest register which I signed.

I remember an automobile accident I had where my neck smashed a large "V-shaped" indentation into the fiberglass steering wheel. It lowered the register of my voice by a couple of octaves for a week or so, but otherwise did no lasting damage. Chalk it up to youthful resilience.

I remember climbing through a cold fog with Rick Owens. On the final difficult stretch to the top of Mt. Kenya, we encountered a very steep, snow covered slope. We lacked any equipment, and it appeared we were stymied. But my ever resourceful companion proposed that we make our ascent of this difficult section by proceeding backwards while kicking out steps with the heels of our boots. It was laborious and exhausting but it worked. Thirty minutes later we stood arm in arm at the peak.

I remember the three and a half years I spent commuting to Indianapolis where I dreaded Mondays and worked 9 to 5 in a cubicle under fluorescent lights while Muzak played in the background. I suffered through petty office politics, dreaded hearing the phone ring, and spent a fair amount of time watching the clock. It wasn't all bad though. There were some good-hearted people around (thank God there always seem to be), I tried to be helpful in my work, I saved some money, bought a house, and had fun on the weekends. I was glad to have had the experience, but even more glad to leave.

My Life as a Hooker

I WAS ABOUT HALFWAY through my Bachelor's degree when I ran into Organic Chemistry and temporarily lost heart in going to school. I needed a break and didn't have much money, so I decided to go up to Gary (in Indiana it's referred to as "The Region") and work in the steel mills. It seemed kind of macho, and back then maybe I felt like I had something to prove. It was a tough place. The "murder capitol of America." For someone like me who had grown up driving my father's sports car and playing golf at the country club, it was a jolt. I surely needed it as I was an awfully pretentious young guy back then. I'm not proud of that.

It was the dead of winter and the grim looking city was covered in filthy snow, but the mills were hiring and the pay was good. I applied for a job and a few days later found myself in the great warehouse of Republic Steel working as a "hooker." It was my job to work beneath an overhead crane and hook-up giant bundles of cold-drawn steel so they could be moved around in the mammoth warehouse or loaded onto semis or train cars. The steel bundles were banded together, stacked in adjoining bins, and oiled down with lubricant to keep them from rusting. I had to get down on my belly to find the pair of chains that rested beneath each oil-soaked bundle. They dangled between the bins, often tangled in knots. I'd disentangle them, attach them to the boom of the crane, get out of the way, and signal to the crane-man to take the load up. We had a lot of hand signals, but I only remember that one.

The oil penetrated everything. It went straight through my clothes to my skin where it clogged my pores and formed blackheads. Coming home from work on the bus, people wouldn't sit next to me.

The guys in the mills seemed to feel I was harmless, sort of amusing even. I didn't have any enemies. With two and a half years of college I was dubbed "the doctor" or alternatively "professor."

My favorite work-mate was John Henry. He was a small, powerful black man with flashing eyes and a tremendous laugh. He was a lay minister in his local church and he'd also lost a finger or two. Lots of people had. Time passed quickly with him. We found something to laugh about with each other all day long. I remember hearing him talk to someone about me. "Cocksuckah! Da perfesser don' wear no hard hat, don' wear no safety goggles, gonna get hisself keeled!"

About once a month, Smitty, my crane man, and Horace, the guy who worked the scales, would split a fifth of whiskey. That meant trouble. Smitty always thought it didn't affect his skills and would even try to concentrate extra hard. Not long into the shift though, he'd start dropping loads onto the floor. Some of them weighed ten thousand pounds. My career as a steel worker lasted only six months and luckily I emerged from it fully intact.

One night, we were working the graveyard shift and the weather was about as bad as it gets up there, which is *real* bad. It was minus ten degrees with a tremendous howling wind whipping off of Lake Michigan. Then the lights went out. Through the great wall of windows that formed the entire east side of the mill, we could see the problem. All the wires connected to the huge transformer that supplied the mill with electricity had come detached due to the wind. Like an insane octopus, the giant lines were smacking every which way, emitting fountains of sparks.

Every man who has ever worked in a steel mill has a tremendous respect for the chief millwright. He's the man responsible for repairing everything in the mill. He was going to have to handle this.

We all watched as three men— the millwright and his two assistants— walked out into that terrible night. It took them thirty minutes. Suddenly the lights were back on. Then something happened which I've never seen before or since. As the three men emerged through the door into the mill, every man in that cavernous building stood up and, without a word being spoken, applauded.

Returning to Vietnam

In 1988 I went back to Vietnam. It was to be the first of two such trips. It wasn't any kind of a pilgrimage, or at least it didn't seem like one. I like Southeast Asia; I always have. I'd traveled through Thailand, Laos and Cambodia, and I'd been in Vietnam too, but of course I'd not been free to come and go as I wished. I'd never even seen Saigon.

By chance, just before I arrived, the United States renewed normal trade relations with Vietnam. It was a news story, but not a very exciting or dramatic one. Nonetheless, there were lots of reporters there to cover it. As an ex-Vietnam veteran I was much in demand for interviews. A few carefully edited quotes or sound bites from me would add a little color to their stories. They were all over us. The interviews were lousy. They all wanted to put words in my mouth. They'd made up their own minds on the subject, and all they wanted from me were some colorful quotes to fill in the spaces. (One of the few good interviews I ever gave on my experiences in Vietnam was for Jeff Wolin who was doing a project on Vietnam veterans that was later turned into a book, *Inconvenient Stories*. He had no agenda. He just wanted to know what it was like.) The reporters I met wanted to know what it felt like and I kept telling them that it felt much like other countries in the area that I'd visited. That didn't make good copy.

At the time I was with four other people who wanted to tour the country. We pooled our money and rented a van and a driver. There's only one good road in Vietnam. It goes up the spine of the country. We saw lots of pretty sights. It's a very lovely place.

One day we arrived late in the afternoon at a medium-sized town. There was an American guy sitting in front of our little hotel, and there was something quite curious about what was going on. He had a kid on his lap and about a dozen Vietnamese of various ages were grouped around him listening to his every word. The feeling of love was palpable.

He was a Vietnam vet and, as always happens when two of us meet, we immediately got into a very intense conversation. It lasted well into the night. They often do. He had been badly torn up by a mine. I don't remember all the specifics, but arms, legs, and face were involved— lots of trauma. He told me that when he went home after the war he was angry— ANGRY— all the time. Out of desperation he had come back to Vietnam. He said he felt at peace here. He was working on a project to bring solar power to a hospital in the area. He claimed it wasn't doing much good, but that wasn't what I saw. Here was a man replacing hate with love.

We both had to get up in the morning, so at some point we were cutting it off. As we were parting he said, "I've got one piece of advice for you."

"Shoot. What is it?" I asked.

"Go to My Lai."[9]

The next day about fifty km up the road, we came to a junction where a gravel road led off to the right.

"My Lai is down that road. Do you want to go?" our driver asked.

As I said, there were five of us. Two voted yes, two no. I was the deciding vote. I voted yes. I guess I don't have much imagination. I've never been interested in historical sites. I'm sure I wouldn't have gone if not for the previous night's conversation.

A few miles along the road we passed a picturesque little village. One of the women wanted to stop and take pictures.

"Not that village," our driver explained. "Some Scandinavians stopped there recently and the car was stoned. They mistook them for Americans."

Most Vietnamese have forgiven us everything, but not everyone has. That would be asking a lot.

---

[9] For those too young to remember, American soldiers killed an entire village of unarmed civilians here.

195

We reached My Lai. There was a large gateway in front of the site. I walked in under it. Stretching out in front of me was a field of intensely bright orange flowers. I just started crying. The woman I was with asked if I wanted to be alone and I nodded, yes. I couldn't stop crying. I had no idea that I even had this feeling in me. I just couldn't stop. There was a reporter there as well, a very sweet woman from New Zealand I think. She had a video camera and a sound system, so maybe the tape is out there somewhere.

The One Who Brings Light

I HAVE SEEN MY Guru wince with pain from back problems. It will sometimes take him an hour to walk down a short corridor lined with devotees as he may want to say a little something to each soul. After several nights of talking to hundreds of the millions of Nirankari saints until two or three in the morning, he looks tired. All it takes is a wedding, or dancing, or a joke, or meeting a great saint he hasn't seen for a while though, and his eyes are sparkling again.

He leads a normal family life, has a wonderful, gracious wife and three lovely daughters. I learned recently that though he eats strictly vegetarian his wife chooses not to. He owns an auto-parts business which provides him with his livelihood. He lives comfortably but not extravagantly. He does every normal human thing, but this is where the resemblance ends. My dear friend and mentor, Prof J.S. Puri once told me that there were many things in this world that you can understand but that you will never understand the Guru.

Baba Hardev Singh is my Guru. The word itself means, "The one who brings light." He revealed God to me, as did his father, Baba Gurbachen Singh. I lost God-consciousness between times, which was entirely my fault. I took this most precious of gifts for granted. If you are ever so supremely fortunate as to receive the *Gyan,* or "Knowledge," don't repeat my mistake. After its revelation, God Knowledge can be cultivated through Satsang (congregation) Simran (remembrance of God) and Seva (service).

My beloved Guru wears a Sikh turban. This is his way. He doesn't ask you to adopt any particular mode of dress or diet. On the contrary, diversity of diet and dress are seen as normal, and any attempt to impose uniformity amongst humankind is both impossible and undesirable. Unity, not uniformity, is the goal. What he asks is that you be tolerant of others' diet and dress. This is one of the five pledges you make when you become a Nirankari. All are the kinds of things any reasonable person would agree to. As with everything else, there is a website: www. Nirankari.org. You can check the five pledges out for yourself.

When his father was murdered by Sikh fanatics, many Nirankaris wanted swift retribution. Baba-ji quickly quashed all talk of this. Instead, he had them set up blood drives with the Red Cross, and all the Nirankaris in the area who were able went and gave. He declared the day of his father's death, Manav Ekta Diwas (Human Unity Day) to commemorate the day Nirankaris throughout the world would be asked to donate blood instead of spilling it.

If you are ever so fortunate as to meet him, you will see how shy and modest he is. What he says to you may be simple or he may just smile. Don't underestimate the importance of his words due to their simplicity. Even if, for example, he graciously says, "Have something to eat," *do it*!

Riding the Rails

(This story originally appeared in The Ryder Magazine in a less ribald version)

As you sit there in the dark you can hear the hissing sound of the engine pressuring the long line of interconnected pneumatic hoses beneath the cars. That's the first indication that the freight you're riding is about to leave the yard. The pressure in the hoses releases the brakes of each car sequentially, ensuring that if any car should become derailed, the hose will come uncoupled, taking the pressure out of the system and immediately slamming on every brake in the train, minimizing the mayhem.

Then far up the line, you hear the engine rev up and start to pull. A small, pencil-wide jet of sand spits out on the track just ahead of the engine's wheels to give them greater traction. An almost imperceptible clicking sound of the first cars being jolted into motion begins to make its way down the train towards you, perhaps a mile back from the straining engine, gradually getting louder— chunk, Chunk, CHunk, CHUnk, CHUNk, CHUNk— with ever increasing thundering violence— CHUNK, CHUNK! Then it hits you with a terrific jolt, enough to throw you off your feet if you're standing, and suddenly you're moving.

It's best now to move out of the doorway of your empty boxcar (called a deadhead) where you've carefully laid out your sleeping bag on a collapsed cardboard box. No one minds that you're riding, but if, say, the assistant yard-boss and his boss see you at the same time, then they'll be duty-bound to throw you off, albeit apologetically. The idea is to not be too obvious. In the old days, I was kicked off only when

I was too brazen— dangling legs out of the car, waving at everybody. Really I was just showing off.

I found the guys in the yard almost unfailingly courteous. They'll help you pick out a train that is going your way or maybe one going somewhere like New Orleans that you hadn't considered until that moment. Wherever the train is stopped, it is always a good idea to scare up the brakeman to make sure your car isn't getting put off on a siding. Cars near a caboose are generally preferable, since cars going shorter distances tend to be placed in the front of the train where they are easier to set off.

The first time I jumped a freight was close to forty years ago. I was on my way to my home in Bloomington, Indiana from Rochester, New York, where I had worked at a toilet factory during the summer. It was my freshman year at IU, and I wanted to make this trip different. My girlfriend, Toni, whose father owned the factory I'd been working in, dropped me off at the yards outside Rochester. Filled with apprehension, I stole along the tree line paralleling the tracks. The first car I saw that looked rideable was a gondola car with a giant earthmoving shovel lashed to its floor. I flew up the ladder and dived into the bottom of the car and stayed there until the train left the yards. As we picked up speed, grit and cinders whipped into my eyes. I could see that the steel belting that held the imposing shovel in place was beginning to strain under the rolling motion of the car. If it wrenched loose I'd be crushed. I was learning things the hard way.

First lesson: don't ride an open car.

Second lesson: never ride with loose freight.

When I was a graduate student, I occasionally took friends on the old Monon Line— usually the stretch from Bloomington down to the Big Three Yards in Louisville. We'd find a clean-looking boxcar on the main track in the yards off Grimes Lane, near the old RCA building. If we were really lucky, we might be invited to ride up in the engine.

Soon we'd be passing the bluffs along Clear Creek, the most beautiful part of our county to my mind. Though the bluffs continue for miles along the now abandoned tracks, only the more accessible Cedar Bluffs are known to most Bloomington residents. During one trip with a friend— now a perfectly respectable doctor— and his wife, we brought a quiche lorraine and a bottle of good champagne. Now that was a fine trip! Near the end of the ride, you cross the mighty Ohio River and marvel at the engineering of a bridge so strong it could easily support a fully loaded freight train with one hundred-fifty cars. A wonderful sight.

I'll never forget the night I first crossed the Continental Divide. For hours we laboriously crawled our way up through tunnel after tunnel, some of them many miles long. Trains are far more sensitive to gradients than cars or trucks. That's why there are so many tunnels and trestles needed to even things out. As we neared the Divide, we were going so slowly that I easily could have hopped out and walked beside my car. Then, when we crossed it, there was that perceptible moment when we seemed perfectly balanced on a pinnacle, just before the train's immense mass began to lend itself to the gathering momentum as we began to inexorably hurtle down the other side of the mountain range. Soon the train was highballing, barreling down through more pitch black tunnels. My car, which now seemed toy-like, was swaying alarmingly from side to side. I held on in fear, but I remember it as a fear mixed with a joyful awe.

Most of the time riding the rails, though, you're going about forty mph— cruising along listening to the clickety-clack, feeling the sway, playing a harmonica, reading a book or maybe just gazing out a boxcar doorway bigger than any picture window. I remember once, as a joke, late at night doing it doggy-style with a young lady in the open door of a boxcar as we went through some tiny northern Indiana farm town with the crossing bell going Ding Dong Ding Dong Ding Dong. What a shock to their consciousness that must have been for somebody. The lady I was riding with that night has not been mentioned in this book and shall forever remain anonymous.

Unlike traveling by automobile where everything faces the road—houses, stores, billboards, in a train you cut straight through the countryside; you catch it unawares, so to speak. When you go through a city, you cut right through its industrial heart—steel mills, stamping plants, coke ovens, monstrous and inhuman, but with their own aesthetic. Like Benares on the Ganges, awful in its ugliness, awful in its beauty.

I was once aboard what was purported to be the heaviest train in the world. I looked out to see four of the biggest engines I'd ever encountered as we started our ride from Nouckschut, the capitol of Mauritania, to be deposited eight hours later two-hundred-fifty miles out in the Sahara, near the iron ore mine. I had good company for the trip: along with the locals, there were Gambians, Senegalese and a couple of intrepid Dutch girls.

We sang a lot, something I've found that people who don't have radios, CD players, and Walkmans tend to do. I first noticed this on a camel trip across the desert in Rajasthan. Our driver sang four or five hours a day— a pretty common phenomenon in the "underdeveloped" world. In the "developed" world we have professional singers to sing songs for us, athletes to play games for us, and actors who can have adventures and love affairs for us. After all, these people are professionals and can do a much better job of it than we could. We've become an intimidated society, afraid that our voices won't be sweet enough, our performances not good enough.

When I speak of freight train riding I speak of the past. Even when I started riding, the golden age of hoboing was already over, and the real roadmen were fast disappearing. I once was lucky enough to meet the real thing out in Grand Junction, Colorado, but I squandered the opportunity. He'd set up a little hobo camp with his dog on the edge of the yards. With my train pulling out, I invited him to come with me so I could spend some time with him, to learn a little bit about his life and to hear a few stories, but he said he had just started reading a good book and didn't want to move for a while. So that was that. A changing world left him behind.

It was on a freight car that I saw my first barcode, a bit of technology that changed things forever. Now, computers use them to monitor which cars are filled and which aren't, eliminating the need to leave doors open, thus shutting out the would-be rider. Personal injury lawyers have bred a fear of liability in corporations. They in turn have passed it on to their employees. You can no longer expect a friendly welcome in most freight yards in America. All this means that no longer can you ride up front in the engine and be invited to blow the whistle at the "W" signs at crossings. For that matter, no one can hitch a ride across the desert in the cab of an 18-wheeler and see the lit up spires of the Mormon Tabernacle in the distance. You can't even spend a carefree summer day swimming in the beautiful quarries surrounding my hometown anymore. We're all a little safer these days. But I like the old ways better.

A Postscript: Since writing this article a few years ago, I've learnt that riding freights isn't dead yet. There's a new generation of freight train riders, and I've met a few of them. They're a stouthearted bunch. It's harder for them than it was for me. There aren't so many open boxcars these days. They're still out there doing it though. I won't go into details since some things they do sound riskier than I would advise. If you are really driven to explore it, you'll find the people to talk to and you'll find a way. Be careful and God Speed.

Advice to Travelers: Get a Haircut

ONE OF THE SMALL pleasures of living in a third-world country is going to a local barbershop for a haircut. This varies from country to country of course, but generally you pick your "do" from a chart on the wall of twenty or so possibilities. You point to the one that suits you, then sit back and relax. Everything will be done in the most leisurely and human way imaginable. All kinds of potions, powders, astringents, and mysterious sweet smelling liquids are applied at appropriate times.

In Thailand while having your hair clipped, you can simultaneously get a manicure and a pedicure. For a hundred Baht during the next twenty minutes, you'll be made to feel like the king of Siam. In India, you used to be able to have your ears cleaned while you sat in the chair. They used long sharp tools that resembled knitting needles. This is no longer possible (sidewalk ear-cleaners will do it for you though), but you can still get a great scalp and face massage.

My favorite haircut was in Guatemala City. The process involved being draped with various steaming hot and cool towels— sybaritic. For a dollar or two, I sauntered out an hour later feeling like a million bucks.

Be Careful of Nicaragua

ABOUT SIXTEEN YEARS AGO I was running into very serious problems with my first marriage. I don't want to go into the details— those are private issues— but both of us could have done better. Things were falling apart, but I had some hope that they could be turned around. I hatched the idea of going to a paradisiacal spot where Elena could finish work on her PhD, the kids would be in a friendly atmosphere, and we'd be surrounded with natural beauty. After much thought I decided that Costa Rica would be the right place. I was in Delhi with Baba-ji, so naturally I asked his advice.

When I asked him what he thought of the Costa Rican idea, he didn't appear to be that taken with it, but he didn't veto it either. Then he said something that should have struck me as peculiar. "Isn't Nicaragua near there?"

"Yes, Baba-ji," I answered, "It's the country just north of Costa Rica.

"Ah," he said, "I'd be careful of Nicaragua."

A few months later, we arrived at the most beautiful spot on a beach of the Nagoya Peninsula in that small gem of a country, Costa Rica. The family we rented rooms from raised bees. Outside our back window was lush green jungle, and large flocks of parrots in tight formations often passed by. A perfectly clear little stream emptied into the sea not far from us. The local chipmunks would eat peanuts from your hand. It was a peaceful place. The kids were happy and we home-schooled them under a giant tree next to the house. Elena was plugging along with her dissertation. I won't say there wasn't friction, but we were making it.

I had a beat up ten-year-old Ford pick-up truck that I'd driven down from Indiana with most of our belongings. Our personal visas were all in order, but the truck had paperwork that could only be taken care of outside the country. I had two options: Panama to the South or Nicaragua to the North. I'd been to both countries, so neither would be a complete novelty. Nicaragua sounded like more fun. The Sandanistas had been in power there, which made it more interesting, if less comfortable. I decided to go to Nicaragua.

It took a couple of days but the paperwork went through without a hitch. I met several interesting people as I'd hoped I would. Next day I was happily on my way home to see my family. That's when things started to go south. As the old truck strained to climb the hill on the outskirts of the capital, its timing belt snapped. It was an automobile part that, up until then, I didn't even know existed. I quickly learned that it's crucial. Without one, you're dead in the water. The U.S had enforced an embargo on little Nicaragua that had only recently been lifted. What that meant from my point of view was that there was not a single timing belt for a ten-year-old Ford truck in the entire country. Believe me, I saw the inside of every grimy auto parts store in Managua. I would have to order the belt from the U.S and have it delivered by Fed Ex. I won't go into the long, boring details, but it wasn't until three weeks later that the part finally arrived. As soon as I had it, a skillful mechanic slipped it into place, and I was on my way.

Next day when I arrived back at our little house by the sea, I was greeted not by my children's happy cries, but instead by the saddest sights. All our collected stones and shells had been discarded out the window. Jacques' lovely artwork of local birds and plants had been taken from the walls and discarded. There was a note from Elena. She had taken the children and wanted a divorce.

I don't remember when I finally made the Nicaragua connection in my mind. It might have been years later.

More to Life in Hong Kong

CHINA HAS FAR SURPASSED America in its enthusiasm for capitalism, its icons of avarice and consumerism. The malls of Hong Kong are constructed in such a way that it's difficult to find your way out of them. I once wandered around for an hour before asking a young couple I thought might speak English where an exit was located. It's similar to casinos where there are never any clocks and sometimes they play this peculiar indescribable music that appears to put gamblers in a kind of timeless trance. Everyone walks around with this strange look in their eyes.

Having escaped the mall, I was walking through the brightly lit streets at night, still dazzled by the city but on the verge of being a little numbed by all the commercialism. A small procession of young people came marching past me chanting and pointing to the sky. A polite young woman of about eighteen stopped and asked me if I knew what they were saying. "No," I said, "I haven't the foggiest."

"We're saying that there is more to life than buying things."

Best Things in the World

- The ancient monasteries of Ladakh perched on lonely flanks of mighty mountains.

- The Temple of the Living Goddess in Katmandu. Every few years through an elaborate selection process, a young girl is chosen to be the goddess. There are various trials of one kind or another she has to go through to prove that she is worthy of the honor. For example, I believe that in one of these trials she must spend a night in a room horribly decorated with dead carcasses. Once she's proven herself, she is moved to a beautiful miniature, hand-carved palace situated in Durbar Square. She reigns here until her first menstruation, at which point, a new virgin is selected. If she happens to be looking out her window and sees you, it's supposed to be a great blessing. The goddess saw me there. Our eyes met and she smiled the loveliest smile.

- It surprised me that I was so moved by my first sight of the Taj Mahal. It makes the list, as does The Mona Lisa.

- Bolivian chocolates. Who would have expected they'd be so great?

- The horse farms surrounding Lexington, Kentucky. Once, I was standing next to a fence surrounding a pasture there when a thoroughbred spontaneously broke loose and tore across the field just for the joy of it.

- A hotel in Goa whose name I won't tell.

- Encountering giant elephant turds with a bore size as big as your leg on a path in Periyar National Park in India.

- The ancient city of Saana at night. As we walked through the dark narrow streets, mud towers six and seven stories tall surrounded us. Each house had stained glass windows shaped like half-moons inset in their walls. They glowed from the light within. Each family designs and makes its own windows. Every Yemeni is an architect.

- At a flea market in Germany a few years ago I bought a "Ten Billion Deutsche Mark Bill" printed in the thirties. I paid one DM for it. This kind of hyperinflation that took place at the time of the Weimar Republic made the rise of the Nazis possible.

- The groovy looking swami in dark shades and skimpy loin cloth at a temple on the outskirts of Katmandu who makes his living picking up a fifty-pound rock with his penis. It's a great photo op for $1.

- Riding on top of the bus in Nepal. We traveled up through forests of rhododendrons in bloom. Snug in our sleeping bags late in the afternoon, we caught the first sight of the Himalayas at sunset.

- Marcel Proust in small doses.

- Sedate coffee houses in Vienna. Some of the habitués have their mail delivered to their favorite table at one of these rather than to their homes.

- I was seated at a tea ceremony in Japan when I realized that the cookie I was about to eat was imprinted with a volcano and a tree; exactly the landscape before me.

- Travelers who bring their guitars with them.

A Fish Story

ABOUT TWENTY YEARS AGO I took a *National Outdoor Leadership School* course up in the Wind River Range in Wyoming. For forty days we were surrounded by beauty constantly. There was only one intrusion: a battered-up old jeep that had tortuously made its way up there to drop off supplies to us half-way through the course. As it came into view, wheezing and farting, I remember thinking that it gave the appearance of some kind of noisy oversized iron horse, ugly and out of place.

After two or three weeks up in the mountains my dreams had changed. Instead of telephones, wastebaskets, airplanes and ice-cream cones, they had to do with rocks, streams, stars, flowers and moose. Indian dreams.

It was a wonderful experience. I got in tremendous condition (If I'd have been a smoker I would have had to quit since no tobacco or alcohol was allowed). I learned skills that have stayed with me my whole life. To top it off, I even got four hours of graduate school credit for taking it. I'd recommend it to anyone.

Towards the end of the forty days, we burned all of our food. It was time to use the survival skills we had learned. We would have to live off the land for the three day trek back to the trailhead.

Next morning, we split into three groups, wished each other well, and set off. Each group would take a different route to the pick-up point. I was to lead one of them.

For the next two days hike, the scenery was incredible, but about all we had found to eat were tiny, wild blueberries. They were sweet but so small and scattered that they barely repaid the effort of gathering them. A little family of quail (a mother and half a dozen chicks) passed directly in front of me once. As always, I was carrying my ice ax as a walking stick... But they were just too adorable. I let them be.

Practically every conversation we had as we walked along together seemed to inevitably gravitate toward food. Suppose I was telling a story about holy men in India. As soon as I'd finished, the first question would be, "What kind of food do they eat over there?" Only half-jokingly we had a rule that no one could talk about food for more than five minutes an hour. For two nights we went to bed hungry.

Just before sunrise on the third day I quietly snuck out of my tent and gathered up my fly rod. The water of the pond was limpid and still on the surface as I made my first cast. I felt a quick shock of joy when a small rainbow trout suddenly rose and took the fly. An hour later, I had landed a dozen beautiful little things just like him.

I had loved fishing as a kid. Over the years, I had gradually found it less and less interesting. This was different. This wasn't just fun. My friends and I were hungry, but this morning we would eat.

The War through Vietnamese Eyes

THIS YEAR I WAS back in Vietnam once more. Two years ago I had been interviewed as one of fifty other American Vietnam veterans in an excellent book called, "Inconvenient Stories," by Jeff Wolin. When I first got my copy, I read it cover-to-cover in one sitting. Finally there was a book that accurately portrayed what it had been like. One thing was missing though: there was nothing about our opponents. I emailed Jeff and told him I thought the Vietnamese soldiers should have their say as well.

He agreed, and six months later we found ourselves braving the anarchic motorcycle traffic of Hanoi. For two straight weeks, day after day we spoke with veterans and heard the most incredible, heart wrenching stories. I hardly know where to begin. Everyone we spoke with lost friends and relatives. Everyone contracted malaria. Practically everyone was wounded, usually numerous times.

I met a man by chance— the owner of a little business where I bought a few pieces of furniture— who lived through a B-52 bombing raid in the jungle. As the bombs fell from the sky, trees all around him were suddenly uprooted and flying everywhere. He had no idea where he was. Everyone with him that day was killed. He was the only survivor.

Sitting quietly together in his store, I could only dimly imagine the horror and total chaos he described. I had experienced a B-52 carpet bombing only from a distance. Even from about five miles away it was terrifying. Clouds of smoke and dust advanced at great speed across the horizon. The ground shook and all the windows around me rattled. I looked up into the clear sky and couldn't make out a speck. When the

212

crew released their bomb-load, they were many miles up. When the bombs finally reached the ground, they were far away. Perhaps they were already thinking about what they'd be doing that evening back in Thailand.

Many years later, speaking with old VC and NVA veterans, I found that they'd joke and laugh about many things that happened to them during the war. Nobody joked about the B-52's.

We met a couple who married during the war. She had been a nurse in a hospital just across the border in Laos. He had been a patient. He was involved in transporting supplies across the border, so after his recovery, they were able to see each other from time to time. I asked her to describe the wedding. She said it took place in a cave. About a hundred of their comrades attended, some brought flowers from the jungle, and they all sang songs together. I asked her if she remembered the lyrics.

"Yes," she said, "Our favorite was about keeping Highway 9 open to defeat the imperialists."

I met a musician who wrote a music composition about a bombing raid he survived in a shallow tunnel with forty two men (forty died). One wall of his apartment was lined with speakers made from beer kegs cut in-two with sound equipment inserted. The piece went on for ten minutes and consisted of pounding, crashing, tortured, piano discordance, with a woman's voice screaming, imploring, and weeping in the background. I've never heard anything so disturbing.

He was wounded three times. Once from a machine gun mounted on a helicopter. Normally, the NVA kept under cover of the jungle, but he was crossing a river one day and a chopper caught him totally exposed on a sandbar. The pilot and the door gunner were toying with him, firing just behind him, then just in front of him. He was hit once. Figuring he was as good as dead, he turned around, faced the helicopter, and defiantly waved to them. The pilot waved back then abruptly wheeled off to the side and a moment later was gone.

Earlier in this book I described the defenses surrounding a base and how impenetrable they seemed. I met the member of a sapper team who described to me how they breached them.

"First," he explained, "We were masters of camouflage. At nightfall, we removed all our clothes and coated ourselves and our rifles and satchel charges totally with mud. Lying on my belly ten feet from you in broad daylight, you wouldn't have seen me.

"We came crawling through in a delta formation," he continued. "Anyone killed or wounded was dragged back out by one of the team, but the rest of us just kept moving forward. Usually the barbed wire obstacles had already been cut through by your own bullets, but the lead man still had to carefully look for flares and disable them without setting them off as he came through. If the wire wasn't severed we'd put sticks beneath them, raise them a bit, and crawl beneath them."

Another example of the resilience and resourcefulness of the Vietnamese soldiers was their intricate tunnel systems. During the war there was a small band of American GIs referred to as "Tunnel Rats." They were legendary, and perhaps a little mad. When a tunnel system was discovered a couple of grenades would be tossed in. Then the tunnel rats (all were volunteers and all were short) would be dispatched down the hole. Armed with pistols, often in pitch-dark, deep underground, they explored the branching passageways. Sometimes they encountered Viet Cong soldiers.

During my stay in Vietnam I was shown through some of the surviving tunnel systems by Viet Cong veterans. They were very gracious to me as they showed me underground hospital wards, cisterns, camouflaged ventilation shafts, common areas where plays were performed. They were so ingenious and so determined. We were never going to beat them, nor should we have.

They told their stories simply and without rancor. They treated me as just another old soldier who had been fortunate enough to make it through. I don't normally drink alcohol, these days, but there is a time for everything.

Muy Hombre

CERRO RICO (RICH HILL) is located in the town of Potosi in the highlands of Bolivia. It has been mined for three hundred years and has, by now, been thoroughly honeycombed with tunnels. Over the years, it has produced more silver than any place on earth. It financed the building of "The Invincible Armada," the Escorial, and most of the paintings in Del Prado and made Spain the dominant power in Europe for a while.

But twenty years ago, the mine was finally played out. Commercial companies could no longer turn a profit so they left, but most of the miners remained. There was nowhere else for them to go; this was the only life they knew. Their only alternative was to attempt to scratch out a bare existence planting potatoes and working the thin dusty soil of the altiplano. Out of desperation, they discovered that by organizing themselves into independent cooperatives of twenty to thirty workers they could still eke out a living as miners.

When I got to Potosi I found that it was possible to arrange to have someone take you down into the mines for a fee. First, though, I had to go to a small local store and load my pack with the staples needed by every miner: coca leaves, 100% alcohol,[10] and blasting caps. These were to be given to the miners as gifts.

---

[10] I no longer drink alcohol (almost), but as a sort of souvenir I brought home a bottle of this stuff as a present to some young friends I thought might enjoy it. Naturally, it knocked them on their asses, but most interestingly, they reported that from the moment they swallowed it until their body eliminated it, they always knew exactly where it was.

Early next morning, I got to the site and joined up with a guide and a handful of hardy travelers. With no preliminaries and not much conversation we suited up, threw on our packs, donned scratched-up, bright yellow hard hats with headlamps, and walked through the cold, thin air outside and into the dark mouth of the mine.

Inside, there were no lights and no ventilation system, just a tunnel with narrow gauge tracks. From time to time we'd hear a rattling sound from the darkness ahead of us and we'd have to jump to the sides and hug the walls as cars of ore, rushing pell-mell, careened past us, all determinedly pushed by grim-faced Indian women. We walked a few hundred meters down the shaft and emerged into a small room brightly lit by naked light bulbs. It was a very peculiar sort of shrine. Through some kind of contorted logic the miners believe that if Jesus and Mary govern above ground, then evil Tinto, or "uncle," must rule down here. Tinto was represented by a statue of a red guy wearing a surly expression, naked, and with an enormous erection. He looked pretty much like a devil to me, but I was told he's never referred to as such. Cigarettes were offered to the statue, and a bit of 100% alcohol was ceremoniously poured onto his pecker for luck. Then we headed down again.

We crawled on our bellies and slipped down chutes; we turned into tunnels to the left and right, climbed up and climbed down, until I was completely lost. Outside the mine it was chilly, but down here it was becoming hot— very hot. The air was stale, dead still, and seemed to contain no oxygen; we were constantly out of breath. Everything was silent except for our muffled conversation and the crunch of our boots.

Walking through the inky darkness, we came to a place where two men were loading ore into the cars. They asked me if I wanted to try my hand at it. After no more than three minutes of shoveling, I was totally out of breath. We left them to their work and continued deeper into the mine.

After another twenty minutes of scrambling up, down, and every which way, we finally reached a room located just behind the working-face, the business end of the mine where the actual tunneling and blasting was taking place. A group of miners was sprawled around, resting up. We collapsed on the floor beside them and took a breather as well. Everybody, including me, had a fat, puffed-out cheek full of coca leaves. In addition, the miners would sip from a bottle of alcohol which every man carried with him.

Our guide told them that I was a wounded veteran, which they all seemed to appreciate. They spoke Quechua. As we sat huddled there, he translated their conversation for us. To my surprise, it consisted almost entirely of jokes, all told totally deadpan. They were mostly about how shitty things were and what a dog's life it was down there.

Life underground is full of intrigue and treachery. Men have died over the discovery of a promising vein of ore. Every once in awhile someone would find some huge nugget, strike it rich, get out of the mine, and never look back. It happened the year before. The guy bought a couple of buses and married a fifteen year old girl. Stories like that keep these men going.

I could hear intense hammering in the next room and crawled in to see what was happening. Both the heat and the weight of the air were stifling. The dust filled my lungs and I could hardly breathe. I was blind at first, and then my eyes adjusted and I made out the shape of a man. He was pounding away with a sledgehammer and a steel bit. There was something terrifying about how he went at it. He looked like a man possessed.

Panty Raids

A LOT OF STORIES don't get told because people are embarrassed that they ever happened. I want this to be an accurate account of my life so... Here goes. Speak, memory, the truth, the whole truth, and nothing but the truth.

Back in the early sixties when I was a freshman at Indiana University, there was a kid called "The Birdman." Every evening at six o'clock sharp he would lean out his window and let out a piercing, insane cackle. As his fame spread, larger and larger crowds began showing up in the courtyard beneath his window to hear him. One evening a sort of critical mass was achieved. Whether it was pre-arranged or spontaneous I don't know, but someone yelled, "*Panties*!" and it didn't take long for everyone to take up the chant. Things began to happen quickly. Hundreds of guys with testosterone coursing through their veins came screaming out of the dormitories and surged down to the natural destination, the giant girls' dorm, *Read Center*.

I was in my dorm room feeling smug and too mature for this kind of nonsense (at the age of sixty I'm happy to report I've grown considerably less mature). A river of young guys was noisily passing beneath my window. Like locusts, the majority of the male student body (fifteen or twenty thousand people) was on the move. They swiftly coalesced into a boisterous swarm outside the fortress-like women's dorm. All doors were ordered locked, and the young women inside were sternly told to turn off their lights. Despite my haughty maturity, I excitedly telephoned my girlfriend, Louise, who had a suite in the dorm. She filled me in about what was going on there.

Down below in the darkness, a sea of faces looked up hopefully, laughing, and of course chanting for underwear. Despite strict orders that no one should oblige them, a few young ladies threw some lacy stuff down to the adoring masses. No real harm came from it, though I think the Birdman was expelled for a semester. If you are twenty years old, your grandfather may have been in the crowd, chanting for panties. Maybe grandma threw him a pair. I hope you won't think the less of them. It was just the Zeitgeist.

The Splendid Splinter

I'M AN INDIANA UNIVERSITY basketball fan. IU is my alma mater. I've watched "The Hurryin' Hoosiers" for as long as I can remember. Basketball is a passion in our state. In the 50s almost every house in Indiana had a hoop tacked up somewhere on the premises. We spent hours tossing up shots. We all played.

Back when I was in high school, there was a kid playing for IU named Jimmy Rayl. I had a particular emotional bond with him: we were both six feet two inches tall and we both weighed one hundred forty-seven pounds. He was known as "The Splendid Splinter." Some people think Jimmy was the greatest natural shooter in the history of Indiana basketball, and *that* is saying something. He grew up in Muncie, Indiana, which was once identified by a sociologist as the most average town in America. He made them feel special. In high school he led The Muncie Central Bearcats to a state championship. What a year that must have been for them.

The evening I'm about to describe took place on a cold winter night in the old Fieldhouse of the IU campus. Outside the great limestone building, snow was falling gently from the heavens. As always, we arrived early. As we passed through the doors, the band was pumping up the crowd with "The IU Fight Song;" the excitement was palpable. The mighty hall (it seems sadly diminished when I pass by it these days) was packed to the rafters. My dad was President of the Varsity Club back then, so we had great seats: twenty rows up, right at mid-court.

Bloomington was smaller then. Everyone knew everyone else. Old family friends (doctor and dentist families mostly) surrounded us. They greeted us warmly as we climbed the stairs of the green painted wooden bleachers, removed our heavy coats, and shuffled down the row and into our seats. Everyone was talking excitedly about the game, assessing our chances, throwing statistics back and forth about field goal percentages, turnovers, possible match-ups between the two lineups, etc. Conversation in our small town had consisted of little else for the week leading up to this crucial game. We were playing the Ohio State Buckeyes. The Buckeyes were always tough and what happened tonight might determine who would take the Big Ten title and go on to the NCAA.

But all chatter was cut short when the PA announced, "Ladies and gentlemen, will you please stand for our National Anthem." The lights dimmed except for a single spotlight that focused on the great flag emblazoned with its 48 stars. As it rose slowly and majestically above the polished wooden court, we stood solemnly shoulder to shoulder with hands clasped closely to our hearts. Proudly and full-voiced, we belted out "The Star-Spangled Banner." Our united voices filled that cavernous space.

Then the first whistle blew and the crowd roared to life as the ref threw the ball into the air at mid-stripe for the starting tip-off. From that moment on, madness prevailed. It was an old fashioned barn burner. Nothing was held back. These former farm boys were transformed; now they were like gods in our eyes. Scrambling after loose balls, players went flying off the court and into the crowd. Laughing fans picked themselves up, helped the kids to their feet, got them back out on the floor, and the battle resumed. The lead see-sawed back and forth a dozen times; it was anybody's ballgame. The excitement and joy of that night seemed almost timeless, but finally the clock ran down to the last minute.

IU had a one-point lead, but OSU was in possession. The Buckeyes were playing control ball. It was maddening. Methodically, they worked the clock, dribbling out on the perimeter as they attempted to spread the defense. They were stalling, holding off for one last shot. The fieldhouse was on fire. We stomped our feet, thrust our arms to the roof, and cheered our Hoosiers on. *"DEfense! DEfense! DEfense!"* Things were desperate. We had to get a steal and rob them of a chance to score. Then, with only three seconds to go, their point guard set a perfect pick and in a burst of speed, the other guard drove the line.

He faked, stopped short, and took a quick jumper. It rattled in. The Buckeyes were up by one point. Ten thousand desperate curses rang out from ten thousand throats.

The game seemed all but lost. But there was one thin hope, and we all knew what it was. The pass was in-bounded to Jimmy at the far end of the court. The fans were out of their minds. There was no time to travel the full length of the floor; Buckeyes were all over him. Somehow, he broke the press and sprinted to the ten-second line halfway down the court. There was no time left, and even at that unbelievable distance, he had to shoot it. It was our only chance.

He let it fly.

Ten thousand fans were on their feet. The buzzer sounded and we held our breath. It was in God's hands now. The ball was in the air, arching on its trajectory. It seemed to hang there forever.

Then...

SWISH...

NOTHING BUT NET!

Best Things in the World

- Once, long ago in India, I heard a phone ring and realized that I hadn't heard that particular sound for three months. I didn't like it. Cell phones are everywhere now, and like so many things, that's a double-edged sword.

- Discovering that a perfect cantaloupe in Japan costs a hundred dollars.

- Old time music from impromptu groups that spring up spontaneously in the dusty parking lot of the Beanblossom Music Festival in Beanblossom, Indiana.

- Sneaking into *The Starlight Drive-in* in the trunk of a car with my date back in the 60's when I was a college student.

- Going through a local market in Indonesia with a native of that country to help explain everything unfamiliar to me. I learned that the old lady with a glop of shredded goo on her forehead was being treated for a headache and the tiny white worms in the bamboo case were for feeding caged songbirds.

- Friday night on Long Street in Cape Town. Music pours out of every door, the pubs and restaurants are hopping, and beautiful people of all races are strutting down the avenue.

- Peace Corps volunteers – God bless them. Almost invariably they'll tell you they're not having much effect. I beg to differ.

- Neuschwanstein and all the other castles in Bavaria built by "Mad Ludwig."

- *The Oscar Mayer Wienermobile.* It's impossible to see a hotdog on wheels drive by and not break into a grin.

- Sky-diving. I let go of the airplane wing and for three seconds all hell broke loose... then, abruptly, the parachute opened. Gently swaying beneath its canopy, I felt like a piece of dandelion fluff gently drifting to the earth. I can remember clearly hearing a dog barking far below me. As I neared the ground, I realized I was coming down much faster than I'd expected. The instructor on the ground was yelling for me to "look up" so I wouldn't stiffen in anticipation of the impact. A few moments later I hit the ground like a sack of potatoes thrown from a roof.

- Morning yoga lessons on a palm tree lined beach in Goa. Our instructor taught us how to fashion small pillows of sand to support our necks while executing shoulder stands.

- The waiters at Leopold's Restaurant in Bombay where I started this list. In a single stroke a new manager fired every one of them.

- The French edition of the "Guide Michelin." It's a big book with tiny print and an exhaustive glossary of symbols. Every hotel and restaurant listed is a testament to L'arte de vivant—the art of living— and a culture that values these things.

- The dozens of ingenious magicians, mimes, comedians, and musicians who perform on the plaza in front of the *Pompidou Museum* in Paris.

- The Roman ruins in Palmyra, Syria. Standing in the middle of the main street and looking along the long corridor of pillars that framed the thoroughfare, I suddenly realized that this ancient desert city must have been far more beautiful than any modern city I'd ever seen.

- Modern dance.

It Takes a Village

WHILE WORKING OUR WAY around the world, my wife, son, and I spent one three month segment on Lamu Island a couple of miles off the northern coast of Kenya. We rented a pleasant little place that looked out on the ocean. Near by was the friendly village of Shella. In the morning after breakfast we sat outside on our big front porch and went through Jacques' lessons with him. Normally it took about two and a half hours. It's amazing how little time it takes in a one-on-one situation for a child to learn what they need to learn to stay even with their contemporaries back home.

After school it was time for a quick lunch and then Jacques would set off with Suzy, his little brown donkey, to go visit his friends. Everyone in the village looked after my son as they did for all the other children. They were good at it, too. Economists are always telling us that people in poor countries have more children for various social and economic reasons. What they never seem to mention is that most people in non-industrial countries just plain *like* children more than most westerners. If you go to a party with your two year old in India or Indonesia or Ecuador, as opposed to America, you'll see what I mean. In America and Europe parenthood is a solitary duty. In the third world, it's a shared joy.

For the rest of the day, Jacques would stay busy with his buddies, fishing, swimming, boating, and visiting at each other's houses. Occasionally, they'd all come to our house, and when they did, we tried to do our part and be good hosts as well.

Whenever we walked across this tiny village, every single soul knew my son. In high spirits they all laughed and shouted out his name as we passed by.

If raising a child has become a burden to you, or if having a child seems like it might be a burden, consider moving to an "undeveloped" country.

The Jaguar Birdman

JACQUES VAN KIRK IS unaware that I have a son named after him. Perhaps the two will meet someday. I met Jacques while traveling in Guatemala in the Peten about thirty years ago. At the time, it was the densest jungle in Central America. A lot of it has been cut down since.

I arrived by bus in Sayaxche, the end of the line. I checked into a small hotel. I was the sole guest and indeed the sole foreigner in this tiny river town at the end of a mud road. That evening, after asking around a little bit, I found an Indian guide, Don Jose, who was willing to take me up the river. Since I didn't know how to describe to him what I wanted to do (which was really nothing more than to experience the jungle), I just told him that I wanted to see animals. We talked briefly over beers, but things were cut off when, at ten o'clock, they turned off the generator and the lights went out all over town.

Early the next morning, we filled a large spare gas tank and set out in a long dugout canoe powered by a small outboard motor. I was perched in the front and Don Jose steered our craft from the rear. Huge trees along the narrow channel shaded us. We traveled at a slow pace through the still green water of the river for several hours, not speaking much, and hardly encountering anyone. At a spot where an ancient Mayan trail split off from the river, we tied off the craft and set out by foot. Everything was so overgrown that it was almost impossible for me to make out the path. My guide knew what he was doing though. From time to time he would even clear a little space with his machete to reveal a thousand-year-old well.

Once he slipped a carbine out of a burlap sack and used it to dispatch a tiny deer with a single shot. I hadn't even been able to discern what he was aiming at when he pulled the trigger. He smiled as he threw the limp body of the little creature over his shoulder, and we set out again. Walking steadily through the heat of the day, we only stopped in the afternoon for a smoke. Since starting along the trail, we hadn't seen a person, so when Don Jose told me there was a gringo living nearby, I was surprised to say the least. I wanted to meet him.

About an hour afterward, we arrived at a beautiful, small, crystal clear lake with a creek flowing out of it. I later learned that freshwater dolphins lived there. A winding path led up the hill to a neat little house roofed with palm fronds and built on stilts. There was a cooking area beneath and bedrooms above. At our approach, Jacques Van Kirk strode out of the house with arm outstretched and a broad smile on his face. We were welcomed in. The two of us hit it off immediately. He lived way out there with his wife, Parny, and their two daughters, Gayle and Parny Lynne, aged ten and fourteen. We soon discovered that both Jacques and I had plans to go into Guatemala City sometime within the next few days, so it was agreed that I would stay with the family until we could both leave together. I paid Don Jose and he left soon afterwards for Sayaxche.

Jacques' older daughter, Parny Lynne, kept chickens and there was a plentiful garden. Of course, the jungle and stream provided food as well. Parny was a great and ingenious cook. We ate some sumptuous meals out there in the middle of nowhere— always laced with a lot of good conversation. One evening, after finishing off a delicious main course of turtle cooked in a sort of marinara sauce and followed up with a mincemeat pie made with homemade mincemeat, Jacques described what he considered the tastiest meat to be found in the area: a kind of giant jungle rat. I'll have to take his word on that, but I have no doubt that Parny could have made something tasty from the dead carcass of a rodent.

Jacques explained that he had once been a top trainer of Arabian horses, but that gradually he had grown tired of the "mink and manure set." One day something happened at work that pissed him off and he stormed out. When he walked in the door of his home, the first thing he said was, "Honey, I've decided to give up this life and start over. I want to be either a Formula One race driver or a white hunter, you choose."

Parny pondered this for a couple of minutes, then responded, "white hunter."

A few days later, Jacques, Parny, and their two infant children arrived in Guatemala City. A week later they were in the heart of The Peten with a tent, a rifle, a few supplies, and no money. Somehow they had not only survived, but as I could see from looking around me, prospered.

One evening, we were sitting in the kitchen area under the house having a wide-ranging conversation that included everything from Jacques' experiences in the Marine Corps (He was always getting busted down to private), to what it's like when army ants march through your property (Get out of the way, it's hopeless to resist. On the positive side, they get rid of all household pests). At one point, he locked his eyes on his remarkable wife. "John," he said, "I hope that someday you are lucky enough to find the second best woman in the world. I've already found the best."

Another evening I remember sitting around the table by the light of a gas lantern reading the family encyclopedia. One of Jacques' former clients had given it to them. The whole family eagerly combed through the pages sharing what they were learning. I only spent a week with this remarkable family. Every one of those days and nights is a vivid memory.

One of the many ways that Jacques made money was by doing charcoal rubbings of Mayan stele that he sold when he went into the capital. One day he asked me to accompany him to an archaeological site deep in the rainforest that had probably only been seen by a dozen white people before us. Jacques and I approached the site in a dugout canoe. We tied off in a clear pond and then ascended an adjacent hill. Near the top was an arched stone bridge traversing a ravine. The jungle was thick, but all around us we could make out the shapes of temples, entirely engulfed in vegetation. For some reason I'd always thought that all sites like this had already been excavated. Here, however, excavation had only just been initiated and then had been abandoned, at least for the time being.

At the center of the temple complex was a clear, flat area where archaeologists had uncovered a single large stele. It depicted the Jaguar Birdman resplendent in a headpiece made of jaguar skins, quetzal feathers, and deer feet. Some people have described these as "space helmets." Perhaps I don't have a good enough imagination; it didn't look like that to me. There was one striking feature that did catch my attention though. Emerging from his mouth was a single mysterious word-glyph in the shape of an 'o.'

Once, Jacques told me, he'd been working on a rubbing like this when he chanced to look up and saw a jaguar taking him in. The big cat wasn't on the prowl. He appeared to be there, just quietly watching Jacques, out of simple curiosity.

Back home that evening we got out Jacques' well worn copy of Morley's, *The Ancient Maya*, hoping to discern the carved date at the bottom of the stele. It was a fascinating intellectual adventure. The Mayan numerical system is similar to ours in that numbers have both place and numerical value. Where our "decimal" system is based on ten (associated with ten fingers) the Mayan system is based on twenty (fingers and toes). Reading through the book, we discovered the date in our Gregorian calendar that corresponded to the zero point of the Mayan calendar (by their reckoning, the date of creation) and we extrapolated from there. The number at the bottom of the stele represented the days counted forward from that zero point. According to our calculations, the stele was roughly one thousand years old, consistent with the time of the "Classical Mayan Era."

Several years later in Nepal, I was trekking with a young American post-hippie lady named Cecilia who had spent a year in Guatemala. I told her the story of an eccentric American who lived out in the jungle with his family. Halfway through the story, she exploded, "That must be Jacques Van Kirk!" Then I learned the next chapter of the story. A few years after I had visited, the government of Guatemala turned the area surrounding Jacques' house into a national park. He had no title to the land, and really no right to be there, so they evicted him without compensation. Shortly afterward, he found himself back in Guatemala City with his family— broke again. It didn't get him down. He went right to work and established an advertising agency. Within a few years, he was a very wealthy man.

The Fetishist

A FEW YEARS AGO in Goa, I met a woman of about twenty-five whose boyfriend had just left for London. She felt abandoned. We struck up a conversation. Neither of us had ulterior motives. We just enjoyed each other's company. I agreed to accompany her to a little thatch-roofed seaside bar that evening where we thought she might hook-up with someone interesting. It was a quiet, relaxed place with nice music and open to the breeze that gently wafted through the palm trees. There was no flooring, just the sand. Many of the customers sipped their drinks lying around in the hammocks that were strewn about the place.

My companion was very shy and not pretty by any conventional standards. I remember dirt under her fingernails. But she was ever so lovable.

She didn't meet anyone, but we both had a good time. At one point that night, I asked what you always ask, "What do you do for a living?" It turned out that she was the editor of a new fetish magazine in England. She said she would let me see the first issue if I liked. What man with blood in his veins could say no to that. The next day she gifted me with a copy. I read it cover to cover, including every ad. It surely made my sexual proclivities seem plain vanilla by contrast. Next day she was gone. I never saw her again.

Three Churches

My brother Richard was once living in a small town in Ohio when he decided that, as an experiment, he would attend every church within the city limits on succeeding Sundays. I think it's a wonderful idea. I'd recommend it to anyone. I've never been that systematic myself, but sometimes I do like to attend different places of worship. There's always something to learn. It's an adventure of sorts.

Many years ago, I was working for the Veterans Administration as a Vocational Rehabilitation Specialist. I didn't have a window and I spent an awful lot of time in that job filling out forms and listening to Musak under fluorescent lighting. But it wasn't all bad. My boss, Don Back, was a big-hearted guy, and our overall mission of reeducating disabled veterans was something worth doing.

There was a lively, young black woman working there in the janitorial staff. She had a cheerful buoyancy to her. When she came by to empty wastebaskets, we'd usually chat for a few minutes. Several times she mentioned her church to me. She urged me to come sometime. "Instead of going out to a bar on the weekends, I like going to my church. It's joyful."

Sounded good to me, so one Sunday evening, I arrived with three friends at her little church in the middle of the black ghetto of Indianapolis. The place was brightly lit and beautiful music poured out the door to meet us. Everyone was friendly and welcoming; we immediately felt right at home.

Things seemed to be well underway as they ushered us in. The congregation was standing up, singing, clapping hands, and swaying to the music. We joined right in. Standing along the walls of the church were women in starched white uniforms. They appeared to be nurses.

About ten minutes after we arrived, a man in the pew directly in front of us suddenly went into what appeared to be an epileptic fit. His glasses fell from his face. He stamped on them, shattering the lenses. His arms and legs started flailing uncontrollably. He looked as if he might harm himself. Two of the white-clad women rushed over and quickly restrained him. They gently cradled his head and soothed him. A couple of minutes later, his quivering receded and he was able to lie back and recover. He appeared exhausted. In the course of the night this happened to different members of the congregation perhaps a dozen times. No one seemed alarmed.

Various musical groups and choirs performed throughout the evening. It was glorious stuff. You couldn't help but be moved. Sometimes when the chorus started swelling, I felt it might take the roof off. I'd never thought of a church as somewhere to go to have a rip-roaring good time. This was a place to celebrate.

After two or three hours, things quieted down a little. The preacher came to the lectern, and my friends and I settled back and prepared to listen to the sermon. He stood there for a moment. Then he cried out, "I'm a fool! I'm a FOOL! I'M A FOOL FOR JESUS!" With that, he stepped down and the music started cranking again. That was the sermon. It's probably the only sermon I've never forgotten.

෨

There's an unadorned but attractive Friends church on the edge of Bloomington. Friends, also known as Quakers, believe in simplicity. Sometimes they're financially well off, but you'll find no Ferraris parked out in front of the church.

I'd never attended a Quaker service. I learned later that there are two basic types. In one there is a traditional preacher, and in the other the congregation meets in silence until someone feels moved. Then they stand up, say their piece, and sit down. The meeting I attended was of the second type. Some of what was said at one service or another rang so true that it still remains with me. I came out of curiosity and wound up attending for several years, off and on. I spent a lot of time thinking over things people said in meeting but also a lot of time just contemplating the weather outside the windows.

No one ever asked me to become an official member. That was one of the things I liked about it. Some people, like me, spoke every few weeks; others, never. The ideals of Quakerism are simple but profound: justice, equality and peace. Quakers worked for the abolition of slavery back when that goal seemed an impossible dream. Today they work passionately for world peace, which today appears equally far away but may yet be attainable. The Quakers of that congregation who I came to know lived these ideals every day. I respect them. I love them.

ഊ

I was interested in the phenomenon of mega-churches. I'd read that they tend to be fundamentalist in doctrine but modern in every other respect. Politically, fundamentalist Christianity has remade the American political landscape. I knew all that, but I hadn't had any direct experience of what a service might be like.

By doing a Google search I discovered that the seventh largest church in America was located just two hours drive south of us in Louisville. Next Sunday, brother Richard and I drove down to attend. The building itself was enormous. There were acres of parking and lots of facilities including a coffee house, bookstore, voter registration area, and plenty of meeting rooms. The main auditorium had comfortable seating in tasteful colors— no hard wooden pews of yesteryear. It could accommodate twenty thousand. There were huge video screens all around. People were friendly and courteous, not pushy and preachy. There was a nice racial mix.

Before the service started, we spoke briefly with one middle-aged married couple sitting next to us. They told us that they had met at a church function here. They seemed content and well matched. In the attractively laid out bulletin, we read about bicycling tours, golf outings, singles get-togethers, all kinds of activities. We noticed in the bulletin that around half a million dollars had been collected. My brother didn't think that was very much until we realized that that was the take for the week.

There seemed nothing unusual about the service. Someone in the front "signed" the sermon so the hard of hearing could follow it.

That was thoughtful. I enjoyed singing the hymns while following the dancing dots on the screen, karaoke-style.

Then the minister introduced a gentleman from the "Jews for Jesus" organization. He was a great speaker and very funny. He soon had the congregation in the palm of his hand. People were laughing and applauding. A snippet of a recent appearance of his on *The Larry King Show* was shown on the many screens situated around the auditorium. There was wide approval of this. Then the tone changed. He began to speak of the "approaching end times." He quoted from Revelations. He described in vivid detail the coming cataclysm in Israel that would presage the ending of the world. A roar of joyful anticipation started to come up out of those plush seats. It began to build in intensity. People were cheering now like it was a rock concert. The parishioners were on fire! They wanted it! They yearned for it!

Trying to Die in Bed at 95

Two things have struck me as I've written this book. First, how many different women I've been with. Though I've learned something from all of them, lovely as they all were, this is not what I would have wished, and I'm trying to learn from my mistakes.

Secondly, I'm struck by how often I've almost died. It's almost laughable. I've been held up at gunpoint at night on the road in Guatemala and shot with a machine gun in the chest and shoulder in Vietnam. I came close to drying up in the Sahara and freezing to death in the Himalayas. I nearly came a cropper from Malaria and Typhoid Fever in Ethiopia and Hepatitis in India. There have been accidents involving motorcycles and automobiles. I've had close calls involving lions (twice), elephants (three times) and a rhino (once).

Whatever there is to be learned from all this, I'm trying like the Dickens to learn. I know I'm mule-headed, but maybe if I can learn lessons the easy way I won't always have to learn them the hard way.

I believe that we're free, and nothing happens that shouldn't happen as a result of those free choices. I've abandoned most of my vices and I'm trying to be more careful. I've got no illusions about how holy I've become, though. God's forgiveness is my one and only hope.

One way or another, we're all circling the plug hole. My aim is to die in bed at ninety-five. I've heard that the first ninety years of life are the hard part; after that, it's smooth sailing. I like to picture my grandchildren tearfully gathered around for my (hopefully wise) last words.

Advice to Travelers:
Every Paradise Has a Lifespan

TODAY I AM GAZING across the Betwa River, beyond a medieval looking wall to the temples and palaces of Orchha. It's a small paradise. This peaceful little town was recommended to me by a fellow traveler. Almost all paradises are passed on by word of mouth.

No paradise lasts forever. The tiny fishing village next to a pristine beach where I first stayed in Goa thirty-five years ago is now filled with noisy rickshaws and hard-eyed hustlers. I'm sure the Costa del Sol was once a place of transcendent beauty, but it isn't now, nor is my previously tranquil beach. The "development" of a paradise is perhaps inevitable. But sometimes it may be guided a little. I give, as an example, a beach named Arambol, near the village where I stay in Goa these days.

When I first saw Arambol thirty-five years ago, there were only two tiny shacks selling candles, sardines, and the like. Walking across some rocky headlands in the late afternoon, I found a small path that paralleled the sea coast. As I topped the ridge on the far side, I was shocked by the beauty lying before me. There was a clear freshwater lake enclosed by jungle. In front of this was the ocean and a broad stretch of sand. The sun was going down, coloring the sea orange and purple. There were scattered groups of naked young people meditating on the beach. Some travelers were living in tents amidst the banyan and palm trees that grew luxuriantly around the periphery of the lake. Others just slept on mats under the stars.

To keep this account honest, I should also add that amongst all these free spirits there were a fair number of junkies (mostly from

Marseilles and southern Italy). They were easy to identify. You had to keep an eye on your stuff.

The beach has changed both for better and for worse. The junkies are mostly gone. Indian cops took care of that. These days there are Chinese restaurants, Mexican restaurants, Israeli restaurants, Dutch restaurants, vegan restaurants, Italian restaurants, and there's a new sushi bar in town. There are over a hundred stores selling Rajasthani, Nepali, Ladakhi, and Kashmiri goods, as well as bikinis and rave gear. It's a very different kind of place now. I still like it. But of course, I've changed too.

Recently the beach has begun to attract a community of creative and artistic people from dozens of countries. A carnival with a jungle theme was in progress not long ago. Some of the town's citizens dressed as gorillas, others as palm trees. All kinds of silliness was going on. My friend Zouzou is very much at the forefront of all of this funny business.

The community now has any number of reiki masters, acupuncture practitioners, singing bowl healers, tarot card readers, herbal healers (cures for piles, cancer and "sexual weakness"), a yoga instructor who lusts after sexy Danish babes, a tai chi master who plays kick-ass mouth organ, and several local Indians who, for a few rupees, will play the flute while their cow dances.   Every possible school of massage and meditation is well represented. You can hear great Rock and Roll, or listen to Sufi music played at beachside restaurants where beautiful Russian girls dance ecstatically.

Lots of writers, poets, artists and craftsmen come here. Not long ago, at a weekly jam session at The Loeke Bar, I met a lady who has made a project of creating lovely carnation-like flowers from discarded trash bags. Somehow she scented them to smell like real flowers. In a country like India where discarded bags often thickly litter the landscape this is an especially clever thing to do. I know of one German fellow who polishes the seashells he finds in Indonesia, makes jewelry from them, and sells them at the weekly hippie market here. This is his sole source of livelihood. This year, he looked as if he was doing so well that I felt no need to buy the lovely jewelry that makes his idyllic lifestyle possible. He appeared to be doing just fine without me.

Paradises have a lifespan. Arambol is still delightful, though it's very different from when I first saw it. It can never go back to how it was. For those searching for totally untouched beaches, there are more than a hundred miles of clean white sand and palm trees just north of Goa in Maharastra. If you want to live where there are no foreigners, you could stay with the fishermen and never see one.

How I Might Have Been a Chief in Samoa

MANY YEARS AGO, WHEN I was a young man crossing the Pacific, I flew into Pago Pago, the magnificently situated capital of Western Samoa. For what it's worth, the city is pronounced as if it had "n" in it: "Pango Pango." I took a bus into town, but when I arrived, I found all the hotels were far too expensive for me. Undeterred, I walked a short distance to the market area. Here I found a flat wooden cart. I unrolled my sleeping bag on top of it and slept blissfully through the night. When I awoke next morning, there were people all around me bustling about, setting up fruit and vegetable stands.

I'd recently read Margaret Mead's classic book, *Coming of Age in Samoa*, and I was intrigued by it. As a result, one of my aims in traveling there was to experience village life. I soon struck up a conversation with a friendly local guy who graciously invited me to visit his village which was situated on the far side of the island. We hopped on a rickety old bus that stopped periodically whenever the driver saw a palm frond, like a hitchhiker's thumb, indicating that someone needed a ride.

In the late afternoon we arrived at our destination, a tranquil village on a perfect white sand beach surrounded by limpid blue water and sheltered by a coral reef. There was a small, empty house amidst the coconut palms. I moved right in.

Life moved slowly, almost timelessly, in my village, one day drifting naturally into the next. We all shared in everything that came from the communal gardens and the sea. None of us worked very hard. We had what we needed.

When I think of that place and time, one particular day always comes to mind. I paddled out to the reef with some friends in the bright sunlight in the most delicate little outrigger canoe. It was so light you could pick it up with one arm and it didn't have a nail in it — a perfect work of art. Joking amongst ourselves, we felt so happy. The sheltering sky above us was heartbreakingly blue, the sea below sapphire and perfectly transparent. We were suspended there between two pristine firmaments.

About once a year the various chiefs would meet in a large, open, circular building to conduct village business. The building was supported by wooden poles, each one designating the status of the chief who sat in front of it. While I was there, a meeting was held, and they generously allowed me to attend. I sat solemnly with my back braced against my assigned pole with what I hoped was perceived as great gravitas.

At the beginning of the gathering, the village virgin chewed kava for us. The results were then passed around the circle in a small bowl from which we all took a sip. I remember the liquid had a slightly stimulating effect while at the same time numbing my mouth like Novocain.

I must have made an acceptable impression because, after the ceremony, my friend told me that it could be arranged for me to become a minor chief and remain in the village for a week, a month, or the rest of my life. It was a beautiful offer, but I had been traveling for over three years and was itching to return to my homeland. Still, I was tempted.

The Optimist

I WAS SITTING ON the front porch of our little house on the island of Lamu just off of the north coast of Kenya shortly before the start of the rainy season. Over the course of a couple of days, I had been watching a swallow laboriously build its nest under the eaves of the porch from tiny droplets of mud which she carried in her beak. The potential nest site was above me at a juncture where the ceiling met the wall. When, after getting a dozen or so dabs to adhere to the surface, upon adding the thirteenth the whole thing would fall to the ground. This happened three times. The fourth time, when the bird was just ready to apply the next piece to her construction, the whole thing collapsed again. She eyed the newly bare spot and, with apparent disgust, threw the small bit of mud she had brought in her beak to the porch floor and flew off. An hour later though, she was back and, with newfound optimism, was at it again. Finally it was complete.

Next day, so quickly I couldn't stop him, the caretaker of our house took a broom and, in a moment, flicked down the entire creation.

Best Things in the World

- Intricate Jain temples with attached bird hospitals. Jains have a reverence for all life and the hospitals are a reflection of this. Before entering, you must remove leather shoes and belts. Jain saints will often cover their mouths and nostrils with gauze to avoid ingesting bacteria. They carefully sweep beneath themselves to avoid sitting on some tiny creature. They filter all drinking water. It's a radical attempt to do no harm.

- The friendly bars in Lightning Ridge, Australia, the town where fire opals are mined. The stones were fragile, so when someone wanted to show-off a large opal at the bar, one of his mates would hold a hat beneath it to make sure it wouldn't drop and shatter on the floor.

- Bollywood of Bombay and Honkywood of Hong Kong.

- Syrian flower-tea served up to us by the owner of an "antique shop." He lost a little of his credibility when one of the dusty, Grecian antiquities he showed us was the figurine of a kangaroo.

- A traditional inn, or Ryokhan, in Kyoto, Japan. Its simplicity and tranquility inspired my normally messy, seven-year-old son to speak softly and meticulously fold his clothes.

- Walking on the beach in Goa one night and turning around to see my footprints glowing due to the bioluminescent bacteria in the sand.

- The giant three-story water-clock made of multi-colored glass in the atrium of "The Children's Museum" in Indianapolis. Crowds gather for "hour changes" when a full line of five small, water-filled containers labeled for ten minute intervals and nine still smaller containers labeled for minutes tilt over and gurgle down into a larger container labeled for the hour.

- Perfectly-sculpted tea plantations that contour the sensual curve of the hills in Sri Lanka.

- The great spherical stones scattered apparently randomly all over Costa Rica. They seem unrelated to any other archaeological sights and are undated. I've never heard an explanation of them that satisfies me.

- Lying on my belly with a friend, clearing a small space in the grass and quietly observing the little creatures passing across this small stage.

- Houseboats in Kashmir. You can sit up on the top deck as various small boats glide by with merchants selling everything you might need from flowers and candy to birth control pills.

- Driving across the vast Serengeti Plains as the sun was about to dip below the horizon. We weren't far from Olduvai Gorge where the oldest human bones were found. It didn't seem strange that it had been here. The land felt ancient.

- The yak herders in Nepal who took me in and saved my life. For the twenty four hours I spent with these dear people regardless of what was going on, they were either laughing or smiling every single minute of the time. The only exception to this came when I took out my camera to film them. They suddenly grew solemn as puritans. As soon as I put it away though, they immediately broke into radiant smiles again.

Working Off-Shore

THERE WAS AN OVERLAND route to India back in the sixties and seventies that was later termed "the hippy trail." It began in Istanbul and you met up with people, jobs, lodgings, rides, etc through the bulletin boards at common stops. The Pudding Shop was a popular one. Through a scrap of paper on another bulletin board at the Amir Kabir Hotel in Tehran, I learned about a job teaching English on an oil platform in The Persian Gulf.

We got to the platform by a thirty minute chopper ride from Lavan Island. Even a few miles out, as we approached the platform, we could see the hundred foot tall flare of natural gas that they kept burning 24/7. A fantastic sight, but considering the hundreds of them across the gulf, a colossal waste of energy, and what must surely be a large contributor to greenhouse gases.

This was one of the better jobs I had. I remember many a night drinking wine, swapping jokes and playing liar's poker until early in the morning with the deep-sea divers. I love people with stories to tell and God knows these fellows had plenty of them. They were the kind of guys who blow into Cairo and rent out an entire whorehouse for a weekend.

The monstrous spidery legs and understructure supporting the platform acted like a coral reef. As a result, we were always surrounded by lovely tropical fish life. I would have expected the marine environment surrounding us to have remained fairly constant, but in fact it changed radically from week to week. I once saw a 25-foot hammerhead shark pass directly beneath us— slow, sad, and deliberate.

I had been working on the platform for three months. It was utterly fascinating for awhile, but after a month or two things can begin to get pretty boring, and people get into all kinds of trouble trying to avoid boredom. I was no exception. One day I spotted a school of sharks swimming and hunting not far off. I ran to my room, put on my swimming suit, climbed down a ladder to a metal platform and went for a swim. The sharks were near but didn't approach me. Five minutes later I crawled out of the water. There are billions of people in the world and probably billions of sharks as well, yet less than 50 people a year are eaten by sharks. I have a greater belief in statistics than anecdotal information. I thought I ought to put it to the test. Sharks must not be as dangerous as people think they are. Still, I have to admit, it was a little nuts.

A few days later I found myself on an airplane headed for Tehran with my pockets full of cash. I was all cleaned up and looking forward to seeing a beautiful Iranian girl I'd met the last time I was in the city. I would be the first man ever to see her naked breast.

Winter in the Hindu Kush

As soon as Afghanis had a weapon that a single man could hold and knock out a helicopter and a weapon that a single man could hold and knock out a tank, the occupying Soviet army was in a hopeless situation. For more than a thousand years Afghanis have lived by pillaging or demanding payment from caravans going back and forth to India. They're indomitable— the toughest people on earth.

The national sport of Afghanistan is Buskashi. A description of it will tell you a lot about the country. The playing field is almost featureless, roughly the size of ten football fields, with single posts at opposite ends of the plain. At the center is a shallow pit. Usually there are about twenty horsemen on a side. The horses are beautiful, thick-muscled, swift creatures; they're high strung and bred for fearlessness.

The game is played with a beheaded goat. The object is to take the goat's body around your opponents' post and return it to the hole. Firearms and knives are forbidden, but anything involving whips, feet and hands, and pummeling with sticks is permitted. There are no officials. To begin play, a swirling, stomping mass of horses and riders pack densely into the center. Then the carcass is tossed into the central pit and total anarchy breaks loose.

The land itself is equally extraordinary. Within its borders, the Pamirs, the Himalayas and the Hindu Kush all meet in a wild collision of mountains. The climate is harsh and vegetation sparse. When the rains come, rivers destroy everything in their path. Bridges are washed away without a trace. In summer much of the land looks like a rugged moonscape, but spots of blue or green, when they appear, can be intense.

I once saw a lake near Bandi Amir (which means land of silence) whose color was the same deep blue as a flawless piece of lapis lazuli.

I arrived in Kabul on a cold winter day aboard a jolly looking, red double-decked London city bus that had been fitted out for overland travel. The company, *Top Deck Travel*, ran about a dozen of these overland buses for the month long run to India. The bottom floor was mostly devoted to baggage, spare parts, supplies and cooking equipment. The topside was outfitted with mattresses and pillows. We lounged about gossiping, smoking hash (purchased from the Afghani border guards), listening to rock music, and reading groovy, uplifting spiritual books and pamphlets as we rolled on toward the mysterious east.

Sharing the ride with me was a bunch of good-natured, shaggy, unkempt, foul smelling, long-haired young travelers headed for India. As soon as I got into town I looked up my life-long friends (we're related as well, but I can never remember quite how), Lois and Jules Hendricks. They had been working on an educational project in Afghanistan and were living in the capital. The American government was paying their salary and expenses. As a result, these unpretentious folks were living in a veritable palace. The house was made of pink stucco and was surrounded by a large enclosure with stout eighteen-foot walls. One of their four devoted servants stood as an armed guard at the gate. They graciously invited me to stay.

Lois and Jules were wonderful hosts and I immediately felt perfectly at home. I had been traveling rough. Hot water and a comfortable bed were a welcome change. I reveled in all this luxury, but early on I told them that after a few days rest, I hoped to explore up into the Hindu Kush. Being too polite to tell me it was a dangerous and slightly crazy idea, they nonetheless recognized that they were going to have to do something to protect their impetuous young friend. Between the two of them they came up with the idea of sending me with one of their servants. This man had family living in a small mountain village far up in the north.

Jules owned the most beautiful rifle I've ever seen. He had acquired it while on assignment in Austria with the O.S.S shortly after the Second World War. It was really a piece of work. The stock was inlaid with bone or perhaps ivory. I remember it as portraying a medieval Teutonic hunting scene, replete with stags and wild boar. He felt that having it would guarantee me a warm welcome— Afghanis love a good gun.

We left Kabul at night in a small rickety bus. It was bitterly cold. The name of the Afghani man accompanying me is lost to my memory. Perhaps it was Mohammed. Let's assume it was. The bus was cramped, but being packed in shoulder-to shoulder helped with the cold. The ceiling was low enough that, while sitting in my seat, the top of my head rested directly against it. I felt every bump. My other companion was an American fellow, a veteran of the US Special Forces. He was a tough kid, and I never heard a complaint out of him. He traveled with a guitar and wound up lugging it through a lot of deep snow that trip.

There was no way to judge the exact temperature, but I believe it was around minus fifteen degrees Fahrenheit. There was a young Afghani riding on the back of the bus whose job it was to put luggage on and off the roof (guarding it from theft as well). Unbelievably, he rode through half the night clinging to the steel ladder with bare hands as we wound our way along the snow packed road.

The bus could only get so far up into the mountains before snowdrifts brought it to a halt near a wayside inn. We disembarked, and the three of us went inside and prepared to spend the remainder of the night there. Mohammed carefully unrolled my sleeping bag, fluffed it up a little, then laid it out neatly. It dawned on me that he had assumed that, for the trip, he was to be my servant. I was taken aback. It went against my grain.

Then he taught me a lesson. From his manner I could see that there was no question that, as men, he saw us as equals. We just had different roles to play. I had to hold up my end of things and maintain a certain dignity. Anything less would reflect badly on him. That was the unspoken contract between us.

That night I slept with the rifle clutched to my chest inside my sleeping bag. The next morning after a hot breakfast, the three of us struck out along a snow trail up a long narrow valley under a clear blue sky. Mohammed led the way. Sometimes we had to wade through waist high snow. I was bearded at the time and remember later seeing a picture of myself with the beard frozen solid with ice. At one point we stopped for a break. I got out my canteen but couldn't get a drink. The water in it was frozen rock-solid. There was little we saw that day that differed from what Marco Polo would have seen.[11] It has been said that Afghanistan is a country poised on the verge of a jump into the Sixteenth Century. Trudging through the snow, we felt as if we'd been transported to another age.

We reached a little village in the late afternoon. The Kuchi dogs that live here on rough terms with their owners came out as if to attack us. I picked up a rock as big as a baseball which made Mohammed laugh. These huge, half-wild dogs wouldn't be threatened by anything that puny. He picked up a rock as big as his head, and at that point the pack grudgingly backed off and, snarling all the while, allowed us to pass into the village. The local people welcomed us in and, like Muslims everywhere in the world, were wonderful hosts. Next morning we went out above the village with the rifle and fired off a few rounds into the cold cloudless sky. That pleased everyone to no end just as Jules had predicted.

Today, especially with the war happening, Afghanistan is even wilder than it was back then, and if you're looking for this kind of adventure, it's still there. My son Jacques is serving in the army over there, five miles from the Pakistan border. He's an adventurer like his old man, and I love and respect him for being there.

---

[11] One seemingly incongruous touch: from time to time in Afghanistan I've passed by a primitive mud village and caught sight of an elegant Afghan Hound proudly prancing along, looking as if it might equally well belong on Fifth Avenue in the entourage of some fashionable heiress.

I Remember

I REMEMBER HOW THE TV cowboy heroes of my youth were so quick on the draw and such great marksmen that they took care of bad guys by shooting their pistols right out of their hands. Not just sometimes— *always*.

I remember a dream that I told to my dear daughter, Thea, when she was a young child. It must have moved her deeply as she'd ask me to repeat it to her over and over again.

I was on a great open, treeless plain, standing alone. A herd of giant buffalo, each one the size of a house, was rumbling toward me. I turned to run but immediately realized it was hopeless. They were far faster than me. Instead, I turned, faced them, then slowly and confidently began to walk towards them. As soon as I did that the great beasts were magically transformed into the cutest little puppy dogs. Whenever I told her the dream, Thea would ask me to go on about how cute they were, how they licked my face, and how they jumped all over me.

I remember a sign in Botswana: "Private Clinic, Catering Service, Bar and Kindergarten." Just down the road was the "3-Way Divorce Club."

I remember being on board a ship crossing the Mediterranean Sea from Algiers to Marseilles. I had only a little over $2 left in my pocket. I needed to make it all the way across Europe to Amsterdam where more money would be waiting for me. I met a nice looking Norwegian girl on board and the two of us quickly agreed to hitch together. Catching a ride anywhere in the world is a whole lot easier when you've got a pretty young woman with you.

I climbed up to the top deck and sat out under the stars, feeling the ocean spray on my face for an hour or so, feeling great. Imagine my dismay when I came back down to find my faithless, would-be lady friend, passionately making-out with a young German guy. Next day in the afternoon sun, a swarm of raggedy, blue jeans clad travelers disembarked and lined up along the grassy embankment beside the road— over 100 of us. We all stuck out our thumbs. Southern France is a hard place to catch a ride anyway. My situation seemed hopeless. But just before nightfall a small miracle occurred. A sweet young French kid in a Deux Chevaux pulled over and gave me a ride.

I remember teaching Junior High School students in inner city Washington, D.C. It was the hardest job I ever had. Not long afterward I found myself in combat in Vietnam. It was a great relief.

I remember dining on the upper terrace of a magnificent palace called the Sheesh Mahal in northern India. My dinner companions were delightful: two physicians from Australia and a cultured and beautiful lady from Paris who organized street performances.

After dinner I brought out my telescope and we looked at Jupiter and its moons. Raj, with a very acute eye, was able to make out the fourth one, which was very close to Jupiter itself. The conversation was congenial, wide-ranging and refined— the poetry of Vikram Seth, Mughal architecture, and mom's cooking. At one point the lights went out, and for several minutes, our party was bathed in moonlight.

The Truth Cannot be Killed

In April 24th, 1980, my beloved Guru, Baba Gurbachen Singh-ji, was murdered by a religious fanatic. He had warned us that it was coming. As the time grew near he reassured us that, "People think that by killing me they can kill the truth. But the truth cannot be killed."

When it happened, the full responsibility of the Mission fell on the young shoulders of Baba Hardev Singh-ji. His first act was to declare that there were to be no retaliations. The blow would not be passed on. The assassination date would henceforward be called Manav Ekta Divas (Human Unity Day). To further commemorate it, in 1987 Nirankaris were requested to initiate blood donation camps. Blood would flow in veins, not drains.

When I next met Baba Hadev Singh-ji in Bombay he treated me with every possible kindness and sweetness. It touched me, so I don't quite know how to put this. There was a tiny little space in my mind that said, "I know his father was the true Guru; I know it as much as I've ever known anything. But is his son?"

Baba Hardev Singh-ji was leaving Bombay. Just before he left, he asked me my plans. I told him that I expected to return to America soon. He shook his head in acknowledgement and then said, "Perhaps you should stay in Bombay for a short while."

A couple of days later, I was invited by some local Nirankaris to take dinner that evening at their home. They were so noble, so kind-hearted and so hospitable, that even though it meant a drive of several noisy hours in a three-wheeler through the city's truly unbelievable air pollution, I knew I had to go. First I was taken to the house of a devotee. The wife of one of the men accompanying me washed my feet in a metal basin. This is always difficult for me. They were the great souls, the holy ones, yet they were washing *my* feet.

Then we got back in the three-wheeler for another ninety-minute ride. I was completely lost by now. We came to a halt at a nondescript concrete apartment building amidst hundreds of other nondescript concrete buildings. We mounted the stairwell, walked down the dark hall, and opened the door to be greeted by the most joyous scene. Kindness and human warmth reached out and engulfed us. There must have been three-dozen souls within the walls of the small apartment, all singing, dancing, laughing and conversing in high spirits. From the kitchen came the smells of a sumptuous Indian feast. It was to be a memorable evening.

As we sat around after the delicious and lovingly prepared meal, the little children sang devotional songs to us with the sweet voices of angels. Exactly what happened next I don't entirely recall. One of the men was saying something. Perhaps it was that Baba-ji had broken down all barriers between us. Whatever it was, I was suddenly thunderstruck by it. I found myself on the floor at the feet of this great soul. The circle of men and women surrounding me looked on with profound and loving eyes. One said, "We're so happy that this happened to you while you were still in India."

Best Things in the World

- One night we were camped under a great tree on an island in the Okavango Delta in Botswana. The Milky Way was magnificent and I finally felt confident identifying the Southern Cross. When I awoke in the middle of the night to pee, I could hear hippo bellowing, while a multitude of birds, toads, insects, and God-only-knows-what creatures called out into the darkness. Not a single one of the sounds was familiar.

- Watching border collies work a herd of sheep at the Indiana State Fair. Such joy in motion! I'd love to have a dog like that as a companion if I ever settle down a little.

- Dancing one night in India with a joyous, bright-eyed 108-year-old Nirankari woman.

- Working long days and nights through October for the Kerry campaign in Ohio. Idealistic people had gathered here from all over America for one reason: we knew the election was going to be close, and felt it might be decided here. In the middle of our gritty, little headquarters building was a board that we all signed. It read, "Columbus, Ohio: Center of the Universe, Tipping Point of the Campaign." It almost happened.

- The Okeefenokee, where you can paddle in by canoe and pitch a tent on one of the large platforms scattered throughout the swamp. At night you can hear the bellowing of dozens of alligators surrounding the campsite.

- The many churches and monasteries that have been lovingly

restored, in the great and magical fifteen hundred year old city of Kiev. Beneath a bright blue sky on a clear winter day, their onion domes glitter with encrusted gold – it thrills your heart to see them.

• Listening on a small short wave radio to the familiar opening music of the BBC World News Service when I was alone at night in the middle of the Sahara.

• Parrillas in Buenos Aires. A Parrilla is an all-meat restaurant with giant slabs of beef spread-eagled over open charcoal pits. Don't let anyone tell you corn-fed beef is superior in taste to grass-fed — it isn't.

• A magnificent and joyful Indian wedding party Marcia Anderson and I attended where the family rented out the entire "Field Museum" in Chicago for the night. Glorious four-foot-tall flower arrangements were set on each of the dozens of tables. The dance floor was set-up beneath the enormous skeleton of a T. Rex.

• The Archaeology Museum in Cairo. Back in the old days, sand leaked in through the overhead glass roof and littered the marble floor below. But the place was filled with the most amazing things.

• Taking a night ferry in Bangladesh across the immense, roiling Brahmaputra River, swollen with monsoon rain on a moonless night. We were far from either shore and plunged in total darkness. The beam from the great searchlight on board encountered no forms as it sliced off into complete darkness.

Queen of the
Ecuadorian Prison System

IF YOU'RE EVER OVERSEAS in a big city with time on your hands, you might consider visiting someone in prison. I was in Quito, Ecuador a few years ago and, on a whim, I took a taxi to the prison on the outskirts of town and asked if I could see an incarcerated American. I'd brought fruit and chocolate along with me.

I was surprised to discover that the prisoner they chose turned out to be an attractive, blonde haired, thirty-year old young woman. She had been convicted of smuggling cocaine and was in for ten years. Her dream had been to become a movie star. Before this sad turn of events, she had lived in Hollywood. One wall of her cell was artfully covered with maps, pictures, and letters from friends to remind her of that exotic, far away place.

Surprisingly, her situation wasn't quite as dire as I might have expected. Her cell was no worse than my hotel room. She had negotiated a franchise with a local ice cream company to sell their products out of her cell and business appeared to be brisk. Previous to that, she had operated a beauty parlor, an enterprise that had also done well.

Latin Americans love beauty contests. Even the prison system had one, and the previous year she had been crowned queen. When an important local politician attended her coronation, she pulled out all the stops to get herself freed, but it wasn't happening.

It was a bright blue day and we sat outside next to the basketball court and talked. She told me that the prison population was split between the non-violent (prostitutes, drug users, etc.) and the violent (murder, armed robbery, etc). She did her best to stay clear of the latter bunch. She seemed cheerful— not ground down by her fate. I respected her for that.

I gave her the fruit and chocolate anyway, but she obviously didn't really need them. I'm glad I didn't bring her ice cream.

Recovery

On the first day of basic training our drill sergeant announced to us, "I'm going to make you guys so tough," a long pause, "You're gonna have muscles in your shit!" It worked, but by the end of the war we weren't fit to go back out into the world. I recall a conversation I had with some young guy in the hospital in Japan where we were all recovering from our various wounds. He'd stepped on a mine. We talked about going home and looking for some sweet, peace loving hippy girl. We needed it bad.

I remember one nurse who worked in a hospital near Long Binh where they flew me shortly after I was shot. It wasn't long after my initial surgery. I must have been pretty out of it. She would finish all her nursing duties on the ward then she'd sit with me, hold my hand, and wouldn't say anything. It wasn't sexual. She wasn't looking for a boyfriend; she was just being a true human. Those women were like angels to us.

There was the physical part of the recovery too. For one thing we needed to be cleaned up. Our clothes had been taken and burned, but our bodies were still filthy. They could give us sponge baths, but the calluses on the soles of our feet wouldn't come clean; they were imbedded with dirt. One day an orderly came to my bed with a bucket of water and razor blades to scrape them off. He didn't get everything though. I picked up some kick-ass foot fungus during my tour of duty that didn't clear up for twenty years.

I had so many bones broken and organs out of place that my doctors advised me to just "lie quietly" for the first month and a half. That was fine with me. I was completely out of pain and was, in fact, fast becoming addicted to Darvon.

A couple of months on, I was flown to a bigger hospital in Japan. The weather was mild, and though I couldn't go out, it was pleasant to watch the small children, neatly dressed in school uniforms and baseball caps passing beneath our windows on their way to class. Our ward was antiseptic and starkly utilitarian, but bright with sunlight. The television was left on ten hours a day, and I remember seeing more Kabuki drama than any non-Japanese should ever have to endure.

A few weeks after I got to Japan, a doctor came in and asked me to move my arm. Somehow, I had assumed this would be no problem. Being a young man, I'd never been hurt to the point where I didn't eventually get better. At that age it seemed the natural course of things. But this time my brain sent the message to my arm to move and… nothing. I couldn't believe it. It wouldn't move one millimeter! The doctor made no comment. He made a small note, and moved on to the next bed. Then it hit me. The arm was paralyzed. It was going to hang there useless, atrophied and dangling for the rest of my life. My first thought was would some woman ever love me again? I felt sick. It will put the next scene in perspective.

Two months after being shot I was told to report to the PT (physical therapy) lab to meet my therapist. I don't remember what he looked like, but I remember that he was a no-nonsense kind of guy. The first thing he asked me was, "How high can you raise your left arm?"

With some effort I placed my right hand on my left elbow and strained to get it to about even with my shoulder.

"Oh no," he responded, "you can get it a lot higher than that."

And with that he wrenched my left arm up another full twenty degrees. It hurt like fury. A small trickle of blood actually flowed out of the bullet wound just above my left nipple. The message was delivered. There would be no pity, no fucking around, and no halfway measures in this room.

We went at it *hard* every day. Today I can do pushups, pull-ups, practically everything with that arm. I thank God for sending that tough son of a bitch my way. I'm plenty grateful to him.

Hanging over the bed just above my head was a sort of trapeze swing. Thousands of times I'd looked at it and tried to will my left arm up there. Then one night I tried it and, like magic, my arm seemed to float up of its own accord. There was no pain, no real effort. I grabbed the bar firmly with both hands. It was late. The ward around me was dead silent, but my heart was swelling with joy. I knew with certainty that this would always remain as one of the happiest moments of my life.

One other soul I want to pay tribute to: She was an elderly Japanese lady and spoke no English. I saw her only once. She arrived one day and moved slowly down our ward from bed to bed, not speaking, but folding exquisite origami fish from bright colored ribbons. It was always hard to feel sorry for yourself in this place. If you'd lost an arm, someone down the row had lost a leg. If you'd lost two limbs, somebody else had lost three. Of course there was one guy in the ward who was the most fucked-up of all. In the case of our ward, there was one man who'd lost three limbs. His remaining arm and part of his face were badly chewed up with shrapnel as well. In this peculiar little fraternity of ours, he was awarded a certain kind of status. The lady made two fish for him— big ones. Thank you, dear woman, and may God bless you. You'll never know how you helped us.

Five and a half months later I was pretty well patched up. Christmas was coming on, so they pushed my paperwork a little and I made it home for the holidays with an honorable discharge. Sometimes it was said that people treated veterans cruelly when they returned. That wasn't my case. I'm grateful for that. People didn't understand, and they almost always asked the wrong questions, but they were kind and that was the main thing.

Shortly after I got home I remember driving a cab around town with my brother Richard riding shotgun one day. Some little smart ass student tried to screw me on a fare. I turned to him in a terrible rage. I screamed at the poor bastard for five straight minutes. As I paused to catch my breath, he fearfully handed over the correct change with trembling hands and quickly jumped out of the taxi, grateful to be out of the clutches of this madman. My brother looked me square in the eye, "Look, you're home, it's over, OK?" I felt a little hardness melt out of me. It helped. Not everyone had someone to say things like that. One way or another we all needed it. Maybe still do.

Around the same time period, I was watching a pretentious "art" movie with my three brothers; I think it was called *If*. The plot had something to do with an English boys' school taken over in a sort of revolution by the students. The Headmaster was the villain. Porcine in appearance, he had been written into the script as pompous and mean. He was being set-up to die in order to satisfy the dramatic logic of the film. That's fair enough; everyone gets their comeuppance, especially in the movies.

Toward the end of the film, there was a scene where the schoolmaster was thrown from a tower. As he fell we were invited to see the terror in his eyes. People around me were laughing, some were applauding. It pissed me off, I couldn't stop myself. I cried out in a loud voice, "That's not funny!" My brothers wanted to crawl under their seats, and I guess I did too after I'd said it. It seemed obscene to encourage an audience to enjoy someone else's pain. It sickened me.

The last step to my recovery was forgiveness. This was a much longer process than the gun shot wound. The bullets we were firing were intentionally made to wobble slightly in the air. As a result, when they encountered human flesh they would start to tumble. The entrance wound to my shoulder was relatively small. The exit wound took out much of my scapula. In the same manner, the entrance wound in my chest is relatively small but the hole in my left lung is the size of a racquetball. Weapons like this are referred to as "anti-personnel" weapons.

A wise old man from Mali once asked me who was responsible for the Vietnam War. Frito just screwed up, there's nothing that needs forgiveness there. But I fully and truly forgive Mr. Kennedy, Mr. Johnson, Mr. McNamara, the man (I picture these people as men) whose insight led to the tumbling bullet and the man who invented the term 'anti-personnel.' I forgive myself. None of us truly knew what we were doing.

A Slum Tourist in Calcutta

I WAS IN CALCUTTA thirty-some years ago. It has always been my idea to hunt out whatever is most characteristic of a place. The dominant characteristic of Calcutta is *not* poverty, but that was my thought when I first went there. Searching for the most destitute in "The City of Darkest Night," I became a "slum tourist." I searched out a man who fed the poor and asked if he would take me with him on his nightly rounds through the outlying *bastis*.

He had taken on the task of feeding about three hundred poor people a night, all of whom had been identified as especially in need of help. This man raised all his own funds and worked independent of any organization. That night we crawled through the dark, muddy streets on the outskirts of the city in a Land Rover that had been donated by the network commentator David Frost with a great aluminum vat of stew rattling around in the back. We stopped periodically and ladled out food. They came ghost-like out of the dark to meet us silently on the street with dented, tin bowls.

At the end of the night I gave him a small donation. It is important that you understand that I'm not denigrating this great soul, but he was a real misanthrope. God bless him, he didn't much care for anybody, especially those he was feeding. He'd say things like, "I don't like it but it just needs to be done."

To round out my tour I went to see one of Sister Teresa's clinics for abandoned infants. These babies had, sometimes literally, been cast onto trash heaps after birth. But here they were cared for in a sun-filled room by a troupe of bustling, cheerful nuns, constantly making the rounds from one meticulously clean crib to another.

263

I know it's been said so often that people may not want to hear it again, but I'll say it anyway. There was no feeling of duty; there was love in that place— overpowering love.[12]

---

[12] Mother Teresa and Princess Dianne died at about the same time. There wasn't a breath of anything negative written about the Princess at that time. That was as it should be. My only comment here is that roughly one third of the stories reporting the death of Sister Teresa included snide comments somewhere in the text. Sister Teresa deserves the same respect and love accorded to Diana.

My House

ONE OF LIFE'S LITTLE pleasures is owning your own home. I've always been a traveler, but I was no different from anyone else in one respect: I wanted to own a tiny little corner of the world and make it familiar and comfortable.

Eight or nine years ago, I bought a place on the west side (the poor side) of our little college town, Bloomington, Indiana. Almost everything about the house was ugly and unlovable. A non-descript, 1920s style bungalow, it sat on a featureless plot like all the others on the block. The exterior was sheathed in piss-yellow aluminum siding. Inside was worse. Fake pine paneling made of particleboard lined all the walls. The ceilings were low, office-like, and made of acoustic tile and lit by harsh fluorescent lighting.

There were some redeeming features. First and foremost, it was cheap. Second, the plumbing, heating, and electrical systems were in place and functional; I wouldn't have to mess with the basics. Structurally, it was okay. I also liked the location, which was walking distance from downtown and my favorite restaurant, "The Uptown." Here I could eat a leisurely late breakfast of andouille sausage omelettes, cottage cheese pancakes, and cafe borgia served up by a tattooed, pierced, and friendly waiting staff.

The house was bicycling distance from our lovely Indiana University campus and its stately old buildings. I liked the demographics of my neighborhood. There was a nice racial mix, a fair number of retirees, and a sprinkling of bohemians and radicals. We favored eccentrics. On the street next to mine, a neighbor had a circus net spread over his backyard so he could practice his trapeze act. Houses had names like

"The Orphanage" and "The House of a Thousand Daggers." Sometimes wars broke out and elaborate tactics involving feints, ambushes, giant squirt guns and barrages of water balloons were clandestinely plotted late at night over marijuana and cheap wine.

We had our politics too. One burning issue was whether or not chickens could be raised in backyard pens. Yes, it was resolved— but no roosters.

It was early fall when Marcia and I moved in. The house was still very much in the midst of chaotic renovation. Without complaining, that dear woman put up with a lot of discomfort. For a month, the sole clean spot was our bed. We were only able to keep it so by stretching a plastic sheet over the area first thing in the morning. This drop was usually covered with a thick layer of drywall dust, ceiling insulation, and other debris by evening. At bedtime, though, we rolled the drop cloth back to find surprisingly clean sheets and covers.

When we started, I had no overall plan. Things just evolved a step or two at a time. First, the acoustic tile came down revealing spacious ten-foot plaster ceilings. All were seriously cracked. We dry-walled over this and inserted canister lights. In the living room we just kept going up. The plaster ceiling was torn out, releasing an avalanche of filthy, coal-dust laden insulation, thus revealing the roof beams. We erected a spiral staircase and turned the remainder of the attic into a loft.

Marcia and I were housepainters. The majority of our time at work was spent putting various shades of white on walls, especially classic off-white ("cow" to those in the trade). We yearned to do something over-the-top, so the living room was done in purple and red with a silk moiré finish. We did a sort-of "aged Etruscan-plaster" look to the bathroom walls and applied a tortoise-shell faux finish to the trim. The kitchen windows were done in a pink and yellow crackle finish. On the north wall is a bookcase with eleven coats of paint that I'm still not satisfied with.

As the project proceeded, I grew progressively more reckless. At one point I decided to knock out a hole in the bathroom wall and put in a giant periscope. With the help of my buddy, Pete Schreiner, we constructed it from two large PVC pipes set at 90-degree angles with an elliptical mirror inserted at the joint. This reflected the light coming in from above. Clouds and sky could then be seen entering through a porthole-like window on the wall above the toilet. Marcia wisely vetoed an idea to attach the cockpit of a salvaged airplane to the wall with its windscreen piercing the roof. I had pictured myself in front of the lit control panel, joystick in hand, gazing out onto Sixth Street.

Now the artwork and doodads could be put up. After twenty-five years of collecting oddities and geegaws, I finally had somewhere to put them all. Toy boats from Cote D'Ivoire, Kenya, Germany, and India. Calligraphy from Damascus, Tibetan mandalas, erotic Persian miniatures, a South African wedding hat, a Dutch map of Brazilian fortifications, a huge metallic mobile dangling from the ceiling. It was a real mishmash of styles that, charitably, might be called eclectic. Around the lights I glued up little brown plastic geckos to give the place a tropical ambience. A large plastic model of the Michelin Man ruled over the kitchen. In the end, the house looked half Metropolitan Museum of Art, half Peewee's Playhouse.

I had ideas to start with for the outside of the house. Many years ago, when I was working on a roof, I was struck by the view from up there. It seemed an unused and expansive space. That winter when I left for India, I sketched out the plan for a wooden roof-deck on the back of an envelope. I gave it to Pete and thought no more about it. When I returned in the spring, it was built and was even more fun than I had dreamed. There were steps leading up the roof to an elevated area with two Adirondack chairs facing out over the back yard. Behind that was an indented pit where you could lie out under the sky, unseen and *au naturale.* Just before evening, it was possible to watch swallows circle the chimney then suddenly drop like stones into the opening. It made me happy to learn from a bird book that these elegant little creatures I was cohabiting with wintered in the Amazon Basin.

I edged the backyard with flowering trees, honeysuckle, and trumpet vines. Wisteria covered a trellis over the ground level deck and sheltered it with hundreds of heavy purple blossoms in springtime and dense shade in the summer. The vine took off like a weed, climbing up the roof (and under the shingles if I neglected to periodically trim it back).

Now it was time for the pond, and there would be no halfway measures. I wanted it to fill the entire backyard. The excavated dirt had to go somewhere, so it became an island. Around the sides were various hillocks. Siberian iris, hasta, and pond lotuses flourished, but a transplanted cattail from a nearby lake failed after a year. The biggest successes were the goldfish and frogs. A bag of feeder goldfish grew into glorious creatures. A glutinous mass of frog eggs transplanted from a woodland pond one spring spawned a noisy colony of amphibians that serenaded me all summer and never failed to over winter. One problem has persisted. When we were installing the liner, it was threatening rain and we hastily lined up the edge, estimating it by line-of-sight. Now, when the pond is full, a strip of plastic is revealed along one side.

People were surprised when I sold my house this year. Perhaps someday I'll build another one. Still, when I'm far away, sometimes I imagine myself on my back deck lying on an Indian prayer carpet. A pillow I bought in Bombay is pushed up behind me, I'm listening to sitar music, reading "The Adventures of Augie March," and gazing occasionally at a dragonfly or the fish swimming dreamily amidst the lotus blossoms.

Worst Hitchhiking:
Six Days of Bad Luck in the Sahara

I HAD COME DOWN on the back of a truck through Morocco and had crossed the border into the country that used to be known as Spanish Sahara. The Sahara from Sidi Ifni to Aaiun is the most beautiful stretch of desert I've seen yet. It has everything— perfectly formed sand dunes, immense wide spaces, great salt flats, and air so clear that you feel you could see for a thousand miles.

I stayed a couple of days at a cheap hotel in Aaiun to rest up for the next leg of the journey. Refreshed and ready to move on, I walked to the outskirts of town, sat down on my pack, and waited for a truck to pass by. The sun beat down on me mercilessly; there was no shade. In this bleak spot, nothing grew and no one lived.

There is only one road between Aaiun, the capital of Spanish Sahara, and Nouakchott, the capital of Mauritania, and I was on it. All wheeled traffic had to go this way. By evening, I still hadn't had any luck so I pitched my tent by the side of the road. I remained there for a week. Not only did no one pick me up, but no one even *passed* me. I finally gave up and took a short hop over to the Canary Islands where I got pleasantly hung up on a lovely beach for a couple of months. From there I caught a tired old tramp steamer from Las Palmas that, ever so slowly, crawled down the coast of West Africa to Mauritania.

Best Hitchhiking:
La Dolce Vita in Algiers

I had just crossed the Sahara and was in northern Algeria not far from the coast. Some bad water I drank on the trip had finally gotten to me. I was feeling pretty uncomfortable. I didn't have much money and needed to get to Algiers to catch the ferry to Marseilles. As usual, I was hitchhiking to save money. The sun was hot and there was only the occasional date palm tree for shade. By mid-afternoon after two short rides, I'd only gotten about ten kilometers down the road. Despite my limited finances, I was seriously considering paying for a bus or train.

Then a small miracle occurred. A guy driving a tiny car with two Italian women stopped. They threw my pack in the trunk and I gratefully hopped into the back seat. Then the women sitting next to me reached over, peeled me a fig she had in her lap, and popped it into my mouth. That bonded us. Things were looking up for the lonesome traveler.

When we got to Algiers, it was nighttime. The Italian fellow who was driving suddenly got into a fiery argument with the woman in the front seat. I have no idea what it was all about, but in the end he wound up kicking us all out and driving off in a huff. So here I was on a very warm night in Algiers with these two extraordinarily beautiful young women. They were wearing white pleated blouses quite low; their breasts were clearly visible through the fabric. They were wearing miniskirts. You have to imagine these scantily-clad women walking through Algiers in the middle of the night, especially in those days:

There were only men on the street—a hundred on every corner— and all were eyeing us. Also, all the hotels were full.

I can't remember what the disagreement was, but somehow the three of us got into one of those slightly daffy, Italian altercations that are secretly so much fun. No one was really angry, but all of us stood there passionately arguing and theatrically gesticulating. Playing my part well, I finally blew up indignantly. In response, the girls played their parts to a "T" and soon I was soothed back to normal. God, what fun it must be to be born Italian.

Very late that night, I finally found a "hotel" for us in a dodgy section of town. It had a room that came available at three in the morning. We took it.

By the next day, things were sorted out a little better and the woman who had been abandoned by her boyfriend now proposed that we make it a *ménage a trios*. The other woman who I was now with would have none of it, which resulted in some hard feelings. Why I didn't throw my full diplomatic skill into patching *that* up I'll never know, but as I say, I have a few regrets in my life.[13]

---

[13] Keeping with the theme, I wanted to do the best and worst roads. They happen to be the same road. It tortuously winds its way through the Himalayas from Srinigar to Leh passing ancient Buddhist monasteries along the way. Our driver was a real S.O.B. Regardless of whether everyone had made it back onto the bus or not he'd just start driving slowly out of town while hapless passengers had to high-tail-it to catch up and clamor on board. But the scenery was out of this world.

Thanks, Xaxa

THIS BOOK HAS BEEN tremendous fun to write. At this moment, I am striding back and forth a little pompously under some palm trees on the bank of the Chapora River. XaXa is jotting it all down in a notebook. It's a pleasant scooter ride along the ocean, through tiny towns and past rice paddies to get here. There is a small, untouched village not far from us which looks like Goa did thirty-five years ago. Occasionally, one of the villagers will come by, mostly out of curiosity, and I'll try to make conversation in my laughably poor Hindi. After a few minutes they smile and drift off. On the far horizon I can barely see waves breaking onto the shallows at the mouth of the river next to Chapora Beach. Nearby, we can just make out the sounds of three fishermen who are working the water with their nets.

Our other writing site is walking distance from my place. Some days we sit together there beneath an ancient vine covered tree that we have learned is considered holy by the villagers. Most Goans are working hard at this time of year. But during the mango season, there is very little to do, and they will sit with their friends under it and eat the luscious fruit that falls from the trees.

Did any writer in all of history ever have it this good? Xaxa and I have become good friends in the course of writing this book. She's an artist, quite beautiful, and wonderful company. I'm grateful to know her. She lives with her boyfriend in a sweet little house surrounded by a flower garden. They have a boisterous, delightful circle of young friends who like to party.

I've come much closer to death, but I'm sixty years old and probably a lot easier to kill off these days. Three weeks ago I had a recurrence of malaria that I had contracted six years ago in the Omo Valley of Ethiopia. As I lay in my bed, feverous and soaked in sweat, a picture of Jesus smiled down at me from the wall above. That and the picture of Baba Hardev Singh to my other side seemed in total harmony. It occurred to me that perhaps things were coming to the appropriate close.

When XaXa dropped by to see me, she had such a lovely sparkle in her eyes. That and a few small things she said made me feel as if there were things which needed doing, and that they might be fun as well.

Advice to Travelers: Making it Work

If you've decided that you want to be a traveler, give some thought as to how you will support yourself. Financial concerns are some of the biggest reasons why people never set out in the first place. For the most part I've just picked up work as I've gone along. Eventually I learned the trade of house painting which worked fine for me, though being an electrician, or even better, a plumber would have paid more.

Many people teach English as a second language (Taiwan and Korea are especially good paying countries for this, but almost any non-English speaking country will also work). Importing can be a good hustle, as well.

You can rent out your home while you're gone. Over time, inflation should make the house more valuable and increase rental fees. When you return from a trip you can buy a new home and keep the previous house as a rental. Continue doing this and you'll eventually acquire several rental properties.

These days there are any number of jobs you can do via computer from any location in the world. If you have the training necessary, and have penetrated their network, NGOs will hire you on short term contracts.

Seasonal jobs of all types allow you to travel. Some jobs like nursing are so much in demand that you can work a year, then take off three years without problem.

In general you should work in rich countries and spend time in poor ones (though most of Sub Saharan Africa is fairly expensive). If you can take jobs where your employer pays for your room and board (e.g., mines and cruise ships) you'll save much more money.

You may learn that many of life's problems are more easily solved by thinking globally. Retirement in Bali costs a fraction of living in the crummiest trailer park in America. Pharmaceuticals cost almost nothing in India, operations and dental work are cheap in Thailand, etc. Hopefully you'll learn that all the busting your ass every day so you can have a few status symbols which supposedly will get you more respect is a fools game anyway. No traveler will think more of you because of your extraordinary backpack or fancy sleeping bag.

The first time I set out, when my life as a traveler really got started, was when my first disability check arrived. It was more than I'd expected. I looked across the room to my brother and said, "Richard, we're going to Europe." For the next two and a half months we climbed mountains in the alps, saw all the great European museums, ate French food, met some terrific women and, in general, had more fun than I'd ever thought possible. Not that there weren't hassles. There were unending hassles, we just didn't care. I arrived back at JFK airport 700 miles from home with $2 in my pocket. It didn't trouble me in the least. I knew I'd make it. After that, if I ever was bored or depressed, I always knew there was a way out.

And the biggest hurdle always is believing that it's possible and acting on that belief.

The secret to living an adventurous life is:

A. Have a dream

B. Research it enough so you know it's doable

C. The hardest step — Do it. Buy the ticket to Mongolia. When you get to Ulan Bator go to the market and buy your horse and supplies. Head out. I have no idea what will happen to you, but you'll make it work. And it will be something you'll remember your whole life— a story your grandchildren might want to hear.

Tokyo Skyline

TOWARDS THE END OF our six year journey around-the-world, my first wife, my son, and I spent a few days in Kyoto. It was springtime and the cherry trees were in bloom. The gardens expanded my mind. There was something about that beauty…

At the end of our stay we were faced with the business of getting back to Tokyo. Everything in Japan is expensive, so we thought we'd try to save some money by hitching a ride. Hitchhiking is not a Japanese custom, or wasn't at that time, so people were curious as to what these three Gaijin were doing out on the side of the road at the edge of town. A stout workingman driving a giant truck ground to a halt next to us.

He spoke no English, but we conveyed the idea that we were trying to get back to Tokyo. He was going there as well, so he motioned for us to hop up in the cab beside him. The truck was a curious affair with a large tank made for transporting live lobster. Every hour or so he would stop, jump down, go round to the side of the truck, and peer through glass portholes to see how the creatures were doing. No communication other than smiles of mutual good feeling and hand gestures passed between us for the entire journey. The sun was setting magnificently as we highballed it along the elevated freeway above that great skyline. He let us off at an exit close to our destination and, with many bows and expressions of goodwill, we left this good-hearted man and walked down into the city.

An Affair with a 300 pound Go Go Girl

As for the rest, take life as it comes, live dangerously,
dread naught, all will be well

W. Churchill

I WAS HITCHING DOWN to Mexico one time back in the sixties. My last lift had left me on the outskirts of a dreary looking town somewhere in Oklahoma. Night was starting to fall out there on those brush-covered flatlands.

It's hard to catch a ride after dark, so when a gregarious young fellow picked me up and offered to let me spend the night at his place, I jumped at it. First though, we thought we'd knock down a few brewskies. One thing led to another and the next thing I knew, we were hanging out with a few of his pals at a bar with some high-spirited dancing girls. I've got no clear recollection of exactly what went on for the next couple of hours, but somehow when the place shut down for the night, he left with a good looking babe and I left with her three-hundred pound friend.

We retired back to his place for a few more drinks, and again one thing led to another. I gave it my best shot, trying to woo her with words that I thought would have melted the heart of a vulture, but to no avail. In the end nothing was consummated.

Not to worry. The next morning with a hearty breakfast of flapjacks under my belt, I was back out on the side of the road with my heart filled with love for the world and my thumb pointed toward Texas.

Election Day

WE WERE DOWN TWO points in the polls, and when I awoke at 5 a.m., rain was pouring out of the dark, greasy looking skies. A bad sign: this was definitely Republican weather.[14] I pulled on my clothes, ate a hurried breakfast, and picked up my rucksack full of election day materials where I had left them the night before by the front door. Ten minutes later I was ascending the stairs of our fine, ornate, old courthouse. The polling place for my precinct (Bloomington 2) was set up amidst the marble splendor of this spacious temple of democracy. Walking through the massive doors and emerging under the great overhead dome sent a curious thrill through me, as well as an almost holy sense of responsibility. I felt grateful to be here, humbled to be a tiny part of what would happen that day.

My first job as precinct captain was to check that the polls were, in fact, open and running smoothly; they were. Everything and everyone was in place and ready for business. As I fumbled through my bag searching for the poll-watchers credentials that entitled me to be there, some handouts I was carrying spilled out onto the floor. The poll judge was on me in a moment. He could see I meant no harm, but sharply warned me nonetheless that no campaign materials were allowed to be displayed inside the polling area. Suitably chastened, I moved my chair down the hall a bit and sorted out my paperwork. By this time the first water-soaked townspeople were starting to straggle in to cast their vote before going to work.

---

[14] For whatever reason, anything that makes it harder to vote tends to hurt Democratic Party turnout.

There didn't seem much more for me to do at the courthouse, so I walked back outside to my pickup and drove to my precinct, located on the near-westside of town. Over the past month or so I'd spent many days knocking on doors and identifying supporters. All that work was paying off now. I knew who was a "day sleeper," who had voted early, who was undecided, who might be persuaded to vote Democratic instead of throwing their vote away on a Libertarian. I knew the Republicans too. Best to just let them be.

The rain was slowing substantially until it was just a light mist. Definitely a good sign. At first I just walked down the still dark streets, quietly hanging reminders on door handles that informed people of where their local polling places were. As lights started to go on, I rang a few doorbells, encouraging people, telling them that it was a crucial election and we were in a fiercely contested race that might determine which party would control The House. The response was encouraging. Almost everyone I talked to either had voted early or assured me that they would vote sometime today.

I kept pounding the pavement all through the morning and early afternoon. At three o'clock I called Marcia Anderson and the two of us had the pleasure of driving some disabled people living at a rest home to the polling place. Marcia was her usual jovial self, and soon we were all laughing and chatting together on our way to the courthouse. Helping a feeble but determined little old lady make it laboriously up all those stairs to cast her vote... It doesn't get much sweeter than that.

By 4:30 I'd knocked on every Democratic door in my little precinct. The polls were set to close at 6:00. At 5:00 I got a call from John Yaggi our local campaign leader. This kid had worked his heart out for the campaign. He'd been logging 18 hour days for weeks. He was always encouraging, always upbeat; it was inspiring just to be around him. "People are just getting home from work, this is our last chance to get them— give it everything you've got!" I took off at a jog down West 6th Street, the heart of my district. Everybody had voted. I high-fived my fellow citizens, then quickly moved on down to the next door. My right knee had been hurting me all afternoon but I figured it would be okay for a bit longer.

At 6:00 I'd done what I could do. I drove home, walked in the door, and immediately flopped down on the floor. I just lay there motionless while I described the day in detail to Marcia as Moti, her big black poodle, patiently licked my face.

At 8:00 we drove down to the Democratic Headquarters. It was packed. The place was buzzing, but there was no real news. Marcia and I decided to go grab something to eat. In two hours there were supposed to be some results coming in. Shortly before 10:00 we were back at HQ. It was intense. So much was riding on the results; in my opinion, nothing short of the fate of our nation.[15]

Results started coming in over the TV on the local races. They were good... *very good.* It was beginning to look like a nearly clean sweep. People were yelling, clapping, stomping around. Then at the other end of the room we heard an explosion. Jake heard it first over his earphone connection with the "head shed" down in Jeffersonville. It spread in a moment. *Sodrel Was Conceding! Baron Had Won!* People were leaping up and down, laughing, crying, climbing all over each other. I spotted Yaggi in the crowd and went over and gave him a hug. There were tears in both our eyes. "Someday we'll have forgotten all kinds of things that have happened to us," I said, "but *this* day we'll remember for the rest of our lives."

---

[15] I've got to toot my horn a little here. A month later I got the numbers for my precinct, "The fightin' 2nd." The first day I was assigned my precinct I was told to shoot for 145 votes for Hill. The final tally was Sodrel- 27, the Libertarian guy- 18, and Hill- 464.

Best Things in the World

- Our little volunteer radio station WFHB (Firehouse Broadcasting). There is no top 40 format for these guys. They play it all, from Tuvan throat singing to Hank Williams.

- Riding through the streets of Beijing twenty years ago on a bicycle. There were bicycle traffic jams at major intersections. Back then the sight of a bus was a rare occurrence. It was the quietest city I'd ever experienced.

- The Onion.com. It invariably makes me laugh out loud. Smoove B is a favorite.

- The incredibly ornate rococo-style opera house in Manaus. Caruso was once paid a small fortune to sing in it. The road around the outside of the opera house was covered in rubber so that carriages arriving late wouldn't disturb a performance. The city of Manaus is situated far up the Amazon a thousand miles from the nearest large town and it became fabulously wealthy for a brief time during the rubber boom.

- "Tree Top Flyer" by Steven Stills. It's a song about a Vietnam veteran who smuggles drugs across the Mexican border. The lyrics ring true.

- The incomparable Botticellis at the Uffizi Museum in Florence.

- Charlie Trotter's Restaurant in Chicago. Our dinner was worth every penny of the two hundred dollars and our waiter let us tour the immaculate high-tech kitchen afterwards. We met Charlie back there. He was standing by one of the great stoves with a big clam in his hands, good-humouredly remarking at its size.

- Sumptuous Indian textiles. Benares silk is especially notable.

- Dutch paper money. It has little raised marks so blind people can read the denominations.

- Rajasthani horses, with ears that curve so that the tips almost touch.

- Star Parties. They take place all over the world on moonless nights. Amateur astronomers meet at remote sites far away from light pollution. They're a friendly lot and everyone lets you peek through their scopes.

- High-tech Japanese toilets referred to as "bottom heaven." You sit down to a gently warmed seat. After doing your business, you consult the handset. The first pictograph shows a fountain spraying onto a stylized buttocks. You hit the button and… bull's-eye! There's a gentle, warm, upwardly-directed spray. The next picture shows a fan. Push that button and warm air wafts up at your command. The third picture was unclear (a douche?). I hear that the newest models have a button labeled "powerful deodorizer" and a final option called "tickle."

- Tidal pools anywhere, though the ones in Costa Rica on the Nicoya Peninsula come to mind.

- Fresh pan-fried kingfish served up at a beach shack restaurant in Goa.

- Hamburger Harry's in Hamburg, Germany. It's my favorite store in the world. Harry has a reputation for buying *anything* sailors bring to him. The result is a huge warehouse on the waterfront filled with stuffed animals, Indian headdresses, pornographic magazines, magnificent Tibetan mandalas, African masks, bowling pins, etc. Monkeys, cats, and dogs live within the cavernous, dimly lit rooms. Scattered turds and little puddles of piss are everywhere.

Stowaway

UNDER "SHIP SAILINGS" IN the back of *The New York Times* is a list of departure times for all passenger ships leaving the city. There's always a Bon Voyage Party on board before the ship leaves the dock and thirty years ago you could pretend you were seeing someone off and attend it.

At my first Bon Voyage Party, I met a very amiable, retired Jewish man. We got into an interesting conversation about riding freight trains, which we had both done. He had ridden during the Great Depression. We really hit it off. When they announced, "All ashore that's going ashore," he surprised me by asking if I wanted to stow away for the trip to the Caribbean. My backpack was stored at a friend's house in Brooklyn. I couldn't leave without it, so I reluctantly declined the offer. But it put an idea in my head. I made up my mind to try it the next day on another boat, this time bound for Europe where I was headed at the time.

Next day I found myself ascending the gangplank of the mighty Italian luxury liner, "The Marconi." Despite the fact that I was carrying a large stuffed rucksack on my back, I somehow talked my way past the man in the doorway of the ship and made my way into the party which was in full swing. Unfortunately, it was in First Class and the vast glittering room was filled with garrulous, beautifully-attired Italians. To say that I stuck out would be an understatement. Nonetheless, I hid my pack behind a plush sofa and did my best to blend in. I knew I was going to need help, so I started chatting up a friendly-appearing fellow. Not long into the conversation I let it drop that I was trying to

284

stow away. His face dropped and he moved away as if I'd admitted to having a rare but contractible disease.

By this time though, the gangplank had been taken down and the lines cast off. I sidled up to a window and waved gaily to my friend, Sally on the dock far below. She waved back gamely. What a thrill it was to be on that magnificent ship... *moving out*.

Then things started to go south. I was confidently approached by an impeccably attired young gentleman with a suave, cultured voice, trained from the cradle, who asked me, ever so politely, if he could see my ticket. I readily admitted to being a stowaway, which didn't phase this guy one single bit.

"Well, could you follow me please sir?"

"No problem." I replied with some trepidation.

We left the animated cocktail chatter behind and started descending stairs. Down, down, down into the bowels of this monstrous ship; I have no idea how many decks. There was no more conversation, only the sound of great machines released and bending to the task. He led me down a hallway (I picture it as white with many pipes of various diameters running along the walls) and then opened a heavy steel door that led into a cramped, stuffy, windowless cabin with about a dozen tough-looking sailors standing around. I sat down obediently and the suave, young gentleman left without another word.

Nobody down here looked a bit friendly. No eyes met mine and not a word was said to me. But the alarming point came when they undid the huge bolts that held the heavy steel plate to the outer shell of the boat. The deep green ocean was shooting by just beneath us. My mind was racing like crazy. No way were they going to throw me overboard... It was the twentieth century for God's sake... It was uncivilized... No way!

But why wasn't anyone talking to me, and what was the steel plate doing off? I don't speak Italian, but I do speak rudimentary Spanish, which I figured with a little Italian inflection might get my idea across. "Que pasa?" I asked plaintively.

This broke the ice. The previously surly-appearing seamen suddenly turned loquacious and amiable. One said to me, "The captain knows you're here so we've got to put you off onto the pilot boat."

"If only we'd have known earlier we'd have gotten you a cabin and you would have made it," exclaimed another.

Italians love anarchic behavior. They were behind me 100%. Everyone was slapping me on the back. No longer a hapless stowaway, suddenly I was a hero.

The captain called down to ask if I wanted to pay for my passage. I replied through intermediaries that I couldn't afford it, so when the pilot boat came alongside and the harbor pilot, who had been guiding us, hopped off, I went as well.

As we shoved off I looked up the side of the great ship. Fifty or sixty Italian workers were leaning out of various portholes and waving to me with gusto. One yelled, "Try the Christapho Columbo next week. We know you'll make it!"

Working on the Great Gate

FOR FIFTY-EIGHT YEARS IN Delhi and forty in Bombay the Nirankari Mission has held massive spiritual gatherings, or smagams. To attend one is to see an India that most westerners never experience. It's not Disneyland India. You're no longer in the land of papaya lassis and banana pancakes.

People will treat you with the greatest courtesy. I can assure you of that. Still, the crowds, the heat, and the dust may seem overwhelming. I urge you to persevere.

The size of these smagams has grown over the years, and now between five hundred thousand and a million people attend. All sleeping facilities, food, and medical care, are provided free to devotees. Preparation for the gathering is done by volunteers. At the smagam grounds, tents to house Nirankari saints go off in all directions as far as the eye can see. This year, as with most years, amidst this mighty throng I was the only ghoré (non-Indian). The message of the Mission is universal, so why I am normally the only westerner there is a mystery to me.

At the entrance to the grounds a great gate is erected. Every year a new one is built and every year the design is different. For the past ten years it has been my great joy to work on it with my Nirankari brothers. When I show up at the site on the first day with a clean brush and a spotless new painting suit the crew of fifty guys rushes out to meet me. We shout, "Dhan Nirankar!" (Glory to the Formless), hug each other and touch each other's feet (a Nirankari custom which shows honor to the soul within). Then we step back and take each other in with big grins on our faces, lots of jokes, and enormous good humor. A few days in their company and a peaceful world seems much less impossible.

As the mighty structure goes up, a scaffolding of bamboo is erected around it to facilitate the high work. Previous to climbing on one of these, I had assumed they would feel rickety. In fact they turn out to be flexible but very secure— bombproof.

We laugh a lot up there as we work. Everyone calls each other Maharaj or Mahatma. In the late afternoon with a cool breeze blowing, a slug of pan in my cheek and a giant twelve-inch Indian brush in my hand, life is temporarily as it should be.

A task done well is a form of worship. I feel that as we work together. Sometimes I'll hold a board in place for a carpenter— bam... Bam... BAM and it's done. They never bend a nail. A board sawn correctly is an act of beauty. There's never a wasted motion with these men. A bare foot secures the board. As the sawing hand moves forward the head moves back, maintaining perfect balance. The blade cuts through the board along the drawn pencil line with a steady inevitability.

Plasterers, carpenters, electricians, and painters accomplish their tasks in perfect harmony. No harsh words are ever spoken. Through the work and over the years, we have come to love each other. That was always the real point.

Me, Dick Cheney,
and the Dalai Lama

THE TIME OF A holy personage is a precious commodity. As the Dalai Lama has become more widely known, it becomes harder to meet him in person. When I first came to India, what I am about to describe was possible. Now it would be far more difficult, through no fault whatsoever of this great soul.

My brother Richard and I were in what was then the still tiny town of McLeod Ganj. We had ascended to the village through a pine forest by a footpath from Dharamsala. Going up, we passed some Tibetan monks going the other way. They were part of a funeral. It was curious to me that they were laughing, joking and smiling.

We stayed at a friendly little hotel called The Mount Kailash. Throughout the day and evening, outside our window we could hear the gentle sound of bells ringing, as pious Tibetans turned long lines of prayer wheels in the small square beneath us. The food in the ground floor restaurant was delicious despite the hordes of cockroaches in the kitchen. I met some wonderful fellow travelers in that place. I was sad to hear that it burned to the ground recently.

There was an enterprising young traveler there who had the clever idea of getting thirty of us together and calling ourselves a "group." Then, through the Dalai Lama's secretary, he asked if, together, our "group" might have a brief audience with the great man.

The appointed time arrived. It was a fine fall day. We were given white scarves to be blessed. As I approached the Dalai Lama, we both stretched out our hands and I gave him a brief, perfunctory shake. The dear man looked me in the eye with the message, "How about a real shake, brother?" I complied with this request sent through his eyes and gave him one. It made me like him.

Our little group assembled in a line with His Holiness standing facing us. He had a personal translator, but it soon became obvious that he understood almost everything that was being said. Only a few small clarifications were needed. He asked us all where we had been in India. Normally, he would just nod or say a couple of words in response. When he got to me, I mentioned that I had been to Auroville, among other places. He asked me what the spiritual climate was like in the wake of the death of the "divine mother." This was the name by which the lady who had been in charge of the community was known.

The presumption of this still troubles me some at this very moment. I rattled on for several minutes on the subject. That's all I can remember of that encounter, other than that at least one person in our group felt as if I'd overstepped my boundaries.

I once saw Dick Cheney. We had initially been protesting on the sidewalk in front of The Columbia Club in Indianapolis where he was giving a fund raising speech to some of our local captains of industry when we were discreetly informed that he'd be leaving by way of the back alley, in order, no doubt, to avoid us and others.

I was standing there on the sidewalk holding a hand-lettered sign with a dozen other hapless picketers as his entourage of Cadillac stretch-limousines crept down the alley. He must have found us amusing. Our eyes met. He smiled broadly and gave me a big wave as the driver of the big shiny black Caddy he was ensconced in goosed the accelerator and shot off like a rocket up Massachusetts Avenue.

War Wounds

I WAS SOMEWHERE IN the Middle East having a conversation with an Iraqi guy when he mentioned that he had been injured in the Iran-Iraq war. Close to a million people died with no gains for either side in that ugly little conflict. I could relate.

He described his many bullet wounds to me then stripped off his shirt to point them all out. I enthusiastically ripped off my shirt and displayed my wounds as well. We laughed like crazy, slapped each other on the back, and praised Allah, whose mercy had preserved us.

Best Things in the World

- Back in the days of the Shah, you could visit the vault under Bank Melli in Tehran, where the royal jewels were on display. The space was as big as a basketball court. As I walked through the great steel doors I remember being struck by the shimmering reflections of the innumerable stones on the ceiling. One piece that comes to mind is a globe on a golden stand embedded with jewels. The seas were emeralds, the continents rubies. Iran and France were encrusted with diamonds.

- Daisy chains.

- The curious way Indians sometimes wag their heads back and forth while speaking, indicating friendliness and amiability. After being there for a month or two, I find myself starting to do it, too. In the same manner, Indians lose this charming habit quickly when they come to America.

- Wandering through the art galleries in the Soho area of New York City even if you can't afford any of the work.

- Army underwear designed for the *Rangers*. I've heard them derisively referred to as "Airborne panties" (they are in fact made of black nylon). Like all military equipment these days, they've been well thought out. The nylon insures that they're lightweight and quick drying – they feel good against your skin. They're jockey-style, but there's an inner-layer that gently cradles your bait and tackle. Nothing like it - I bought several pair.

- Back when these things were still possible, my friends and I used to climb radio, microwave and TV towers for fun. Climbing to the top of a TV tower (probably about the height of the Empire State Building) east of Bloomington, I saw my hometown from a new perspective. A tiny train crept through the center of the city and toy single engine airplanes flying beneath me landed at the airport on the far side of town.

- The exuberant roller skating scene that has evolved in front of *Le Musee D'Homme* in Paris just across the river from The Eiffel Tower.

- The delicate swooping patterns described by swallows in flight.

- Banyan trees. The worlds largest is in the botanical garden in Calcutta. The canopy has a circumference of 400 meters. Many small Indian villages have banyan trees as their central feature.

- Walking on fire. As we approached the fire pit, the crowd surrounding it kept chanting, "Yes! Yes! Yes!" and pointing to the fire. An intense young woman, directly in front of the pit, barred my way. She looked straight into my eyes, saying "Yes! Yes! Yes!" then "GO!"

- The music of The Congo. It's smooth, danceable, and complex as a Bach Fugue.

- Getting out my well-worn National Geographic Atlas, spreading out my travel books around me on the carpet, and planning the next trip.

Six Paradises

I'VE DECIDED NOT TO write a complete book about "Six paradises where you can retire comfortably for $500/month" (if you need a cook, a gardener, and a nanny it will cost $1000/month). The places are too small and vulnerable; I don't want to be responsible for their getting overrun. I'll go halfway with you though. I'll tell you where they are. If you're serious about escaping from wherever you are, you'll buy the Lonely Planet Guide, spend a day or two doing Google searches, and you'll have what you need to know. Once you've done that, you're ready for an exploratory visit. Maybe you're not ready for that yet. Just keep it in the back of your mind that if everything goes to hell in your life sometime in the future, you don't need to give up hope; these places can be your get-out-of-jail free card.

I define a paradise as somewhere that's safe, beautiful, has a pleasant climate, good food, adequate health care, a community of foreigners to keep you company, and is, of course, cheap. Here's the list:

1. Lake Atitlan, Guatemala. Talk with the locals and follow their advice about what is safe and what isn't.
2. Any of the many valleys that go up into the Himalayas. I'm most acquainted with the area just north of Almora, but all of the others would work as well.
3. Goa. Find the beach that suits you; they all have different vibes.
4. Pokhara, Nepal. Not dangerous, no matter what the press says, or what you may think. It's where I started the Jomson trail.
5. Lake Toba, Indonesia

6. Bali. Stay out of Kuta Beach, which is awful anyway, and you'll be safer than you would be living in a little town in Nebraska.

I Remember

I REMEMBER WORKING FOR three months as a waiter in a bar. We had two kinds of beer on tap, premium (Budweiser) and regular (Pabst Blue Ribbon). People usually felt strongly about which one they wanted. As an experiment, whichever beer they chose I gave them the other. I served thousands of glasses and pitchers. Not a single person ever called me on it. I find it disconcerting that the images (created by advertising) that people carry around in their heads are usually more compelling than their own direct perceptions. It leads me to believe that we all need to re-learn to trust our personal experience.

I remember when I was a child in school seeing a black and white movie of a nuclear blast shown in slow motion. The film showed a two-story house located one mile from ground zero. As we watched, a shower of tiny flecks flew off the sides of the house. Emotionlessly, the narrator explained that these were paint chips exploding off the wooden siding, an effect of the intense heat radiating from the blast. There was no time for combustion because the next moment the shock wave hit, and an instant later not a splinter of the house remained.

I remember a wealthy family down the street from us was rumored to have a fallout shelter. Secrets like this were deeply guarded. If a nuclear war broke out, there wouldn't be sufficient room, food, or filtered air for everyone in the neighborhood. It seemed prudent to keep a gun in the shelter in case it might be needed to keep out those who hadn't planned ahead.

I remember sitting on the edge of a cliff in Kenya and seeing where two tectonic plates almost touch. Between them they form the Great Rift Valley and all the long thin lakes along its length.

I remember a restaurant in Prague when someone ordered a flambé dessert. As soon as the waiter lit it, a man with a totally dead-pan expression driving a toy fire engine with a screaming siren rushed out of the kitchen, raced to the table and put out the flames with a fire extinguisher.

The Czechs have lost every war for six hundred years. It's a miracle they still exist. But they built Prague, which some people consider the most beautiful city on earth. Their national hero is a sad sack military man named Private Sjvek, who is always being humiliated, but somehow always survives. When I once called him an anti-hero the Czech I was speaking with became suddenly indignant—"He's not an anti-hero, he's our *true hero.*"

I remember learning croquet as a child from my grandfather, Spaine Armstrong. He played a ruthless game.

I remember riding a motorcycle down to Canton, Mississippi hoping to register black voters. It was near the beginning of the Civil Rights Movement. I was going to be an "outside agitator," working for the Mississippi Freedom Democratic Party. I'm afraid I didn't accomplish much, but it was interesting to see how it felt to be somewhere at a historic moment. I find it interesting to read how different organs of the media report such events. You learn who you can trust to get it right.

All the Good Times Aren't Over

I'm sure Paris in the Twenties was wonderful. So was the Summer of Love in San Francisco. I missed Woodstock since I was in Vietnam, but I was fortunate enough to see what some consider the last great rock concert of that era, The Isle of Wight Festival. These days it's remembered mostly as Jimi Hendrix's last concert. It took place in an enormous natural amphitheatre covered in lush green grass perhaps half a mile across. Magnificent chalk cliffs that fell off three hundred feet to the crashing waves of the ocean below framed the southern boundary.

All the great groups of the era were there. It was the first and only time I saw Leonard Cohen. When he asked us all to light a match, the valley was filled with thousands of flickering lights. The things that went on at that concert could fill a book. I met a lot of kind and loving people there. We dropped acid. We had visions. We had a great time. I'll always remember it.

Last year I went to another event: Burning Man. If you have the chance, go there. Once a year it's put on in the middle of the Nevada desert on a windy, desolate, alkali flats that won't even support cacti. The festival has a "gift economy:" no one is permitted to buy, sell or trade anything while they're there. (One exception was a place selling coffee, but people were picketing outside it.) I know you've got to buy a ticket, but there are portapotties and a hundred other expenses to pay for to put on an event like this. To my knowledge, no one's getting rich from Burning Man.

I'm not going to go into great detail about everything that goes on there. Check out the website at www.Burningman.org, or talk to anyone who has been. The Isle of Wight Concert was great, but Burning

Man had more beautiful sights, more naked people, more "knock your dick in the dirt" craziness than anyplace I've ever been.

I remember seeing a very old, conventional looking British couple picking their way through the crowd of revelers at the Isle of Wight. I remember thinking that I hoped to be like them someday. I still aspire to that.

Living in the Himalayas

If it weren't so hard, it would be too easy.

Anonymous

As MARCIA AND I sit in front of our little cottage in the foothills of the Himalayas with the whole day to piss away, the loudest sound we hear is the sound of the bees in the flowers that surround us. There's also the sound of birdsongs, the wind in the trees, the creek flowing nearby and the occasional laughter of children playing. It's a forty minute walk to the nearest road, and it's not much of a road.

We can't quite make out the snow-capped mountains, eighty miles distance from us near the Tibetan border. This time of day, clouds often obscure them. Last night there was a tremendous rainstorm and the lights went out (we're at the tail end of the monsoon season). We built a bright fire in the fireplace and lit candles on the windowsills to read by.

There's a lovely French lady named Armella who dresses like a 1960s magic-lady and lives down the path from us. She grows her own herbs and vegetables and runs a small restaurant. We take a lot of our meals there, but at least half the time we cook our own food.

Crusty fresh bread is delivered to us every other day and milk, still warm from milking, every evening. At mid-morning, Kishan, the part-owner of the cottages, usually drops off a copy of "The Times of India" for us, which he picks up in town when he walks his daughter to school.

Several cottages have been built here amid terraced fields planted with fruit trees interspersed with dozens of varieties of vegetables and flowers. There are many species of birds. We've learned most of their names. We scatter breadcrumbs on our veranda for them, but sometimes the local dog gets them first.

Things are looking up. On bad days I never sink too low, and on good days I don't feel half bad. For the past month or so I've been emerging from a dark hole of depression. It's been unlike anything I've ever experienced. Nothing gave me joy— old friends, a good book, a beautiful day. Some days I wouldn't get out of bed. Faces would come into my field of vision. Often they were friendly and encouraging, but it was as if I were seeing them through a long, dark tunnel, far away and unreachable. When I slept, it was a troubled sleep. Suicide was constantly on my mind. I took a chance coming back to India.

Last night I slept peacefully. I awoke to the sound of my dear Marcia quietly bustling around our room. We snuggled for a while, and then she disappeared into our bright little kitchen and emerged with some hot milk coffee. Outside our window, the sun was cutting through the morning haze, with the village and temple on the hill beyond our small valley clearly visible.

A couple of nights ago I got out a big folding map of Uttaranchal and sketched the outline of a seven-day trek to the base of Nanda Devi and the Pindari Glacier. I'm starting to write a new book about how to retire to a paradise for $500 a month. Next month we hope to see Baba-ji in Delhi.

The past few months have given me many lessons. I've become acutely aware that my body, wealth, and even my mind are a gift. Everything is transient, and anything can happen. It's been humbling. Still, as I sit here gazing off in the distance at the range of snow-capped peaks now cleared of clouds, I can't help but feel a little optimistic.

Best Things in the World
(which I hope to do before I die)

- See the gorillas in Rwanda.

- Walk the streets of Cuzco.

- Travel the length of the Karkoram Highway, the highest in the world. It originates in the ancient Silk Road town of Kashgar in western China, then climbs over the Karkoram Mountains to the mythical Hunza Valley of Pakistan.

- See the gigantic metal shell of The Guggenheim Museum in Bilbao.

- Visit Mongolia, Lebanon, Tibet, Finland, Peru, Lithuania, Estonia and Latvia, Cuba and the Cook Islands.

- Circle holy Mount Kailash in Tibet.

- Gawk at the sights of Shanghai.

- Take the Trans-Siberian Railway. It takes seven days, crosses eight time zones, and is the cheapest way to get 1/3 of the way around the globe.

- Walk through the great square in St. Petersburg and visit the room in the Hermitage that is walled in amber.

- Visit The Sandpaper Museum in Two Harbors, Minnesota.

- Shoot the rapids of the Colorado and the Zambezi.

- Climb the thousand-foot sand dunes in Namibia. (March 2007)

- Trek through the Torres del Paine in Chile (November 2007)

Final Advice to Travelers

By a million schemes you cannot smuggle yourself into the kingdom of God

The Sikh Prayer

DEAR READER, I DEEPLY appreciate that you've given up your time to hear these stories of my life. I've enjoyed putting them down. I apologize for the wooden prose.

It has given me a lot of pleasure to revisit some of those moments. It might have been better if the book was a bit more chronological, but try as I might, I could never be sure of what happened before what.

Soon after I started writing this book I resolved to make it as true as I was able. That has proved to be more difficult than I anticipated. I haven't included everything; it's not a confessional. Parts of the book are like the joke about the bikini— what is revealed may be interesting, but what is concealed perhaps even more interesting.

Friends have disagreed with my memory on a few details. Some of those details I'm very sure of – the dust that caked our faces while riding on an A-Cav in Vietnam, the Sicilian steak I ate in Vientiane, the tortoise-like stare in the opium addict's eyes... Some details, like the flap jacks I may have eaten for breakfast in Oklahoma, well, it might have been swordfish steak served en brochette, or maybe a big bowlful of Cocoa Puffs. All I know is that when I tried to dredge up from my memory what went on that morning "flap jacks" bubbled-up from the murky depths. But all important things are true— by my lights at least.

Judith, an English friend who read some of the earliest stories I'd written, asked if there was any thread tying all of the stories together. A good question. I think there is, but I think it's the same thread that runs through every single soul's life. If we know it or not, deny it or not, every soul seeks the "super soul," enlightenment, satori, or whatever you want to call it. It can never be tricked into accepting anything less. It may seem like a stretch sometimes, but all the antics and monkeyshines in this book are explainable in the light of that search.

The strict analogy of a road that leads there is misleading. It's like being pregnant. You're never halfway there. The only real preparation for being "born again" is to cultivate the same desire for it as a drowning man held beneath the surface of the water desires air.

In the deepest recesses of our hearts the same questions are always asked: Who am I? What is going on here? With every cell in my body, I swear to you there are answers. My final advice is to pursue them while you still have life. Remember your clear moments and intimations. Shun the cynical. Go where you need to go, do what you need to do, knock on every door, try wrong turns until you find that they aren't leading anywhere. It's okay to be discouraged, but never give up. Seek and ye shall find.

Afterward

MY FEAR IS THAT this book will have a negative effect on some people; my sincere prayer is that it will not.

I want to make one thing clear: I have spoken often in these pages about the Nirankari Mission. This is not a Nirankari publication. I am a Nirankari, but a very poor example of one.

True Nirankaris use the five principles as their guidelines in life. They are modest and hardworking, loving parents and good citizens. They are not perfect, but they tend to sleep well at night. It is a testament to their tolerance that despite my many serious failings, there are still so many members of the mission who love me and have continued to be my friends.

There is sex, drugs, and violence in this book. Perhaps I was unwise to have included so much of it. I apologize if I have offended anyone.

In defense of his book *Sexus,* Henry Miller wrote, "If it was not good, it was true; if it was not artistic, it was sincere; if it was in bad taste it was on the side of life."

Acknowledgements

FIRST, I WANT TO thank two people who helped me with encouragement and editing; they're two of my favorite people in the world, Rick Owens and JD Grove. As they've both no doubt noticed, I eventually acceded to about half of the changes we crossed swords over.

Thanks also to my dear old buddy Gary Chumley who read an earlier version of the transcript. He's my oldest friend. I read his books and he reads mine.

Love and thanks to my dear children, Jacques and Thea (Learn from your father's mistakes, ok?). I'm so proud of both of you.

As for my three brothers, Al, Richard and Phil— you guys suck, and you have tiny wienies.

I'm particularly grateful to Peter Bently for his wise insight into the publishing world. He advised me to spend time perfecting the book flap, think long and hard about the first and last sentences to the book, try to find a "unique selling point," and lastly, give the thing some kind of chronological or structural form. I made progress with the first three, but the fourth... I can't seem to do it.

Of all the people I'll mention here, none were more helpful in writing this book than Marcia Anderson. Thanks Moo.

I want to thank Mike Sullivan, a gentleman and a great soul. He's put up with all my screw-ups through the years, ignored my bad qualities, and stuck with me through thick and thin.

Thanks to XaXa Mason, wherever you may be. You were a joy to work with.

The crew at *Bloomington Paint and Wallpaper* read early drafts of the book, seemed to enjoy it and urged me on. Thanks guys, you're the greatest.

Thanks to Nathan Brown and Carlea Holl-Jensen who saved the book from going to print with several embarrassing typos, fragments, and ambiguities.

Judy Comer-Calder (a real writer) read a few early stories. Her encouragement meant a lot to me.

Thanks to Grace Mitchell. Shoulder to shoulder we worked our way through the entire document together, buffing, rebuffing, arguing over words and commas, tightening, loosening, adding, eviscerating, bitching, laughing. Who would have thought editing could be so much fun. You're the real deal, Grace.

Finally I want to thank all my Nirankari sisters and brothers around the world whose daily lives give me something to shoot for.